INSTANT POT RECIPES COOKBOOK
Jennifer Wittman

300 Healthy Mouth-Watering Instant Pot Recipes, Quick & Easy Prepare Recipes For Professional Busy Working People and Your Family

Copyright 2017 by Jennifer Wittman All rights reserved.

In no way is it legal to reproduce, duplicate, or transmit any part of this document in either electronic means or in printed format. Recording of this publication is strictly prohibited and any storage of this document is not allowed unless with written permission from the publisher. All rights reserved.

The information provided herein is stated to be truthful and consistent, in that any liability, in terms of inattention or otherwise, by any usage or abuse of any policies, processes, or directions contained within is the solitary and utter responsibility of the recipient reader. Under no circumstances will any legal responsibility or blame be held against the publisher for any reparation, damages, or monetary loss due to the information herein, either directly or indirectly.

Respective authors own all copyrights not held by the publisher.

The trademarks that are used are without any consent, and the publication of the trademark is without permission or backing by the trademark owner. All trademarks and brands within this book are for clarifying purposes only and are the owned by the owners themselves, not affiliated with this document.

Table of Contents

Coconut Pumpkin Pies	18
Delicious Chickpea Seafood Instant Pot	19
Vanilla Creamy Banana Oatmeal	20
Ham Cheesy Apple Casserole	21
Cheddar Sausage Frittata	22
Nutritious Strawberry Oatmeal	23
Delight Savory Breakfast Porridge	24
Cinnamon Quinoa Vanilla Recipe	25
Sesame Scallion Mix Eggs	26
Onion Carrots and Kale Mix	27
Garlic Drop Of Egg Soup	28
Perfect French Toast Bake	29
Awesome Blueberry Croissant Pudding	30
Butter Poached Up Tomato Eggs	31
Instant Pot Steel-Cut Oats	32
Cinnamon Maple-Syrup Quinoa	32

Instant Pot Buckwheat Banana Porridge	33
Egg Ham Bacon Treat	34
Chia Seeds Oats Combination	35
Cheesy French Styled Soup	36
Spiced Nutmeg Apple Butter	37
Cheer Up Banana Breakfast Bread	38
Instant Pot Hard-Boiled Eggs	39
Apricot Steel-Cut Oats	40
Onion Chicken Porridge	41
Nourishing Butter Carrot Cake Oatmeal	42
Banana Cinnamon Buckwheat Porridge	43
Vanilla French Toast Bake	43
Honey Pounded Carrot Puree	44
Yummy Enchilada Soup Of Chicken	45
Cheesy Onion Crustless Milk Quiche	46
Vanilla Berry Cake with Yogurt Glaze	47
Delicious Stuffed Vegetables	49
Delicious Apple and Maple Oatmeal	49
Chili Garlic Chicken Recipes	51
Instant Pot Spaghetti	52
Sweet Chili Sesame Chicken	52
Butter Onion Chicken Dumplings	53
Oregano Pork Chop With Rice	55
Garlic Potato Bacon Chowder	56
Cranberries Turkey Sauerkraut	57
Garlic Lamb Shanks with Wine	58
Tender Corned Beef	60
Parmesan Chicken Piccata	61
Delicious Spicy Pork Shoulder and Peanut Stew	62
Instant Pot Chicken Noodle Soup	63

Spicy Chicken Pasta In A Pot	64
Mushroom Tender Pork Chops	65
Yummy Pot Roast	66
Indian Chicken Curry	68
Tasty Chickpea Curry	69
Delight Whole Chicken	70
Weekend Treat Baby Back Ribs	71
Classic Sweet-Spicy Meatloaf	72
Instant Pot Orange Roast	74
Simple Delicious Chicken Soup	75
Tender English Lamb Shanks	76
Garlic Butter Steamed Crab Legs	77
Mustard Onion Smoked Brisket	78
Rosemary Bell Pepper Tender Beef	79
Ginger Cola Dipped Chicken Wings	81
Spiced Pork Loin Chops With Pear	82
Rosemary Lamb Chops	83
Instant Pot Beefy Lasagna	84
Apple Cider Cabbage Corned Beef	85
Garlic Oxtail and Vegetables Casserole	86
Mushroom Beef Stroganoff	87
Instant Pot Hearty Beef Stew	88
Tasty Beef Brisket	89
Spicy Shredded Beef Recipe	90
Garlic Worcestershire sauce Spinach Ground Beef	92
Chili Mustard Beef With Beans	93
Instant Pot Sesame Beef Steak	93
Ginger Spicy Beef	94
England Pot Roast	95
Delicious Chicken Dumplings	97

The Best Chop Suey	98
Feta Cheese Tuna Noodles	99
Chicken Noodle Soup	100
Onion Balsamic Beef	101
Italy Pepperoncini Beef Recipe	102
Sesame Mustard Mixed Beef	103
Delicious Spanish Soup	104
Vegetable Beef Shank Soup	105
Instant Pot White Fish With Beer	106
Spicy Lemon Salmon	107
Country-Style Delicious Ribs	108
Garlic Soy Sauce Beef Steak	109
Weekend Treat Steak Roll Ups	110
Instant Pot Shrimp Scampi With Rice	111
Smoked Sausage Seafood Mixed	112
Healthy Chicken Potato Bake	114
Not another Instant Pot Meatloaf	115
Heavy Cream Scallop Chowder	116
Classic Beef Stroganoff with Pasta	117
Wonderful Milk-Braised Pork Loin	118
Light n' Delicious Shrimp Corn Stew	119
Delicious Soy Sauce Broccoli Beef	120
Hearty Beef in Light Sauce	122
Flavorful Applesauce Pork Chops	123
Cheesy Lobster Casserole	124
Garlicky Carrot Shrimp Rice	125
Ketchup Garlic Honey Chicken	126
Buttery Chicken Wings	127
Instant Pot Pork Carnitas	128
Instant Pot Barbecue Pork Ribs	129

Tender Soy Sauce Pork Belly 130
Sweet and Sour Chicken 130
Ginger Mixed Meat Recipes 133
Bell Pepper Carrot Beef Mixed 133
Buttery Ground Meat Mixed Veal 134
Cabbage Jalapeno Cod Fillets 135
Ginger Ketchup Honey Shrimp 136
Dark Beer Sauce Chicken 137
Pork Carnitas With White Pepper 137
Maple Soy Sauce Salmon 139
Garlic Linguine Cheesy Shrimp 139
Instant Pot Soy Sauce Red Meat Rice Dish 140
Chili Ground Beef 141
Apple Juicy Pork Tenderloins 141
Parsley Celery Salmon 143
Red Pepper Butter Shrimp 143
Hot Sauce Mushroom Beef 144
Onion Buttery Scallops 145
Mayonnaise Cheesy Crab Meat 146
Ginger Maple Cooked Red Pork 147
Creamy Broccoli Chicken Rice Casserole 148
Yummy Chicken Taco Salad 149
Buttery onion Broccoli Beef 149
Garlic Mushroom Chicken Marsala 150
Chili Black Bean Pork 152
Macaroni Mixed Beef Casserole 153
Asian Style Garlic Broccoli Pork Chop 154
Summer Italian Chicken 155
Hot and Sour Pork Stew 156
Lima Beans Lamb Chops 157

Recipe	Page
Arrowroot Lemon Garlic Chicken	159
Pork Tenderloin Coconut Rice	160
Marina Sauce Meatballs	161
Barbecue Gravy Classic Meatloaf	162
Delicious Corned Up Beef and Cabbage	164
Yummy Creole Cod	165
Healthy Turkey Veggie Soup	166
Jasmine Rice Congee Chicken	167
Tasty Mongolian Beef	168
Garlic Artichoke Pork Chops	169
Cinnamon Ginger Pork Chops With Cherry Sauce	170
Mozzarella Lime-Salsa Chicken	171
Corn Starch Thai Peanut Butter Chicken	172
Tender Gravy Cornish Hens	173
Ketchup Ghee Garlic Chicken	174
Shredded Flank Pepper Steak	175
Lemon Creamy Shrimp Chowder	176
Yummy Barbecue Pulled Chicken	177
Butternut Squash and Ginger Soup	178
Almond Rosemary Meatloaf	178
Mushroom Gravy Chicken	179
Peppercorn Lamb Curry	180
Creamy Cabbage Beef &Chicken	181
Amazing Chipotle-Chocolate Chicken Chili	182
Buttery French Onion Chicken	183
Hot Sauce Sesame Beef	184
Tasty BBQ-Flavored Pork	185
Buttery Mushrooms Chicken Cubes	186
Walnut Dates Lamb Stew	187
Garlic Stingy Sword Fish	188

Instant Pot Coconut Turkey Curry	189
Coriander Bacon Cheese Beef	190
Delicious Multi-Meat Blend	191
Crab Black Bean Soup	192
Healthy Continental Chicken	194
Tasty Ginger Duck	194
Delicious Pork Fried Rice	195
Mouth-Watering Hawaiian Pork	196
Cashews Thai Chicken	198
Cumin Zucchini Curry Chicken	198
Chili Beef	199
Easy Salsa Verde Chicken	200
Popular Pumpkin Pie	202
Instant Pot Crème Brule	202
Orange Marble Cheesecake	204
Yummy Coffee Espresso Pudding	205
Beautiful Carved Out Of Cherry	206
Raisin Bread Pudding	207
Coconut Samoa Cheesecake	208
Cherry Topping Almond Pudding Cake	210
Fudgy Brownies	211
Chocolate Mix Lemon Pudding	212
Mango Cake	213
Creamy Chocolate Cheesecake	214
California Cheesecake	216
Delicious Oreo Cheesecake	217
Mouth-Watering Apple Crisp	218
Apple Blast Cheese Cake	219
Yummy Red-Wine Baked Apples	220
Crumble Cinnamon Stuffed Peaches	221

Instant Pot Berry Cobbler	222
Mini Lava Cake	223
Maple Syrup Crème Caramel	224
Honey Cranberries Pear Cake	225
Delicious Tapioca Pudding	226
Delicious Orange-Glazed Poached Pears	227
Coconut Cashew-Lemon Cheesecake	228
Vegan Strawberries + Cream Oats	230
Rice Milk Buckwheat Porridge	230
Healthy Vegan Yogurt	231
Yummy Veggies Rice Dish	232
Tasty Asparagus Millet Veggies	233
Instant Pot Garlic Lentils And Rice Risotto	234
Mushroom Curry Lentils Burgers	235
Red Cabbage Black Bean Burgers	236
Healthy Dairy-free Mashed Potatoes	237
Nutritious Soup	238
Mild Chili Beans Mixed	239
Tomato Cilantro Mushrooms Beans	240
Tasty Chili Onion Vegan Polenta	241
Apple Cider Vinegar Spicy Braised Cabbage	242
Yummy Buckwheat Beans Porridge	243
Instant Pot Quinoa Almond Pilaf	244
Amazing One-Pot Artichokes Rice	245
Nutritious Chipotle-Pumpkin Apple Soup	246
Favorite Vegan Curried Sorghum	247
Garlic Lentils Kidney Bean Stew	249
Tasty Chili Taco Mix	250
Mustard Spaghetti Squash Lasagna	251
Healthy Red Cabbage Salad	253

Mushroom Walnut Cabbage Rolls	254
Coconut Black-Eyed Peas + Kale Bowl	255
Special Basil Tomato Zucchini Dish	257
Detox Vegetable Mix Dish	257
Coconut Chili Sweet Potato Peanut Butter Soup	259
Tomato Beans Stew	260
Tamari Tofu & Veggies Dish	261
Ginger Tomato Mushroom Dish	261
Almond Milk Corn With Lime Sauce	262
Rich N' Delicious Vegan Lasagna	263
Curry Pineapple sweet veggie dish	265
Instant Pot Chickpeas Dish	266
Creamy Butternut Squash Soup	267
Thyme Tomato Soup	267
Soy Milk Butternut Pumpkin Soup	268
Fresh Mint Creamy Barley Soup	269
Taco Soup	270
Mustard Seeds Spinach Lentil Soup	270
Turmeric Pumpkin Bean and Chickpea Stew	271
Peanut Potato Stew	272
Kidney Beans Chickpea Lentil Stew	272
Yummy Cannellini Stew	273
Green Chilies Spinach Curry	274
Garlic Carrot and Lentil	275
Masala Curry Potato Chickpea	276
Coconut Mustard Black Chickpeas	277
Ginger Green Peas Masala Curry	278
Thai Coconut Chickpeas Dish	279
Instant Pot Paprika Broccoli Burgers	279
Special Cinnamon Couscous Patties	281

Instant Pot Coconut Creamy Spinach 282
Healthy Almond Vegetable Curry 282
Yummy Opt Squash 283
Sprig Sage Butternut Squash Risotto 284
Onion Asparagus Arborio Rice 285
Delicious Mash Potato 286
Mustard Chili Cabbage Sabzi 286
Tasty Vegan Corn Burger 287
Gluten-free Instant Pot Mushroom Patties 288
Garlic Amaranth Black Eyed Peas 289
Onion Lentil Risotto & Arborio Rice 290
Simple Lemon Broccoli 290
Grilled Zucchini With Chickpeas Quinoa 291
Garlic Mushroom Risotto 292
Instant Pot Lentils Burgers..293
Flaxseed Black Bean Burgers 294
Amazing Mushroom Spinach Lasagna 295
Cumin Moroccan Black Eyed Peas 297
Vegan Sheppard's Pie 298
Mexican Style Corn With Lime Sauce 299
Spinach Sweet Potato Risotto 299
Ginger Moroccan Pumpkin Lentils...301
Garlic Spinach Pasta 302
Kale Pasta with Pinto Beans 302
Delicious Garlic Veggies Dish 303
Simple Vegan Penne Rigatta 304
Mexican Bell Peppers Mixed Beans 305
Simple Potato Salad 307
Chili Ginger Mixed Vegetable..307
Instant Pot Broccoli Carrots Casserole 308

Tasty Red Cabbage Salad	309
Brown Rice Cabbage Rolls	310
Simple Brussels sprouts	311
Delicious Garlic Chickpeas	312
Stuffed Bell Peppers	312
Tasty Tofu Curry	314
Yummy Bolognese Lentil	315
Healthy Plant-based lentil pasta	316
Asian Onion Sesame Tofu	317
Satisfying Parsnip Potato Soup	318
Healthy Rice Dish	319
Vegan Corn Bread	320
Maple Cinnamon Apple Lentils	321

Introduction

I want to thank you and congratulate you for downloading the book, "Instant Pot Recipes Cookbook: 300 Healthy Mouth-Watering Instant Pot Recipes, Quick & Easy Prepare Recipes For Professional Busy Working People and Your Family"

In recent times, there has been an ever-growing need for ways to save time and money. In this respect, the Instant Pot methods are one of the most advanced appliances designed for this very purpose to date. Simmering, boiling, browning and sautéing, instant Instant Pot is a smart cooker that has multiple pre-programmed functions. The outside of the pot often has a control panel by which you can adjust the cooking settings. The pot interior is made from a highly heat conducive material. The pots have multiple layers for differing steaming/cooking style uses, and the lid has a valve that releases steam.

You can make delicious food, easy-peasy with the simple yet effective recipes this book has to offer! Make the most of your Instant Pot!

Thanks again for downloading this book, I hope you find it enjoyable!

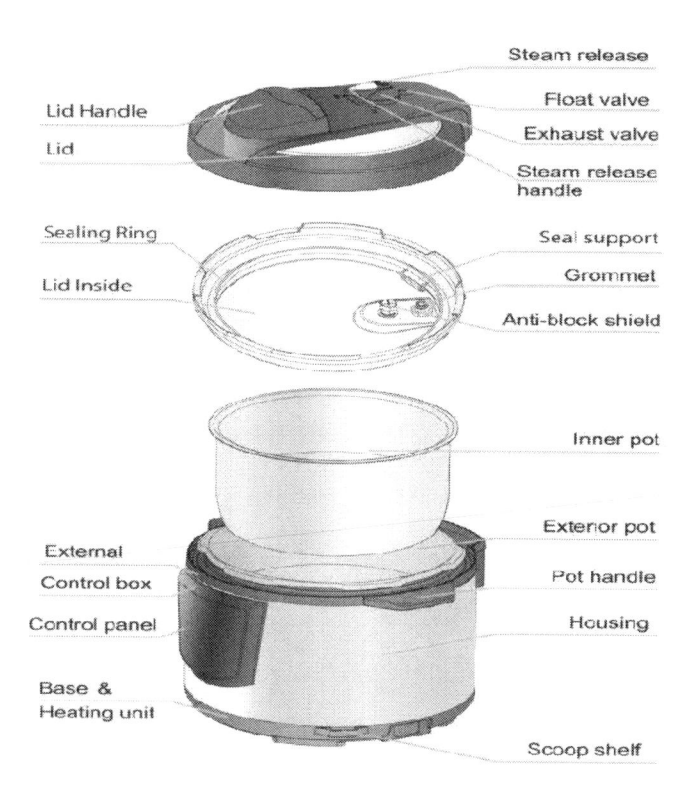

Functions of the Instant Pot

On the Instant Pot control panel, you will see that there are many cooking settings that you can select with pre-programmed cook times for various kinds of food:

- **Multigrain**: This setting is optimal for softening the harder grains like wild and brown rice.

- **Porridge**: Grains and cereals can be turned into oatmeal easily using this setting.

- **Sauté/ Browning**: If you're in need of food sautéing, this setting allows you to cook with the lid open.

- **Beans/Chili**: Beans are optimally cooked under these settings, but just be aware that this shouldn't be used for cooking up meat-based chili.

- **Soup**: This setting can be used for preparing broths and soups.

- **Slow Cooker**: This turns your pot into a slow cooker, but with no pressure.

- **Meat/Stew**: This setting can be used for pot roast, stew, or any type of cooked meat.

- **Rice**: As the name suggests, this setting can optimally cook rice.

- **Steam**: This setting turns your pot into a steamer, which is great for steaming vegetables.

- **Poultry**: This setting is for cooking bird meats.

- **Manual**: In case you don't want to use pre-programmed settings, manual setting is always an option.

CHAPTER 1 BENEFITS OF USING INSTANT POT /PRESSURE COOKER

Once you hear of the advantages to owning an Instant pot, there should be no mistake in assuming you want one for yourself! The various benefits of the Instant Pot are as follows:

- **Saves Energy:** No more excessive gas or electricity bills when you welcome the instant pot into your household. Compared to other household appliances that do the same job as the Instant Pot, you can find yourself saving up to 70% on energy bills. Being innately pressurized, moisture is retained in foods and any water that you put in will stay, thus cutting water needs for cooking.

- **Automated Cooking:** Given that the cooking times are pre-programmed into the pot, cooking now requires minimal effort from you, and will stop once the timer has ticked down to zero. No need to be paranoid about checking your pot anymore!

- **Fast Cooking:** Cooking under a pressurized appliance will make sure the cooking conditions are stable. Because of this, the times needed to fully cook your meal have been cut down significantly. Soon enough, you'll have more time than you know how to deal with!

- **Preserves Nutrients in Cooking**: Since the ingredients aren't cooked in too much excess water, coupled with the pressurized conditions, very little in the way of nutrients is lost in the process of cooking or via evaporation. Also, with little air exposure, food is not as easily oxidized.

- **Quiet and Clean:** Your kitchen has never been quieter! No spills, smoke, smell or noise.

- **Safe to Use:** Instant Pot appliances are UL/ULC certified and has full-proof safety protections.

Chapter 2 Instant Pot Breakfast Recipes

Coconut Pumpkin Pies

Prep Time: 5 minutes
Cooking Time: 10 minutes
Serving: 4

Ingredients
- 2 pound of peeled and diced up butter nut squash
- 1 cup of coconut milk
- ¾ cup of maple syrup
- 2 large sized eggs
- 1 teaspoon of powdered cinnamon
- ½ a teaspoon of powdered ginger
- ¼ teaspoon of powdered cloves
- 1 tablespoon of organic corn starch
- 2 pinches of salt

For garnish
- Sweetened whipped cream
- Chopped up pecans

Directions:
1. First add about 1 cup of water into the instant pot
2. Toss in the squash cubes into the steamer basket and lower down the pressure
3. Close up the lid and let it cook for about 3-4 minutes at high pressure
4. While it is being cooked, take a medium mixing bowl and pour in 4 cups of milk and pour in the maple syrup as well
5. Toss in the cinnamon, eggs, ginger, cornstarch and salt and beat it using an immersion blender
6. Once the squash are cooked, take a fine mesh strainer and stress the cooled squash and keep the pulped juice
7. Gently take the pulp into 2 cups and freeze them
8. Take the pulp and pour them down into the egg mixture
9. In your instant pot, take about 1 cup of water

10. Pour in the previously made mixture into a nice heatproof ramekin and lower it into the cooker

11. Make sure to put the second layer on top of the first layer making sure of balance out the edges of the ramekin below

12. Close up the lid of the pressure cooker and let it cook for about 10 minutes over high pressure. Let the pressure release naturally

14. Take out the ramekins and let them stand for 5 minutes before serving.

Nutrition information:
- **Calories: 143**
- **Fat: 2.3g**
- **Carbohydrates: 2.1g**
- **Protein: 3.3g**

Delicious Chickpea Seafood Instant Pot

Prep Time: 10 minutes
Cooking Time: 15 minutes
Serving: 4

Ingredients
- 1 cup of chopped up scallions
- 1 chopped up carrot
- 1 pound of shrimp
- 2 tablespoon of black pepper
- 2 cups of vegetable broth
- 2 cod fillets
- 1 cup of soaked ad drained up chickpea

Directions:
1. Start off with place all of the ingredients in your inner pot of your Instant Pot
2. Set the pot at high pressure and let it cook for 12 minutes
3. Once done, simply wait for 10 minutes and let the pressure release naturally. Then open up and top it up with some tomatoes and cheddar cheese if you so choose to and serve hot

Nutrition Information:

- **Calories: 268**
- **Fat: 4.2g**
- **Carbohydrates: 25g**
- **Protein: 14.5g**

Vanilla Creamy Banana Oatmeal

Serves: 4
Time: 18 minutes

Ingredients:

2 ¼ cups water
½ cup steel-cut oats
2 very ripe, chopped bananas
½ cup packed light brown sugar
¼ cup half-and-half
2 teaspoons vanilla extract
½ teaspoon ground cinnamon
¼ teaspoon salt

Directions:

1. Mix oats, bananas, brown sugar, vanilla, salt, and cinnamon with 2 ¼ cups and pour into the Instant Pot.
2. When the brown sugar dissolves, close the lid.
3. Select "Manual" and then 18 minutes at "high pressure."
4. When time is up, hit "Cancel" and wait for the pressure to come down on its own.
5. When time is up, carefully open the cooker.
6. Stir in the half-and half, and enjoy!

Nutritional Information:

Total calories - 130

Protein - 12
Carbs – 6g
Fat – 3g

Ham Cheesy Apple Casserole

Serves: 4-6
Time: 22 minutes

Ingredients:
8 ounces of chopped bacon
4 sliced scallions
2 big, beaten eggs
¾ cups instant grits
½ cup shredded cheddar cheese
1 peeled and chopped green apple
2 tablespoons butter
1 teaspoon dried thyme

Directions:

1. Turn your Instant Pot to "Sauté" to melt the butter.
2. Add the ham, stirring, and cook for 1 minute.
3. Toss in the scallions, thyme, and apples.
4. Stir and cook for another minute.
5. Move everything to a bowl and set aside.
6. Hit "Cancel" on the Instant Pot.
7. Wipe down the inside of the pot with a paper towel.
8. Turn "Sauté" back on and pour in 3 cups of water.
9. When boiling, add the grits.
10. Whisk constantly until the grits are thick.
11. Hit "Cancel" again.
12. Move the grits to the bowl with the other cooked ingredients.
13. Let the grits cool for 10 minutes while you clean out the cooker.
14. Pour in another 2 cups of water.

15. Put in the trivet.
16. Stir the cheese and eggs into the grits' bowl.
17. Pour into a greased 2-quart, round baking dish and cover with foil.
18. Lower into the Instant Pot.
19. Secure the lid and hit "Manual," and then 22 minutes on "high pressure."
20. Quick-release the pressure when time is up.
21. Cool before serving.

Nutritional Information:

Total calories - 157
Protein - 12.3
Carbs - 8.9
Fiber -0 .5
Fat - 7.7

Cheddar Sausage Frittata

Serves: 2-4
Time: 40 minutes

Ingredients:

1 ½ cups water
4 beaten eggs
½ cup cooked ground sausage
¼ cup grated sharp cheddar
2 tablespoons sour cream
1 tablespoon butter
Salt to taste
Black pepper to taste

Directions:

1. Pour water into the Instant Pot and lower in the steamer rack.
2. Grease a 6-7 inch soufflé dish.
3. In a bowl, whisk the eggs and sour cream together.
4. Add cheese, sausage, salt, and pepper. Stir.
5. Pour into the dish and wrap tightly with foil all over.
6. Lower into the steam rack and close the pot lid.
7. Hit "Manual," and then 17 minutes on "low pressure."
8. Quick-release the pressure.
9. Serve hot!

Nutritional Info:

Total calories - 282
Protein - 16
Carbs - 1
Fiber - 0
Fat - 12

Nutritious Strawberry Oatmeal

Serves: 1
Time: 20 minutes

Ingredients:

⅔ cup whole milk
⅓ cup rolled oats
2 tablespoons strawberries
½ teaspoon sugar
1 pinch of salt

Directions:

1. Pour 2 cups of water into the Instant Pot and lower in the steamer basket.
2. Mix the milk, strawberries, oats, and salt in a small bowl.
3. Put the bowl into the pressure cooker and lock the lid.
4. Hit "Manual" and then 10 minutes on "high pressure."
5. When the timer goes off, hit "Cancel" and wait for the pressure to go down.
6. When the pressure is gone, open the lid and stir.
7. Serve with sugar and a sprinkle of cinnamon, if desired.

Nutritional Info:

Total calories - 207
Protein - 8.6
Carbs - 18.3
Fiber - 2.8
Fat - 7.3

Delight Savory Breakfast Porridge

Serves: 4
Time: 1 hour

Ingredients:
2 cups chicken broth
2 cups water
4 eggs
4 chopped scallions
½ cup rinsed and drained white rice
1 tablespoon sugar
1 tablespoon olive oil
2 teaspoons soy sauce
½ teaspoon salt
Black pepper

Directions:

1. Pour water, broth, sugar, salt, and rice into the Instant Pot.
2. Close the lid.
3. Hit "Porridge" and 30 minutes on "high pressure."
4. While that cooks, heat oil in a saucepan.
5. Crack in the eggs one at a time, so they aren't touching each other.
6. Cook until the whites become crispy on the edges, but the yolks are still runny.
7. Sprinkle on salt and pepper.
8. When the Instant Pot timer goes off, hit "Cancel" and wait for the pressure to go down on its own.
9. If the porridge isn't thick enough, hit "Sauté" and cook uncovered for 5-10 minutes.
10. Serve with scallions, soy sauce, and an egg per bowl.

Nutritional Information:
Total calories - 214
Protein – 10
Carbs – 20g
Fiber – 1.5g
Fat – 2 g

Cinnamon Quinoa Vanilla Recipe

Prep time: 4 minutes
Cooking time: 11 minutes
Servings: 3
Ingredients:
- Uncooked Quinoa – 1 cup
- Water – 2 cups
- Maple syrup – 1 ½ tbsp.
- Vanilla – 1 tsp.
- Cinnamon powder – 2 tbsp.
- Salt – a pinch
- Toppings: fresh berries, cherries, crushed almonds

Directions:
1. Mix water, maple syrup, quinoa, vanilla, salt and cinnamon in the instant pot.
2. Set the pressure to 1 minute. When the sound beeps, turn it off and let it rest for 10 minutes. Release the pressure and then open the pot.
3. Take out the quinoa in the bowl and serve it with any of your favorite toppings mentioned above. Enjoy!

Nutrition Information:
- **Calories: 155**
- **Fat: 7g**
- **Carbohydrates: 10g**
- **Protein: 40g**

Sesame Scallion Mix Eggs

Prep time: 5 minutes
Cooking time: 5 minutes
Servings: 4

Ingredients:
- Egg – 2
- Water – 1 cup
- Scallions (chopped) – S lb.
- Sesame seeds – 1/3 cup
- Garlic powder – S tsp.
- Salt and pepper to taste

Directions:
1. Get a bowl and mix water and egg in it.
2. Put the scallions, sesame seeds, garlic powder along with salt and pepper in the instant pot. Add the egg mixture.
3. Set the timer on manual for 5 minutes. When the timer goes off, release the pressure of the instant pot. Serve and enjoy!

Nutrition Information:
- **Calories: 100g**
- **Fat: 10g**
- **Carbohydrates: 8g**

- **Protein: 110g**

Onion Carrots and Kale Mix

Prep Time: 10 minutes
Cooking Time: 30 minutes
Serving: 4

Ingredients:

- 10 ounce of roughly chopped up kale
- 1 tablespoon of nice ghee
- 1 medium sized thinly sliced onion
- 3 medium sized carrots cut into half inch pieces
- 5 cloves of peeled and chopped up garlic
- ½ a cup of chicken broth
- Kosher salt
- Freshly grounded pepper
- Vinegar
- ½ teaspoon of red pepper flakes

Directions:
1. In your instant pot, pour down the ghee and let it melt over medium heat
2. Toss into the inner pot the chopped up onions and carrots and sauté them until they are nice and soft
3. Toss in the garlic and keep stirring it until a nice fragrance has appeared
4. On top them, create a pile of kale and then pour down the chicken broth
5. Sprinkle some pepper and salt as seasoning
6. Lock up the lid and increase the temperature to high. After a high pressure has been reached, let it maintain that level for about 8 minutes and then manually and naturally let the pressure release itself
7. Open up the lid and give a swirl to make sure that everything is in order. Pour down the vinegar and sprinkle some more pepper flakes if spicy is what you prefer

Nutrition Information:
- **Calories: 41.1**

- **Fat: 2.1g**
- **Carbohydrates: 5.5g**
- **Protein: 1.4g**

Garlic Drop Of Egg Soup

Prep Time: 5 minutes
Cooking Time: 10 minutes
Serving: 6

Ingredients
- ½ a teaspoon of ginger
- 1 star anise
- 2 cloves of garlic
- 3 fennel seeds
- 1/8 teaspoon of cinnamon
- 2 teaspoon of white pepper
- 8 ounce of cherry tomatoes
- 4 cups of water
- 2 cups of chook broth
- 4 whisked eggs
- 2 chopped up green scallion

Directions:
1. Start off by putting the spices in a tea bell
2. Toss the spices, water and tomato alongside the broth to your cooker
3. Lock up the lid and let it cook at high pressure for 7 minutes
4. Let the pressure release naturally
5. Open up the lid and pour in the whisked eggs and sprinkle some scallions and serve

Nutrition Information:
- **Calories: 187**
- **Fat: 10g**
- **Carbohydrates: 20g**

- **Protein: 47g**

Perfect French Toast Bake

Prep Time: 15 minutes
Cooking Time: 25 minutes
Number of Servings: 4

Ingredients:

- 6 slices day-old bread, cubed
- 1/4 cup sugar
- 3 eggs
- 1/2 cup milk
- 1 teaspoon vanilla extract
- 1 teaspoon ground cinnamon
- 1 cup maple syrup for serving

Directions:

1. Beat the eggs, then whisk in milk, vanilla, and cinnamon. Stir the bread into the egg mixture until well coated.
2. Pour the bread and eggs into a baking dish that fits inside the Instant Pot. Place a trivet inside the pot and add enough water to reach the top of the trivet. Place the baking dish on top of the trivet.
3. Close the lid and set the cook time for 25 minutes on high pressure.
4. Serve French toast with maple syrup.

Nutritional Information:

Calories - 403
Fat - 5.19 g
Carbohydrates - 82.47 g
Fiber - 1.2 g

Protein - 7.82 g

Awesome Blueberry Croissant Pudding

Serves: 7
Time: 40 minutes

Ingredients:

3 big, cut-up croissants
One 8-ounce package softened cream cheese
2 eggs
1 cup blueberries
1 cup milk
⅔ cup sugar
1 teaspoon vanilla

Directions:

1. Put the croissants and blueberries in a heat-safe bowl you know fits in the Instant Pot.
2. In a separate bowl, mix cream cheese, eggs, sugar, and vanilla.
3. Add milk and mix again.
4. Pour over the croissants and rest for 20 minutes.
5. When ready, put the bowl in the Instant Pot and lock the lid.
6. Press "Manual," and then "high pressure" for 20 minutes.
7. When time is up, hit "Cancel" and then quick-release. Serve and enjoy.

Nutritional Information:
Total calories - 263
Protein - 15
Carbs - 10
Fiber - 2
Fat - 10

Butter Poached Up Tomato Eggs

Prep Time: 5 minutes
Cooking Time: 5 minutes
Serving: 6

Ingredients
- 5 large sized eggs
- 5 large sized tomatoes
- 3 tablespoon of melted butter
- ½ a teaspoon of pepper

Directions:
1. The first step here is to place about one cup of water in your inner pot
2. Hollow out your tomatoes by digging out the middle part of the vegetable
3. Take an egg and break it into each of your tomato and place those tomatoes on a dish
4. Place that dish on your Instant pot
5. Choose the pressure cooking mode and let it cook at low pressure for 5 minutes
6. Gently remove the eggs and top off them with pepper and butter
7. Gently serve it with turkey, beef slice or ham as you required

Nutrition Information:
- **Calories: 145**
- **Fat: 2g**
- **Carbohydrates: 0g**
- **Protein: 5g**

Instant Pot Steel-Cut Oats

Serves: 3-4
Time: 6-7 minutes

Ingredients:
2 cups of water
1 cup steel-cut oats
Pinch of salt
Milk
Sugar

Directions:

1. Pour 1 cup of water into the Instant Pot and lower in the trivet.
2. In a heatproof bowl, mix 2 cups of water, oats, and salt.
3. Set on top of the trivet and lock the pressure cooker lid.
4. Select the "Manual" setting and cook for at least 6 minutes, but no more than 7.
5. Heat a cup or so of milk (depending on how much you want) in the microwave.
6. When the oats are done, scoop into individual serving bowls.
7. Pour milk on top and add sugar before serving.

Nutritional Information:

Total calories - 155
Protein - 4
Carbs - 28
Fiber - 2
Fat - 3

Cinnamon Maple-Syrup Quinoa

Serves: 4-5
Time: 11 minutes

Ingredients:

2 ¼ cups water
1 ½ cups uncooked, rinsed quinoa
2 tablespoons maple syrup
½ teaspoon vanilla
¼ teaspoon cinnamon
Pinch of salt

Directions:

1. Add the water, quinoa, maple syrup, vanilla, cinnamon, and salt to the Instant Pot.
2. Select "Manual" and then "high pressure."
3. Choose the 1 minute cook-time.
4. When ready, turn off the pressure cooker and wait 10 minutes.
5. Quick-release the rest of the pressure.
6. Using a fork, fluff the quinoa.
7. Serve with milk, fruit, nuts, and/or more maple syrup if necessary.

Nutritional Information:
Total calories - 213
Protein - 7
Carbs - 41
Fiber - 2
Fat - 3

Instant Pot Buckwheat Banana Porridge

Prep Time: 2 minutes

Cooking Time: 6 minutes
Number of Servings: 2

Ingredients:

- 1 cup buckwheat grouts, rinsed
- 3 cups milk, plus more for serving
- 1 ripe banana, sliced
- 1 teaspoon ground cinnamon
- 2 tablespoons brown sugar, plus more for serving

Directions:

1. Pour the grouts, milk, banana, cinnamon, and sugar into the Instant Pot.
2. Close the lid and set to 6 minutes on high pressure.
3. Serve porridge with additional milk and brown sugar.

Nutritional Information:

Calories - 409
Fat - 12.7 g
Carbohydrates - 25.26 g
Fiber - 4.5 g
Protein - 15.08 g

Egg Ham Bacon Treat

Prep time: 5 minutes
Cooking time: 14 minutes
Servings: 3

Ingredients:
- Eggs – 4
- Milk – 1 cup
- Salt to taste
- Bacon – 3 slices
- Ground Sausage – 1 lb.
- Ham (diced) – 1 cup
- Green onions (chopped) – 3
- Cheddar cheese – 2 cups

Directions:
1. Get a bowl and whisk eggs with milk in it.
2. Add salt to it and then pour it in the instant pot. Mix bacon, ham, and sausage in the pot. Sprinkle green onions and cover it all with cheddar cheese.
3. Let it cook for 14 minutes in the pressure pot. When ready, take it out and serve!

Nutrition:
- **Calories: 155**
- **Fat: 7g**
- **Carbohydrates: 10g**
- **Protein: 40g**

Chia Seeds Oats Combination

Prep time: 5 minutes
Cooking time: 10 minutes
Servings: 2

Ingredients:
- Butter – 1 tbsp.
- Oats – S cup
- Water – 2 cups
- Cream – S cup
- Salt to taste
- Chia seeds – ½ cup
- Strawberries (sliced) – 1 cup
- Brown sugar – 2 tbsp.

Directions:

1. Add butter in the instant pot and select the sauté option. When the butter melts, then add oats, cream, water, chia seeds, brown sugar and salt in it. Mix well.
2. Let it cook on pressure for 10 minutes. When it beeps, take it out and serve with the strawberries slices on it.

Nutrition:
- **Calories: 90**
- **Fat: 8g**
- **Carbohydrates: 20g**
   Protein: 25g

Cheesy French Styled Soup

Prep Time: 5 minutes
Cooking Time: 10 minutes
Serving: 6

Ingredients:
- ¾ of cup extra virgin olive oil
- 4 Vidalia onions sliced up
- 4 pieces of cup
- 1 cup of red wine
- 4 cups of vegetable stock
- Salt as needed
- Pepper as needed
- 4 slice of French bread
- 4 ounce of Swiss cheese

Directions:
1. Start off by pouring the olive oil into your instant pot
2. Sauté your onions until nicely brown
3. Then add in the garlic and sauté for another extra minutes
4. Toss in the thyme, red wine and vegetable stock
5. Lock up the lid and let it cook at high pressure for 10 minutes
6. Let the pressure release naturally
7. Open up the lid and toss in some extra salt or pepper if needed
8. Pre-heat your over to a broil setting and toast your French bread

9. Ladle some soup on an oven protected bowl and place a French toast on top of our soup
10. Slice some cheese and broil the soup until the cheese has melted
11. Serve hot

Nutrition Information:

- **Calories: 137**
- **Fat: 10g**
- **Carbohydrates: 25g**
- **Protein: 33g**

Spiced Nutmeg Apple Butter

Ingredients
- Apples 2
- Water 1 cup
- Cinnamon 5g
- Sugar (as needed)
- Nutmeg 5g
- Pumpkin pie spice 5g

Directions:
1. Fill your pressure cooker to the line with apples. Add 1 cup water.
2. Set pressure cooker to steam setting. Adjust time to 4 minutes.
3. When you hear the beeps indicating it's done, just leave it. Let the pressure return to normal on its own.
4. Open the lid and using an immersion blender, blend until it reaches the apple butter consistency.
5. Put in cinnamon, sugar (use Splenda) to taste. You can also add a pinch of nutmeg and pumpkin pie spice.
6. Put into containers or canning jars with new lids, and into a water bath for 25 minutes.
7. These is a great breakfast treat on fresh baked bread, or over pancakes and waffles.

Nutritional Information
- **Preparation Time: 45 minutes**

- **Total Servings: 2**
- **Calories: 34**
- **Protein: 1g**
- **Total Fat: 0g**
- **Total Carbohydrates: 3g**

Cheer Up Banana Breakfast Bread

Prep Time: 15 minutes
Cooking Time: 50 minutes
Number of Servings: 6

Ingredients:

- 1 stick butter
- 1/4 cup white sugar
- 1/4 cup brown sugar
- 2 eggs
- 3 ripe bananas, mashed
- 2 cups flour
- 1 teaspoon baking soda
- 1/2 teaspoon salt
- 1 teaspoon ground cinnamon

Directions:

1. Grease an aluminum cake pan of a smaller circumference than the Instant Pot inner pot with butter.
2. In a bowl, whisk together the flour, baking soda, salt, and cinnamon. Set aside.
3. With an electric mixer, cream the butter with the sugars. Beat in the eggs one at a time, then stir in the bananas. Add the flour mixture to the wet ingredients by thirds. Pour the batter into the cake pan.

4. Place a trivet in the inner pot. Pour enough water into the pot to just reach the top of the trivet. Place the cake pan on top of the trivet.

5. Close the lid and set the cook time for 50 minutes on high pressure. Allow cake to cool before serving.

Nutritional Information:

Calories - 394

Fat - 17.31 g

Carbohydrates - 54.16 g

Fiber - 2.9 g

Protein - 6.98 g

Instant Pot Hard-Boiled Eggs

Prep Time: 1 minute
Cooking Time: 5 minutes
Number of Servings: 3

Ingredients:

- 6 eggs
- 1 cup water

Directions:

1. Pour the water into the pot. Place eggs in the steamer basket and set the basket over the water.

2. Close the lid and set the cook time for 5 minutes on high pressure.

3. After the pressure naturally releases, place the eggs in cold water. Peel when cool enough to handle.

Nutritional Information:
Calories - 468
Fat - 20 g
Carbohydrates - 3.6 g
Fiber - 10.1 g
Protein - 30 g

Apricot Steel-Cut Oats

Prep Time: 2 minutes
Cooking Time: 3 minutes
Number of Servings: 2

Ingredients:
- 1 cup steel cut oats
- 1 tablespoon butter
- 1 1/2 cups milk, plus more for serving
- 1 1/2 cups water
- 1 cup dried apricots

Directions:

1. Set the Instant Pot to Sauté. Melt the butter in the bottom of the pan. Add oats and toast until oats are lightly browned and smell nutty.
2. Pour in the milk, water, and dried fruit.
3. Close the lid and set cook time for 3 minutes on high pressure.
4. Ladle the oatmeal into pots and serve with milk.

Nutritional Information

Calories - 335; Fat - 12.38 carbohydrates - 20.59 g ; Protein - 16.16 g

Onion Chicken Porridge

Prep Time: 60 minutes
Cooking Time: 20 minutes
Serving: 6

Ingredients
- 1 cup of jasmine rice
- 1 pound of chicken legs
- 5 cup of chicken broth
- 4 cup of water
- 1 and a ½ cup of fresh ginger
- Green onions
- Toasted cashew nuts

Process
1. The first step is to put the rice in a freeze about 1 hour before cooking
2. Take the rice out of the freezer and place toss them down into the inner pot of the instant pot
3. Pour in the broth and water and seal down the pot
4. Turn on the porridge option and let it cook until the default count down runs out
5. Remove the pressure naturally
6. Open up the lid and remove the chicken legs and just take the meat from the legs
7. Put the meat in the soup and keep stirring it until. Add in some salt until a nice flavor has been obtained
8. Pour in bowls and garnish with green onions and nuts

Nutrition Information:
- **Calories: 138**
- **Fat: 10g**
- **Carbohydrates: 12g**
- **Protein: 13.6**

Nourishing Butter Carrot Cake Oatmeal

Prep Time: 10 minutes
Cooking Time: 10 minutes
Number of Servings: 2

Ingredients:

- 1 cup steel-cut oats
- 1 tablespoon butter
- 2 cups milk, plus more for serving
- 2 cups water
- 2 carrots, grated
- 1/4 cup brown sugar
- 1 teaspoon ground cinnamon
- 1/2 teaspoon nutmeg
- 1/2 cup raisins

Directions:

1. Set Instant Pot to Sauté. Melt butter in the pot and add oats. Toast until oats are lightly browned and smell nutty.
2. Pour milk, water, carrots, sugar, cinnamon, nutmeg, and raisins into the pot.
3. Close lid and set cook time to 10 minutes on high pressure.
4. Serve with additional milk.

Nutritional Information:

Calories - 320

Fat - 14.4 g

Carbohydrates - 20.05 g

Protein - 16.57 g

Banana Cinnamon Buckwheat Porridge

Number of Servings: 2

Ingredients:

- 1 cup buckwheat grouts, rinsed
- 3 cups milk, plus more for serving
- 1 ripe banana, sliced
- 1 teaspoon ground cinnamon
- 2 tablespoons brown sugar, plus more for serving

Directions:
1. Pour the grouts, milk, banana, cinnamon, and sugar into the Instant Pot.
2 Close the lid and set to 6 minutes on high pressure.
3. Serve porridge with additional milk and brown sugar.

Nutritional Information:
Calories - 409
Fat - 12.7 g
Carbohydrates - 32.26 g
Fiber - 4.5 g
Protein - 15.08 g

Vanilla French Toast Bake

Prep Time: 15 minutes
Cooking Time: 25 minutes
Number of Servings: 4

Ingredients:

- 6 slices day-old bread, cubed
- 1/4 cup sugar
- 3 eggs
- 1/2 cup milk
- 1 teaspoon vanilla extract
- 1 teaspoon ground cinnamon
- 1 cup maple syrup for serving

Directions:

1. Beat the eggs, then whisk in milk, vanilla, and cinnamon. Stir the bread into the egg mixture until well coated.
2. Pour the bread and eggs into a baking dish that fits inside the Instant Pot. Place a trivet inside the pot and add enough water to reach the top of the trivet. Place the baking dish on top of the trivet.
3. Close the lid and set the cook time for 25 minutes on high pressure.
4. Serve French toast with maple syrup.

Nutritional Information:

Calories - 403
Fat - 5.19 g
Carbohydrates - 32.47 g
Fiber - 1.2 g
Protein - 7.82 g

Honey Pounded Carrot Puree

Prep Time: 5 minutes
Cooking Time: 10 minutes
Serving: 6

Ingredients
- 1 and a ½ pound of roughly chopped up carrots
- 1 tablespoon of butter at room temperature
- 1 tablespoon of honey

- ¼ teaspoon of sea salt
- 1 cup of water
- Brown sugar if need

Directions:
1. Start off this recipe by preparing your carrots by cleaning them up, peeling them and drying them finely
2. Then cut them up in rough small sizes
3. Pour about 1 cup of water in your pressure cooker and place the steamer in your instant pot
4. Place the chopped up carrots in your steamer basket and close up the lid
5. Let it cook at high pressure 4 minutes and then quickly release the pressure
6. Remove the carrots and dry them yet again
7. Take a deep bowl and use an immersion hand blender to blend all of your steamed up carrots,
8. Pour the butter, sea salt and honey for flavor
9. Serve

Nutrition
- **Calories: 143**
- **Fat: 9g**
- **Carbohydrates: 16g**
- **Protein: 2g**

Yummy Enchilada Soup Of Chicken

Prep Time: 20 minutes
Cooking Time: 5 minutes
Serving: 5

Ingredients:

- 1 tablespoon of extra virgin olive oil
- 2 cups of sliced carrot
- 2 cups of sliced celery
- ½ a cup of diced yellow onion

- 2 minced garlic cloves
- S2 tablespoon of taco seasoning
- 1 and a ½ teaspoon of black pepper
- 1 jar of 18 ounce diced tomato
- 2 cups of cubed butternut squash
- 5 cups of chicken stock
- 2 pounds of boneless chicken breast
- 2 teaspoon of lime juice
- Cilantro, lime wedges for serving

Directions:

1. The first step for this recipe is to set your instant pot to sauté mode and on medium heat
2. Pour down the olive oil, celery, carrot, garlic, salt, taco seasoning and pepper and let them cook for about 5 minutes
3. After 5 minutes, toss in the remaining ingredients
4. Cancel the selected sauté mode and close down the lid. Let them cook for about 5 minutes by choosing the soup mode.
5. Once the timer is out, gently let the pressure release naturally
6. Transfer the chicken to a plate and shred it completely. Then transfer the shredded chicken to your instant pot
7. Gently pour the soup into separate bowls and serve them hot

Nutrition Information
- **Calories: 345**
- **Fat: 16.3g**
- **Carbohydrates: 6g**
- **Protein: 13.3g**

Cheesy Onion Crustless Milk Quiche

Ingredients
- Large eggs 6

- Milk 8 tbsp. (120ml)
- Salt 2g
- Ground black pepper 1g
- Bacon (cooked and crumbled) slices 4
- Cooked ground sausage 1 cup
- Diced ham ½ cup
- Green onions 2
- Shredded cheese 1 cup

Directions:
1. Put a metal trivet in the bottom of the electric pressure cooker pot and add 1 1/2 cups water.
2. in a large bowl whisk together the eggs, milk, salt, and pepper. Add bacon, sausage, ham, green onions, and cheese to a 1-quart soufflé dish and mix well. Pour egg mixture over to the top of the meat and stir to combine.
3. Loosely cover the soufflé dish with aluminum foil. Use an aluminum foil sling to place the dish on the trivet in the electric pressure cooking pot.
4. Select 30 minutes cook time. When timer beeps, turn off, wait 10 minutes, then use a quick pressure release.
5. Carefully lift out the dish and remove the foil. If desired, sprinkle the top of the quiche with additional cheese and broil until melted and lightly browned. Serve immediately.

Nutritional Information
- **Preparation Time: 50 minutes**
- **Total Servings: 4**
- **Calories: 291**
- **Fat: 18.8g**
- **Carbohydrates: 12.9g**
- **Protein: 17g**

Vanilla Berry Cake with Yogurt Glaze

Ingredients
For the Cake:
- Eggs 5

- Sugar ¼ cup
- Butter 28g
- Ricotta cheese ¾ cup
- Vanilla yogurt ¾ cup
- Vanilla extract 28g
- Wheat flour 1 cup
- Salt 2.5g
- Baking powder 10g
- Berry Compote ½ cup
- Sweet Yogurt Glaze
- Berry Compote

Sweet Yogurt Glaze:
- Yogurt ¼ cup
- Vanilla extract 3g
- Milk 5g
- Powdered sugar 28g

Directions:
1. Prepare the Berry Compote beforehand, so it is cold and thick. If used warm, it has a tendency to sink to the bottom of the pan. For the Breakfast Cake, generously grease a 6 cup Bundt pan with nonstick cooking spray.
2. Beat together the eggs and sugar until smooth. Add the butter, ricotta cheese, yogurt, and vanilla and mix until smooth.
3. In a separate bowl, whisk together the flour, salt, and baking powder. Combine with the egg mixture. Pour into the prepared Bundt pan.
4. Using 1/2 cup of Berry Compote, drop by tablespoons on top of the batter and swirl in with a knife.
5. Add 1 cup of water to the electric pressure cooker pot and place a trivet inside. Carefully place the Bundt pan on the trivet. Cook at high pressure for 25 minutes.
6. While the cake is cooking, make the Sweet Yogurt Glaze by whisking together the yogurt, vanilla, milk, and powdered sugar, set aside.
7. When electric pressure cooking is done, remove the pan from the electric pressure cooker. Let cool slightly. Loosen the sides of the cake from the pan and gently turn over onto a plate. Drizzle with Sweet Yogurt Glaze and serve warm.

Nutritional Information
- **Preparation Time: 35 minutes**
- **Total Servings: 6**
- **Calories: 440**

- **Fat: 17.5g**
- **Carbohydrates: 27.6g**
- **Protein: 4.5g**

Delicious Stuffed Vegetables

Prep Time: 5 minutes
Cooking Time: 16 minutes
Serving: 6

Ingredients
- 4 red bell peppers with their tops cut off
- 1 cup of white bean soaked up over night
- 1 cup of quinoa
- 1 cup of goat cheese
- 3 cups of vegetable broth
- 2 tablespoon of garlic powder

Directions:
1. Open up the lid of your pot and toss in the quinoa, beans, garlic powder and pour in the vegetable broth as well
2. Let it cook at high pressure for 8 minutes
3. Release the pressure naturally
4. Take your pepper and fill it up with bean and quinoa mixture
5. Wipe out your instant pot and place you're filled in pepper in it
6. Change your instant pot mode to warm and keep it like that for 6 minutes.
7. Take it out and serve hot

Nutrition Information:
- **Calories: 313**
- **Fat: 14g**
- **Carbohydrates: 9g**
- **Protein: 15g**

Delicious Apple and Maple Oatmeal

Prep Time: 5 minutes

Cooking Time: 18 minutes
Serving: 4

Ingredients
- ½ a cup of steel cut oats
- ½ a cup of chopped up dried apples
- ¼ cup of maple syrup
- ¼ cup of sliced almonds
- ¼ teaspoon of ground cinnamon
- ¼ teaspoon of salt

Directions:

1. Start off by opening up the lid of your pot and pour in the 2 and a quart cup of water
2. Toss in all of the ingredients and mix them thoroughly
3. Close up the lid of your pot and let it cook for 18 minutes at high pressure
4. Let the pressure release naturally
5. Open up the pot and serve

Nutrition Information:
- **Calories: 233**
- **Fat: 7g**
- **Carbohydrates: 37g**
- **Protein: 8g**

Chapter 3 INSTANT POT LUNCH RECIPES

Chili Garlic Chicken Recipes

Prep time: 4 minutes
Cooking time: 15 minutes
Servings: 2

Ingredients:

- Olive oil – 2 tbsp.
- Onion (minced) – 2
- Chicken breasts – 4 large
- Tomatoes – 3
- Chicken broth – 2 cups
- Garlic powder – ½ tbsp.
- Chili powder – 2 tbsp.
- Onion powder – 2 tbsp.
- Salsa (any) – 2 tbsp.
- Salt and pepper to taste

Directions:

1. Add olive oil with onion and chicken breasts to the instant pot. Let it cook for 5 minutes.
2. Add tomatoes, garlic powder. Chili powder. Onion powder with salsa in it. Add chicken broth and let it cook for 10 minutes.
3. When ready, sprinkle salt and pepper and serve!

Nutrition Information:
- **Calories: 90**
- **Fat: 8g**
- **Carbohydrates: 20g**
- **Protein: 25g**

Instant Pot Spaghetti

Total Time: 20 minutes
Serves: 6 Servings

Ingredients:
- 1 lb. ground beef
- 2 tbsp. extra virgin olive oil
- 8 oz. spaghetti noodles
- 2 cups water
- 1 jar spaghetti sauce
- 1/4 cup onion, diced

Directions:
1. Add oil, garlic, and onion in Instant Pot and select sauté. Cook onion until softened.
2. Add ground beef and stir well and cook ground beef until all pink is gone.
3. Add water, noodles, and spaghetti sauce. Stir well.
4. Seal pot with lid and cook on manual high pressure for 7 minutes.
5. Release pressure using quick release method then open lid carefully.
6. Stir well and serve.

Nutritional Information:
- **Calories 291**
- **Fat 10.2 g**
- **Carbohydrates 21.1 g**
- **Protein 27.3 g**

Sweet Chili Sesame Chicken

Serves: 4
Time: About 30 minutes

Ingredients:

6 boneless chicken thigh fillets
4 peeled and crushed garlic cloves
5 tablespoons hoisin sauce
5 tablespoons sweet chili sauce
½ cup chicken stock
1 chunk of peeled, grated fresh ginger
1 ½ tablespoons sesame seeds
1 tablespoon rice vinegar
1 tablespoon soy sauce

Directions:

1. Spread chicken thighs flat and place them into the Instant Pot.
2. Whisk garlic, ginger, chili sauce, hoisin, vinegar, sesame seeds, broth, and soy sauce into a sauce.
3. Pour over chicken and stir.
4. Select "Manual," and then 15 minutes on "high pressure."
5. When time is up, hit "Cancel" and wait for a natural pressure release.
6. When all the pressure is gone, open up the cooker and serve the chicken with rice.

Nutritional Information:

Total calories - 428
Protein - 30
Carbs - 52.9
Fiber - 1
Fat – 9

Butter Onion Chicken Dumplings

Serves: 8
Time: 55 minutes
Ingredients:

3 ½ cups chicken broth
8 chicken thighs
4 chopped celery stalks
4 tablespoons butter
3 peeled and chopped carrots
2 chopped onions
2 tablespoons cornstarch
½ cup flour
½ cup whole milk
Salt + pepper
1 ¾ cups flour
1 cup whole milk
¼ cup cornmeal
3 tablespoons melted butter
1 tablespoon baking powder
½ teaspoon salt
¼ teaspoon pepper

Directions:

1. Turn the Instant Pot to "Sauté" and add the butter from the first ingredient list.
2. Season chicken with salt, pepper, and coat in flour.
3. When the butter is hot, brown the chicken in batches on both sides.
4. Set chicken aside.
5. Add onions, celery, and carrots, and cook for 3 minutes.
6. Pour in chicken broth and add the browned chicken back to the pot.
7. Sprinkle with salt and pepper.
8. Lock the pot lid.
9. Hit "Manual" and cook for 11 minutes at "high pressure."
10. Look to the second ingredient list to make the dumplings.
11. Mix cornmeal, baking powder, flour, salt, and pepper.
12. Pour in the milk and melted butter and mix until just moistened.
13. When the Instant Pot timer goes off, hit "Cancel" and quick-release.
14. Pour in milk (from the first ingredient list) and mix.
15. In a separate bowl, mix ½ cup of the hot broth with cornstarch.
16. Pour back into the Instant Pot and stir to thicken.
17. Turn the pot back to "Sauté."

18. In tablespoons, put dumplings into the pot. They should be separated from each other and submerged in the liquid.

19. Cook for 12-15 minutes with the lid on, but not locked. Leave it on a little lopsided, so hot air can escape.

20. When the dumplings have grown twice their original size, they're done.

21. Take the meat off the chicken bones and add back to the pot.

22. Serve!

Nutritional Information:

Total calories - 543
Protein - 25
Carbs - 40
Fiber - 2
Fat - 14

Oregano Pork Chop With Rice

Prep Time: 5 minutes
Cooking Time: 10 minutes
Serving: 4
Ingredients

- 2 tablespoon of olive oil
- 4 pieces of ½ inch t hick bone-in pork loin or rib chops
- 1 large sized yellow onion
- 1 piece of 4 and a ½ ounce canned chopped up mild green Chile
- ½ a tablespoon of dried oregano
- 14 ounce can of diced up tomatoes
- 1 cup of long grain white rice
- 1 and a ½ cup of chicken broth

Directions:

1. The first step here is to set your pot to sauté mode and melt in 1 tablespoon of butter

2. Toss your chops into your pot and cook for 4 minutes

3. Transfer the chops to a plate and repeat to cook and brown the rest
4. Toss in your onions to the pot and let it cook for 4 minutes until aroma comes
5. Then stir in your oregano, chiles and keep stirring for more 1 minutes
6. Finally, stir in your diced up tomatoes and rice and pour in the chicken broth
7. Nestle the pork chops into your mixture
8. Lock up the lid and let it cook for about 10 minutes at high pressure
9. Quick release the pressure
10. Keep it there for 10 minutes to steam up your rice
11. Unlock and serve

Nutrition
- **Calories: 421**
- **Fat: 20g**
- **Carbohydrates: 45g**
- **Protein: 57g**

Garlic Potato Bacon Chowder

Prep Time: 5 minutes
Cooking Time: 10 minutes
Serving: 8

Ingredients
- 5 pound of russet potatoes peeled up and cubed
- 3 stalks of thinly sliced celery
- 1 small diced up onion
- 1 clove of minced up garlic
- 1 tablespoon of seasoning salt
- 1 teaspoon of ground black pepper
- 4 cups of chicken stock
- 1 pound of fried and roughly chopped up bacon
- 1 cup of heavy cream
- ½ a cup of whole milk

- Sour cream, shredded cheddar cheese and diced up green onion

Directions:
1. The first step is to toss in your potato into your inner pot
2. Toss in the celery, garlic, onion, pepper, salt, butter and seasoning and stir gently to combine
3. Toss in the bacon and pour the chicken stock now
4. Lock up the lid and let it cook for about 5 minutes
5. Quick release the pressure
6. Open up the lid and use a potato masher to crush the vegetable if you want, it should give you a nice smooth mash
7. Add some cream and whole milk and stir to mix
8. Serve hot with a topping of shredded cheddar and sliced up green onion

Nutrition Information:
- **Calories: 400**
- **Fat: 15g**
- **Carbohydrates: 49g**
- **Protein: 52g**

Cranberries Turkey Sauerkraut

Prep Time: 10 minutes
Cooking Time: 25 minutes
Serving: 3

Ingredients
- 2 cups of dried sauerkraut
- ¼ cup of raisins
- 3 peeled, chopped up and smashed clove of garlic
- 1 and ½ cup of frozen cranberries
- 1 small chopped up lemon with seeds removed
- 1 teaspoon of ground cinnamon
- ½ tablespoon of dried parsley flakes
- 1 teaspoon of dried thyme

- 1 teaspoon of sea salt
- 1 cup of apple cider (non-alcoholic)
- 1 teaspoon of arrowroot flour
- 2 teaspoon water

Directions:
1. The first step is to toss in the sauerkraut at the bottom of your instant pot and toss in the raisins and garlic
2. Place the turkey in your pot
3. Sprinkle in about 1 cup of cranberries and lemon over your turkey
4. Take a bowl and toss in the ground cinnamon, thyme, parsley flakes, and salt and apple cider. Mix them and pour the whole mixture into the pot
5. Close the lid and let it cook for 30 minutes making sure to set it to the Poultry setting
6. Once the cooking time is over, let pressure be released naturally
7. Gently pre-heat your oven broiler and place the turkey pieces in your oven proof casserole and broil for 5 minutes until a brown texture has appeared
8. Set the instant pot to sauté setting and toss in the other ½ up of cranberries
9. Combine the arrow root flour with water to make a slurry
10. Pour down the slurry into the pot sauce and let it simmer until thickened enough
11. Serve the turkey with the sauce and cranberries

Nutrition Information:
- **Calories: 148**
- **Fat: 7.1g**
- **Carbohydrates: 17.2g**
- **Protein: 2.6g**

Garlic Lamb Shanks with Wine

Ready in: 45 m
Prep 15 mins

Cook 30 mins
Number of Servings: 2

Ingredients:
10 cloves garlic (peeled)
4-ounces chicken broth
4-ounces Port wine
1 tbsp. olive oil
1 tbsp. tomato paste
2 pounds lamb shanks
1 tbsp. butter
1 tsp. balsamic vinegar
½ tsp. dried rosemary
Salt and pepper to taste

Directions:

1. First, cut the excess fat from the lamb shanks. Season the shanks with a little bit of salt and pepper.
2. Heat the olive oil in your pressure cooker. Place the shanks in the bottom of your pot and brown all sides of the meat. If you're preparing a double or triple batch, you should brown the meat in a frying pan.
3. When the meat is almost browned, add the peeled garlic cloves. Cook until the garlic cloves are slightly browned. But, don't let the cloves burn.
4. Next, add the chicken broth and remaining ingredients – except for the butter and vinegar. Stir the ingredients until the tomato paste dissolves.
5. Close the lid on your cooker and bring to full pressure. This should be 15-pounds. Reduce the heat and cook for 30-minutes.
6. Allow the pressure to naturally release and then open the lid and remove the lamb shanks.
7. Heat the remaining liquid to a boil, uncovered, and cook for about 5 minutes or until the sauce has thickened.
8. Whisk the butter and vinegar into the sauce. Pour the sauce over the lamb shanks and serve.

Nutrition Information:
Calories: 620
Total Fat: 25.8
Total Carbohydrate: 17.3
Dietary Fiber: 0.8

Protein: 122.7

Tender Corned Beef

Ready in: 1 h, 10 m
Prep 10 mins
Cook 1 hr.
Number of Servings: 3

Ingredients:
1 bay leaf
1 clove garlic
1.5 pounds corned beef brisket
1 tsp. pickling spices
Water

Directions:
1. Start by placing the corned beef in the pressure cooker. Depending on the size of the corned beef, you may need to cut it in half.
2. Add the seasoning packet that came with the beef. Next, add the bay leaf, garlic clove, and pickling spices. You should add just enough water to cover the top of the corned beef.
3. Turn the burner on and then bring the mixture to a boil. Place the lid on the cooker, along with the rocker. Continue cooking until the rocker starts to rock.
4. Adjust the temperature to medium to keep the rocker moving in a medium to low rocking motion. Cook for 60-minutes and then turn off the burner.
5. Allow the pressure to escape naturally. Carefully open the lid to the cooker and remove the beef. Place the corned beef on a serving platter and allow to cool for five minutes. Cut the brisket into thin slices, cutting against the grain. Serve and enjoy. If you'd like, you can pour the liquids over the brisket.

Nutrition Information:
Calories: 454.6
Total Fat: 24.5

Total Carbohydrate: 1.9
Protein: 31.8

Parmesan Chicken Piccata

Ready in: 42 m
Prep 10 mins
Cook 32 mins
Servings: 6

Ingredients:
4-ounces flour
4 tbsp. olive oil
4 shallots
3 crushed garlic cloves
6-ounces chicken broth
6 chicken breast halves
4 tbsp. lemon juice
1 tbsp. sherry wine
2 tsp. salt
¼ tsp. white pepper
1 tsp. dried basil
8-ounces pimento-stuffed olive
4 tbsp. sour cream
1 tbsp. flour
¼ cup parmesan cheese
1 thinly sliced lemon

Directions:
1. First, dust the chicken pieces with the flour. The easiest way to complete this step is to place the flour in a plastic bag. Place several chicken pieces in the bag, seal the bag, and then shake. Repeat until you've coated all the chicken pieces.
2. Heat the oil in your pressure cooker. Add several chicken pieces to the cooker. Sauté in the oil until all sides are browned. You should use tongs to turn the chicken. Continue browning all the pieces and set them aside on a plate.

3. After you've finished browning the chicken, add the shallots and garlic. Sauté until the onions become translucent. Add the lemon juice, broth, sherry, basil, olives, salt, and pepper. Thoroughly stir everything together.
4. Place the chicken back in the pressure cooker. Close the lid and heat to medium-high heat. The steam should reach high pressure. Reduce the heat to maintain pressure and then cook for another 10 minutes. Next, release the pressure according to the instructions for your pressure cooker.
5. Stir this mixture and then transfer to a serving platter. Cover the chicken to keep the chicken hot.
6. In a medium mixing bowl, combine the sour cream and starch with a whisk. Stir this mixture into the cooking liquid. Mix and then cook over medium heat for 60-seconds. Stir the entire time.
7. Spoon this sauce over the chicken and transfer to serving plates. Sprinkle parmesan cheese and lemon slices over the chicken and serve.

Nutrition Information:
Calories: 317.9
Total Fat: 17.2
Total Carbohydrate: 10.9
Protein: 18.4

Delicious Spicy Pork Shoulder and Peanut Stew

Prep Time: 5 minutes
Cooking Time: 25 minutes
Serving: 4
Ingredients
- 14 ounce of diced tomatoes
- ½ a cup of crunchy natural style peanut butter
- 1 tablespoon of packed fresh oregano leaves chopped up
- ¼ teaspoon of cayenne
- ¼ teaspoon of grated nutmeg
- ¼ teaspoon of salt
- 2 tablespoon of peanut oil
- 2 pound of boneless skinless pork shoulder, trimmed up by cutting the large bits of fat and cut into 2 inch pieces
- 1 large sized yellow onion, halved and thinly sliced

- 1 tablespoon of minced fresh ginger
- 2 teaspoon of minced garlic
- ¼ cup of dry white wine
- 6 medium carrots in 2 inch pieces
- 2 bay leaves
- 2 tablespoon of fresh lime juice

Directions:

1. Start off by whisking in your peanut butter, tomatoes, oregano, nutmeg, cayenne, and salt in a medium sized bowl until the butter has become loosened
2. Put your Instant Pot in Sauté mode and heat up your oil. Add in the meat in batches and brown for 6 minutes
3. Repeat for all of the meat
4. Then, toss in the onion and ginger, making sure to keep stirring it often for about 4 minutes
5. Toss in the garlic and cook for another 10 seconds
6. Pour in the wine then and scrape off the browned bits in the bottom of your pot
7. Stir in your tomato mixture and return the pork to your pot along with any juices on the plate, alongside the carrot and bay leaves
8. Stir and lock up the lid and cook for 40 minutes at high pressure
9. Release the pressure naturally
10. Unlock, discard the bay leave and serve with a dash of lime juice

Nutrition Information:
- **Calories: 405**
- **Fat: 20g**
- **Carbohydrates: 14g**
- **Protein: 26g**

Instant Pot Chicken Noodle Soup

Prep Time: 10 minutes
Cooking Time: 8minutes
Number of Servings: 4

Ingredients:
- 2 boneless chicken thighs, cubed
- 1 onion, diced
- 2 carrots, sliced
- 1 celery stalk, sliced
- 3 cups chicken stock
- 1/2 teaspoon salt
- 1/2 teaspoon black pepper
- 1 bay leaf
- 2 cups uncooked egg noodles

Directions:

1. Combine all ingredients in Instant Pot. Close lid and set cooking time for 8 minutes.
2. Discard bay leaf. Serve hot.

Nutritional Information:

Calories - 311
Fat - 17.31 g
Carbohydrates - 14.68 g
Fiber - 1.3 g
Protein - 20.21 g

Spicy Chicken Pasta In A Pot

Prep Time: 5 minutes
Cooking Time: 8 minutes
Serving: 4

Ingredients
- 1 pound of skinless chicken breast cut finely into ½ inch pieces
- 14 ounce of diced up tomatoes
- 1 and a ½ cup of chicken broth
- 1 cup of drained and rinsed up canned pinto beans

- 8 ounce of dried whole wheat ziti
- 4 and a ½ ounce of chopped up mild green chiles
- 1/3 cup of loosely packed and chopped up cilantro leaves
- 1 tablespoon of ground cumin
- ½ teaspoon of salt
- ½ teaspoon of ground black pepper

Directions:
1. This recipe is very straightforward and will required you to only toss in all of the ingredients into the inner pot of your instant pot
2. Lock up the lid firmly
3. Let it cook for 8 minutes at high pressure
4. Wait for about 10 minutes to release the pressure naturally
5. Open up the pot and serve hot
6. Make sure to stir it gently before serving

Nutrition Information: Calories: 559; Fat: 15G; Carbohydrates: 27G; Protein: 39g

Mushroom Tender Pork Chops

Ready in: 30 m
Prep 10 mins
Cook 20 mins
Servings: 3-6

Ingredients:
3 tbsp. olive oil
1.5 cups water
2 tsp. chicken bouillon powder
6 pork chops
10.5-ounces cream of mushroom soup
12-ounces sour cream
1 tbsp. fresh parsley

Directions:
1. Heat the oil in your pressure cooker over medium heat until the oil is hot.

2. Begin browning the pork chops on both sides. Don't fully cook the chops. You just want to lightly brown both sides. Cook two or three pork chops at a time, depending on the size of your cooker. Place the browned pork chops on a plate.

3. When you're finished browning the pork chops, add the water and chicken bouillon powder. You may need to scrape the bottom of the pan to remove pieces of the pork chops. Stir the powder and water together.

4. Add the pork chops back to the pressure cooker. Close the lid on the cooker and heat over medium heat.

5. Cook the pork chops for 8 minutes and then turn off the heat. Allow the pressure to release naturally.

6. When you don't see any more steam, carefully open the lid. Remove the pork chops, setting them on a platter. Cover the platter to keep the pork chops hot.

7. Add the soup and heat over medium-low heat. Add the sour cream, using the whisk. Heat over low heat. Pay attention to the heat. Don't allow the liquid to boil, as the sour cream will curdle.

8. Stir in the parsley and then pour the sauce over the pork chops. If the sauce is too thin, then add 8-ounces of bouillon before adding the soup. You can garnish the plates with additional parsley. Serve and enjoy!

Nutrition Information:
Calories: 720
Total Fat: 27g
Total Carbohydrate: 10.3g
Protein: 66.7g

Yummy Pot Roast

Ready in: 1 h, 15 m
Prep 15 mins
Cook 1 hr.
Number of Servings: 6-8

Ingredients:
2 crushed garlic cloves
1 tbsp. olive oil
4-ounces beef broth

4-ounces tomato paste
4-ounces water
3.5-4 pounds chuck roast
1 onion (peeled and chopped)
2 tbsp. brown sugar
½ tsp. dry mustard
¼ tsp. sweet paprika
4 tbsp. lemon juice
4 tbsp. apple cider vinegar
1 tbsp. Worcestershire sauce

Directions:
1. First, rub the meat with the crushed garlic. You should use one garlic clove for each side of the roast.
2. Heat your pressure cooker to medium-high heat and brown the roast on all sides. If the meat begins to smoke, then the heat is too high. You don't want to burn the outside of the roast. After you've browned the meat, remove the roast and set on a platter.
3. Add the oil to the cooker, along with the onion. Cook until the onion begins to appear translucent. Then, add the tomatoes paste, beef broth, and water. Stir these ingredients together.
4. Next, add the brown sugar, dry mustard, and paprika. Stir these ingredients into the mixture and then add the cider vinegar, Worcestershire sauce, and lemon juice.
5. Scrape the bottom of the cooker in order to remove pieces of meat. Thoroughly stir the ingredients until the dry ingredients have dissolved and the mixture begins to boil.
6. Place the roast back in the cooker. Use tongs or a large fork to turn the roast, so that you can coat all sides of the roast with the sauce.
7. Close the lid on the cooker and bring to high pressure with medium-high heat. Reduce heat to maintain the pressure.
8. Cook for 60 to 75-minutes. For a 3-pound roast, cook for 60-minutes. For a 4-pound roast, cook for 75-minutes.
9. Remove from heat and allow the steam to release naturally. Carefully remove the lid and check the meat.
10. Remove the meat from the cooker and slice on a serving platter. Use a spoon to scoop sauce over the roast. Garnish with parsley and serve.

Nutrition Information:
Calories: 385.9

Total Fat: 15.3
Saturated Fat: 6.5
Total Carbohydrate: 10.7
Protein: 49.3

Indian Chicken Curry

Serves: 6
Time: 15 minutes + 1 hour marinade

Ingredients:

6 boneless chicken breasts
2 tablespoons olive oil
1 chopped tomato
1 yellow onion
2 teaspoons garam masala powder
1 teaspoon grated ginger
1 teaspoon chili powder
1 teaspoon coriander seeds
Salt
Juice of 1 lemon
2 teaspoons ginger powder
2 teaspoons coriander powder
2 teaspoons garlic powder
1 ¼ teaspoons chili powder
½ teaspoon turmeric
Salt

Directions:

1. Mix the ingredients in the second list and rub over the chicken.
2. Place in a bag and chill in the fridge for an hour.
3. When ready, heat oil in the Instant Pot on "sauté."
4. Toss in the coriander seeds and heat them till a few pop open.
5. Add the chopped onion and cook till they become clear.
6. Add in the garam masala, coriander powder, chili powder, garlic, and ginger.
7. After a few minutes, add chopped tomatoes until they soften.

8. Take out the chicken and sauté to brown them a little.
9. Close the pot lid.
10. Choose "Poultry" and adjust to 8 minutes on "high pressure."
11. When ready, quick-release the pressure.
12. Serve with the tomatoes and onions, and rice.

Nutritional Information

Total calories - 234
Protein - 19.9
Carbs - 5.7
Fiber - 3
Fat - 12.7

Tasty Chickpea Curry

Serves: 3-4
Time: About 35 minutes + overnight soak

Ingredients:
2 cups dry chickpeas
1 can diced tomatoes
1 big, diced onion
4-6 tablespoons olive oil
2 tablespoons masala
2-4 tablespoons lemon juice
1 tablespoon garlic paste
1 tablespoon ginger paste
1 teaspoon turmeric
½ teaspoon garam masala
Coriander leaves
Salt

Directions:

1. Soak the chickpeas in water in a bowl on the counter overnight.
2. The next day, pour 2 cups of water into your Instant Pot and hit "sauté."
3. When the water is boiling, add chickpeas.
4. Boil for 10 minutes.

5. When time is up, pour the peas and water into another bowl.
6. Heat oil in the pot.
7. Add garam masala and diced onion.
8. When clear, add turmeric.
9. Toss in ginger and garlic paste, and stir.
10. Add tomatoes and cook for a few minutes.
11. Add chholey masala.
12. Pour in chickpeas with their water.
13. Sprinkle in a little salt.
14. Close and secure the lid.
15. Hit "Manual" and then adjust to 20 minutes on "high pressure."
16. When the timer beeps, hit "Cancel" and wait for the pressure to reduce naturally.
17. Add coriander leaves and lemon juice before serving.

Nutritional Information:

Total calories - 177
Protein - 5.9g
Carbs – 4g
Fiber - 3.2
Fat -5g

Delight Whole Chicken

Ready in: 30 m
Prep 5 mins
Cook 25 mins
Servings: 4-6

Ingredients:
2 tbsp. olive oil
12-ounces chicken broth
2 pounds whole chicken

Dash of salt and pepper

Directions:

1. Rinse the chicken and then pat dry. Season the chicken with a dash of salt and pepper.
2. Heat the oil in your pressure cooker and then brown the chicken in the hot oil. Brown all sides of the chicken, being careful not to burn it. Remove the chicken from the cooker.
3. Place your rack in your pressure cooker and then set the chicken on the rack. Carefully pour the chicken broth around the chicken.
4. Close the lid on your pressure cooker and increase the pressure. Maintain pressure and then cook for 25-minutes.
5. Use the quick release method to release pressure and steam from your cooker. Carefully remove the chicken and place on a platter.
6. Pour the juices from the pot into bowl. Serve the chicken with the juices. You can pour this sauce over the chicken before serving, to help moisten the chicken, or add a little of the juice on each plate. Serve and enjoy!

Nutrition Information:
Calories: 375
Total Fat: 20
Total Carbohydrate: 0
Protein: 25.1

Weekend Treat Baby Back Ribs

Ready in: 1 h, 5 m
Prep 15 mins
Cook 50 mins
Servings: 4-6

Ingredients:
2 tbsp. olive oil
½ tsp. salt

½ tsp. onion powder
¼ tsp. black pepper
3 pounds beef back ribs
¼ tsp. garlic powder
¼ tsp. paprika
8-ounces beer
12-ounces barbecue sauce

Directions:

1. First, cut the ribs into serving pieces. Mix the spices together. This will create a dry rub. Rub the dry rub into the ribs.
2. Heat the oil in the bottom of your pressure cooker. Add the ribs. Brown all sides of the ribs in the heated oil. Set the ribs aside.
3. Place a cooking rack in your pressure cooker. Add the beer to the bottom of the pan. Place the ribs on the rack.
4. Close the lid and bring to high heat and then reduce the heat. Cook for 35 minutes.
5. Allow the pressure cooker to naturally release pressure.
6. Remove the rack from the pressure cooker. Add the barbecue sauce and heat until it begins to simmer. Simmer for 10 to 15 minutes and then serve immediately. Ribs always taste great with something cold, such as coleslaw or potato salad.

Nutrition Information:
Calories: 228.3
Total Fat: 7 g
Saturated Fat: 0.9
Total Carbohydrate: 10g
Protein: 0.4g

Classic Sweet-Spicy Meatloaf

Serves: 4
Time: About 50 minutes

Ingredients:
1 pound lean ground beef
⅔ Cup bread crumbs
⅔ Cup diced onion
6 sliced black olives
1 egg white
2 tablespoons ketchup
2 fresh, chopped basil leaves
1 teaspoon minced garlic
½ teaspoon salt
Black pepper
¼ cup ketchup
1 tablespoon brown sugar
1 tablespoon spicy brown mustard

Directions:

1. Prepare a round, one-quart dish with a bit of olive oil.
2. Mix everything in the first ingredient list and form a loaf in the dish.
3. In a separate bowl, mix the brown sugar, ketchup, and spicy brown mustard together.
4. Brush on top of the meatloaf.
5. Cover the dish tightly with foil.
6. Pour one cup of water into the pressure cooker and lower in the trivet.
7. Place the meatloaf dish on top and close the Instant Pot lid.
8. Select "Meat/Stew," and then 45 minutes.
9. When the beep sounds, quick-release.
10. Carefully take out the hot dish.
11. holding the meat in place, pour out any excess liquid.
12. Rest the meat before serving.

Nutritional Information:

Total calories - 261
Protein - 25
Carbs - 15.2
Fiber - 0
Fat - 7.5

Instant Pot Orange Roast

Serves: 8
Time: About 50 minutes

Ingredients:
4 pounds bottom roast cut into cubes
1 cup beef broth
5 minced garlic cloves
1 peeled and chopped Granny Smith apple
1 thumb of grated ginger
½ cup soy sauce
Juice of one big orange
2 tablespoons olive oil
Salt and pepper to taste

Directions:
1. Season the roast with salt and pepper.
2. Turn on your Instant Pot to "sauté."
3. When hot, pour in the olive oil and brown the roast all over.
4. Move the meat to a plate.
5. Pour in the beef broth and scrape any stuck bits of meat.
6. Pour in soy sauce and stir.
7. Put the roast back into the pot.
8. Arrange the cut apple, garlic, and ginger on top.
9. Pour in the orange juice.
10. Close the pressure cooker lid.
11. Select "Manual" and then 45 minutes on "high pressure."
12. Hit "Cancel" and quick-release the pressure when the timer beeps.
13. Serve!

Nutritional Information:

Total calories - 492
Protein – 46g
Carbs – 3g
Fat – 17g

Simple Delicious Chicken Soup

Serves: 4
Time: 50 minutes

Ingredients:
16-ounces water
16-ounces chicken stock
2 frozen, boneless chicken breasts
4 medium-sized potatoes
Three peeled carrots
½ big diced onion
Salt and pepper

Directions:

1. Put everything into the pressure cooker, including salt and pepper.
2. Turn on your Instant Pot by selecting Manual, and then 35 minutes on "high pressure."
3. When time is up, turn off the cooker and wait 15 minutes for the pressure to come down by itself.
4. Carefully open the cooker, stir, and serve!

Nutritional Information:

Total calories - 72
Protein – 5g
Carbs – 4g
Fat – 2g

Tender English Lamb Shanks

Ready in: 40 m
Prep 10 mins
Cook 30 mins
Servings: 4-6

Ingredients:
4-6 lamb shanks
4 tbsp. flour
3 thickly sliced carrots
1 chopped onion
1 crushed garlic clove
1 tbsp. freshly chopped oregano
1 tsp. grated lemon rind
6-ounces red wine
4 tbsp. vegetable stock
8 tsp. cold water – helps thicken the gravy
Salt and pepper to taste

Directions:
1. First, peel the potatoes and cut into quarters. Then, coat the shanks in flour. The easiest way to coat the shanks is to add flour to a large freezer bag. Place the shanks in the bag and shake. Shake to remove any excess flour.
2. Heat half of the oil in the bottom of your pressure cooker. Then, brown the shanks. You should be able to add two shanks at a time. After browning the shanks, set them aside.
3. Add the remaining oil to the bottom of your pressure cooker. Next, add the onions, garlic, and carrots. Sauté the vegetables for 5 minutes while stirring occasionally.
4. Add the tomatoes, oregano, and lemon rind. Then, stir in the wine and stock. Bring the mixture to a boil while stirring. Boil for a few minutes.

5. Place the lamb shanks back in the cooker and season with salt and pepper. Use a spoon to spoon some of the liquid and veggies over the lamb shanks.
6. Close the lid to your pressure cooker and bring to high pressure. You may need to adjust the heat to stabilize the pressure. Cook for 25 minutes.
7. Allow the pressure to release naturally and then check the meat. It should be very tender and falling off the bone. If needed, you can cook for a few more minutes.
8. If the gravy is too thin, you can thicken it by adding more flour and stirring until smooth.
9. Serve while still hot. You can serve the gravy on the side or pour it over the dish.

Nutrition Information:
Calories: 620
Total Fat: 25g
Saturated Fat: 15
Total Carbohydrate: 15
Dietary Fiber: 2.9
Protein: 53.7

Garlic Butter Steamed Crab Legs

Serves: 4
Time: 15 minutes

Ingredients:
2 pounds crab legs, fresh or frozen
1 cup water
4 tablespoons salted butter
1 halved lemon
1 big minced garlic clove
1 teaspoon olive oil

Directions:
1. Pour water into the Instant Pot and insert the steamer basket.

2. Put the crab legs inside and lock the lid.
3. Hit "Steam" and 3 minutes at "high pressure" for fresh, and 4 minutes for frozen.
4. Take a saucepan and heat olive oil on the stove.
5. Toss in the garlic and cook for 1 minute.
6. Add the butter and stir to melt.
7. Turn off the heat and squeeze in lots of lemon juice.
8. When the Instant Pot timer beeps, hit "Cancel" and quick-release.
9. Serve the crab and dipping sauce!

Nutritional Information:

Total calories - 346
Protein - 44
Carbs - 2
Fiber - 0
Fat – 7

Mustard Onion Smoked Brisket

Prep Time: 5 minutes
Cooking Time: 50 minutes
Serving: 2

Ingredients

- 1 and a half pound of beef brisket
- 2 tablespoon of coconut sugar
- 2 teaspoon of salt
- 1 teaspoon of black pepper
- 1 teaspoon of mustard powder
- 1 teaspoon of onion powder
- ½ teaspoon of smoked paprika
- 2 cup of chicken stock
- 1 tablespoon of liquid smoke

- 3 fresh sprigs of thyme

Directions:

1. Keep the briskets in the fridge and remove them about 30 minutes before cooking
2. Firstly you are going to create your spice blend by combining the salt, pepper, onion powder, mustard powder, smoked paprika and coconut sugar
3. Using the mixture, gently coat up all sides of the meat nicely
4. Turn on your instant pot and set it to sauté mode. After about 2-3 minutes use your oil to grease the bottom and toss in the seasoned briskets.
5. Let it brown on all sides and pour in the broth and thyme
6. Once browned, close down the lid and let it cook for about 50 minutes under high pressure
7. Release the pressure naturally and serve hot
8. If you are looking for a thicker sauce, then remove the brisket and sauté the sauce for about 10 minutes more

Nutrition Information:
- **Calories: 71**
- **Fat: 5g**
- **Carbohydrates: 2g**
- **Protein: 5g**

Rosemary Bell Pepper Tender Beef

Ready in: 55 mins
Prep 10 mins
Cook 45 mins
Servings: 5

Ingredients:
Olive oil
Italian dressing

2 or 3 pounds sirloin roast
3 garlic cloves
14.5-ounces canned diced tomatoes
2-ounces wine
2/3-cup of finely diced Mirepoix
1/3-cup of chopped frozen bell pepper
½ tsp. dry oregano
½ tsp. rosemary
½ tsp. kosher salt
¼ tsp. ground black pepper
1 tbsp. flour

Directions:
1. Bring the heat on your pressure cooker as high as it will go. Add oil and then sear all sides of the roast.
2. Next, add the remaining ingredients, except for the flour.
3. Close the lid on your pressure cooker and cook for 45 minutes.
4. Use the quick-release or cold-water release method to reduce pressure. Remove the meat and set on a plate.
5. In a small bowl, mix the flour with a dash of cold water. Add this paste to the hot liquid to thicken the sauce. Continue heating the sauce while stirring until it reaches the right consistency.
6. You can also taste test the sauce and add more seasoning. If you want a smoother sauce, you can blend in your blender or a food processor. But, you'll need to allow the sauce to cool and then reheat after blending.
7. Serve the roast with the sauce on the side.

Nutrition Information:
Calories: 298
Total Fat: 7g
Total Carbohydrate: 4.9g
Dietary Fiber: 1
Protein: 5g

Ginger Cola Dipped Chicken Wings

Prep Time: 5 minutes
Cooking Time: 25 minutes
Serving: 6

Ingredients

- 1 and a ½ pound of chicken wings
- 4 crushed cloves of garlic
- 1 stalk of green onion
- 1 tablespoon of sliced ginger
- 200 ml regular coca cola
- 2 tablespoon of light soy sauce
- 1 tablespoon of dark soy sauce
- 1 tablespoon of Chinese white rice wine
- 1 tablespoon of peanut oil

Directions:

1. Start off by heating up your instant pot by putting it in the Sauté mode and pour about 1 tablespoon of peanut oil
2. Toss in the ginger, garlic and green onion and Sauté them nicely.
3. Toss in the chicken wings then and stir fry them for about 2 minutes
4. Once the edges of your chicken starts to brown up, pour in your coca cola and deglaze the bottom with a wooden spoon
5. Add in the sauces specified above alongside the rice wine and mix well
6. Close up the lid and cook at high pressure for about 5 minutes and release the pressure naturally afterwards
7. Season as needed and serve

Nutrition Information:
- **Calories: 309**
- **Fat: 15g**
- **Carbohydrates: 12g**
- **Protein: 18g**

Spiced Pork Loin Chops With Pear

Prep Time: 5 minutes
Cooking Time: 12 minutes
Serving: 4

Ingredients
- 2 tablespoon of unsalted butter
- 4 pieces of ½ inch thick bone-in pork loin or rib chops
- ½ a teaspoon of salt
- ½ a teaspoon of ground black pepper
- 2 medium sized yellow onions peeled up and cut into 8 wedges
- 2 large pears, peeled up, cored and cut into 4 wedges
- ½ cup of unsweetened pear, cider
- ½ a teaspoon of ground allspice
- Several dashes of hot pepper

Directions:
1. The first step here is to set your pot to sauté mode and melt in 1 tablespoon of butter
2. Toss your chops into your pot and cook for 4 minutes
3. Transfer the chops to a plate and repeat to cook and brown the rest
4. Toss in your onion and pears in your pot and let it cook for 3 minutes for until the pears are lightly browned
5. Pour in the cider the and stir the allspice, pepper sauce
6. Nestle the chops in your sauce
7. Lock up the lid and let it cook for about 10 minutes at high pressure
8. Quick release the pressure
9. Keep it there for 10 minutes to steam up your rice
10. Unlock and serve

Nutrition Information:
- **Calories: 318**
- **Fat: 19g**
- **Carbohydrates: 4g**
- **Protein: 31g**

Rosemary Lamb Chops

Ready in: 50 m
Prep 10 mins
Cook 40 mins
Servings: 4

Ingredients:
4-ounces chopped green pepper
2 sliced medium onions
6 lamb chops (large size; trimmed)
Salt and pepper to taste
1 tbsp. fresh rosemary
12-ounces tomato juice or 14-ounce-can chopped tomatoes

Directions:
1. Add a small amount of oil to the bottom of your pressure cooker. Add the pork chops and fry just until brown.
2. Next, add the pepper and onions. Stir until the onions begin to soften. Add the remaining ingredients and stir to combine.
3. Close the lid to your pressure cooker. Bring to pressure and cook for 15 minutes. Allow the pressure to drop and remove the lid.
4. If the sauce is too thin, continue heating, uncovered, while stirring. The sauce should thicken as it cooks. Remove the pork chops and trim the fat. You can serve immediately or store the pork chops in your fridge. If you store until the next day, it will be easier to remove the fat.

Nutrition Information:
Calories: 479.8
Total Fat: 24g
Total Carbohydrate: 9.1
Dietary Fiber: 1.4
Protein: 24.6

Instant Pot Beefy Lasagna

Serves: 6
Time: About 30 minutes

Ingredients:
2 pounds ricotta cheese
1 pound of ground beef
24-ounces pasta sauce
8-ounces of no-boil lasagna noodles
1 package shredded mozzarella cheese
2 big eggs
¼ cup water
⅓ Cup grated Parmesan
1 diced onion
1 tablespoon olive oil
2 teaspoons minced garlic
1 teaspoon Italian seasoning
Salt and pepper to taste

Directions:

1. Pour olive oil in your Instant Pot and heat until it starts to smoke.
2. Quickly add the ground beef, onions, salt, and pepper.
3. When the meat is brown and onions clear, pour in the water and pasta sauce.
4. Stir before pouring out into a bowl.
5. in a separate bowl, mix the ricotta, garlic, Italian seasoning, eggs, Parmesan, salt, and pepper together.
6. Fill the pressure cooker with ¼ inch of water.
7. Layer ⅕ of the beef mixture into the bottom before adding the noodles.
8. Pour in ⅓ of the ricotta mixture, and then more beef sauce.
9. Top with noodles, and keep going until you've used everything. The last layer should be beef sauce.
10. Close the Instant Pot lid.
11. Select "Manual," and then 7 minutes on "high pressure."
12. When the beep sounds, hit "Cancel" and quick-release the pressure.
13. Open the lid and sprinkle on the mozzarella.

14. Cool for a few minutes before serving.

Nutritional Information:

Total calories - 408
Protein - 25.1
Carbs - 27.4
Fiber - 2.6
Fat - 22.1

Apple Cider Cabbage Corned Beef

Serves: 6
Time: 1 hour, 30 minutes

Ingredients:
3 ½ pounds rinsed corned beef
1 ½ cups unsweetened apple cider
8 whole cloves
6 big carrots, cut in half widthwise
One, 4-inch cinnamon stick
1 big cored green cabbage, cut into 6 wedges
¼ cup honey mustard

Directions:

1. Pour cider and put the cloves and cinnamon stick into the Instant Pot.
2. Lower in the steamer basket.
3. Put the corned beef on top.
4. Rub honey mustard on top.
5. Lock the lid.
6. Select "Manual," and then "high pressure" for 80 minutes.
7. When time is up, hit "Cancel" and wait for the pressure to come down by itself.
8. Open the lid and move the meat to a cutting board.
9. Take out the rack as well as the cloves and cinnamon stick.

10. Put the carrots and cabbage into the pot.
11. Lock the lid.
12. Hit "Manual," and then "high pressure" for just 8 minutes.
13. When time is up, press "Cancel" and quick-release.
14. Carve the meat into slices.
15. Serve in bowls with the meat, cabbage, carrots, and broth.

Nutritional Information:
Total calories: 473
Protein: 59
Carbs: 14
Fiber: 4.6
Fat: 19

Garlic Oxtail and Vegetables Casserole

Ready in: 3 h, 30 m
Prep 30 mins
Cook 3 hrs.
Servings: 6-8

Ingredients:
1 medium chopped onion
1 large carrot
1 tbsp. brown sugar
1 can of tomatoes
3 oxtails (cut up)
6-ounces canned tomato paste
3 garlic cloves
Beef stock
Bouquet Garni
Salt and pepper to taste

Directions:

1. Heat a small amount of oil in you pressure cooker. Brown the meat on all sides. Next, add the onion and carrot. Stir this mixture into the oil. Then, add the crushed garlic and stock. Add the tomatoes, paste, sugar, bouquet Garni, and the salt and pepper.
2. Close the lid. Bring to medium pressure and medium heat. Cook for 30 minutes.
3. Allow the pressure to drop naturally. Remove from heat. Allow the mixture to cool. When you open the lid, skim off the top layer of fat.
4. Use a little bit of corn flour mixed with water to thicken the soup. The meat should fall off the bones. If the meat doesn't slide off, then it's not done cooking. Cook for another 5 minutes until the meat is tender and falling from the bone.
5. Serve with steamed vegetables or mashed potatoes.

Nutrition Information:
Calories: 55.2
Total Fat: 4.3g
Total Carbohydrate: 7g
Dietary Fiber: 2.5
Protein: 10g

Mushroom Beef Stroganoff

Prep Time: 10 minutes
Cooking Time: 25 minutes
Servings: 4

Ingredients:
- 2 pounds steak tips, cubed
- 1 teaspoon salt
- 1/2 teaspoon black pepper
- 1 tablespoon butter
- 1 onion, finely chopped
- 1 cup mushrooms, sliced
- 1/2 teaspoon thyme
- 1/2 teaspoon tarragon
- 1/2 cup white wine
- 1 cup beef broth
- 1/2 cup sour cream

Directions:
1. Season steak tips with salt and pepper. Melt butter in Instant Pot set to Sauté mode and add beef. Brown on all sides, then remove to a plate.
2. Add onion and cook until translucent. Add mushrooms and cook until tender. Add thyme and tarragon and coast 30 seconds.
3. Deglaze the pot with white wine, then add broth. Replace meat in the pot. Close lid and set cooking time for 20 minutes.
4. Use quick release to remove the steam. Stir in sour cream. Serve over egg noodles or with boiled potatoes.

Nutritional Information:
Calories - 539
Fat - 22g
Carbohydrates - 9.43 g
Protein - 55.63 g

Instant Pot Hearty Beef Stew

Prep Time: 10 minutes
Cooking Time: 45 minutes
Servings: 2

Ingredients:

- 1 pound chuck beef
- 1 teaspoon salt
- 1/2 teaspoon black pepper
- 2 tablespoons butter
- 1 onion, chopped
- 2 carrots, sliced
- 1 celery stalk, sliced
- 1 teaspoon thyme
- 1/2 teaspoon rosemary
- 2 tablespoons flour
- 1 tablespoon tomato paste
- 2 cups beef broth

- 1/2 pound potatoes, chopped

Directions:

1. Season the beef with salt and pepper. Melt the butter in the Instant Pot on Sauté mode. Brown beef in butter. Remove to a plate.
2. Add onion, carrots, and celery to the pot. Cook until onion is translucent, then add thyme and rosemary and toast 30 seconds. Add flour and stir until everything is well-coated.
3. Add tomato paste, then beef broth and scrape off anything stuck to the bottom of the pot. Add potatoes and replace beef in pot.
4. Close lid and set cooking time to 35 minutes on high pressure. Season to taste with salt and pepper.

Nutritional Information:

Calories - 570
Fat – 21.5 g
Carbohydrates - 18 g
Fiber - 4.5 g
Protein - 50g

Tasty Beef Brisket

Prep Time: 10 minutes
Cooking Time: 1 hour
Servings: 6

Ingredients:

- 1 3-pound brisket
- 1 teaspoon salt
- 1 teaspoon black pepper

- 2 tablespoons olive oil
- 3 carrots, sliced
- 1 onion, sliced
- 1 celery stalk, sliced
- 2 cups beef stock
- 2 tablespoons tomato paste
- 1 bay leaf

Directions:

1. Season beef with salt and pepper. Heat oil in Instant Pot on Sauté mode. Brown brisket on both sides and transfer to a plate.
2. Add carrots, onion, and celery to the pot. Brown lightly, then add stock, tomato paste, and bay leaf. Replace beef in pot.
3. Close lid and set cooking time to 50 minutes.
4. Discard bay leaf and season sauce to taste with salt and pepper.

Nutritional Information:
Calories - 501
Fat – 18.5 g
Carbohydrates - 2.58 g
Fiber - 0.7 g
Protein - 64.9 g

Spicy Shredded Beef Recipe

Ready in: 1 h, 10 m
Prep 10 mins
Cook 1hr
Servings: 4-6
Ingredients:
1 peeled and quartered onion
1 quartered green pepper
2 ½ -3 pounds beef roast
4 to 5 chipotle peppers

8-ounces of fresh cilantro – about 1 cup
6 smashed garlic cloves
3 tsp. cumin
3 tsp. oregano
8-ounces water
3 tsp. salt
3 tsp. pepper
3 tbsp. olive oil

Directions:
1. Begin preparing the meal by adding salt and pepper to the roast. Heat the olive oil in the bottom of your pressure cooker. Add the roast and brown all sides. This should take about 5 to 8 minutes.
2. While the meat is still browning, you can start chopping the onions, green peppers, and cilantro. You can also smash the garlic cloves.
3. The roast should be placed on a platter after it is done browning. Drain the excess fat and oil from the pan. Place the grate in the bottom of your pressure cooker. If you don't have a great, don't worry. You can still follow the resto f this recipe.
4. Add the meat, onions, green peppers, garlic, cilantro, and chipotles. Season these ingredients with the cumin and oregano. Then, add 8-ounces of water to the mixture.
5. Close the lid to your pressure cooker. Bring to high heat with high pressure. You'll need to reduce heat to stabilize. Cook for 60-minutes with 15-pounds of pressure. Allow the pressure to drop naturally after the timer goes off.
6. Next, remove the meat from the cooker and allow it to cool for 5 minutes. You can also discard the vegetables. Though, if you prefer a spicy meal, you can leave some of the vegetables in the mixture. Discard most of the liquid, but reserve a cup or two.
7. Begin shredding the meat using two forks. You should throw away any fat or gristle that you come across.
8. Place the shredded meat back in the cooker, along with the reserved liquid. Warm on low heat until you're ready to add the meat to a burrito or use in another recipe. Enjoy!

Nutrition Information:
Calories: 371.4
Total Fat: 16.5
Total Carbohydrate: 7.1
Dietary Fiber: 1.8

Protein: 50.4

Garlic Worcestershire sauce Spinach Ground Beef

Prep time: 6 minutes
Cooking time: 19 minutes
Servings: 2
Ingredients:
- Ground beef – 1 lb.
- Onion (chopped) – 1
- Garlic (minced) – 2 cloves
- Tomato sauce – 2 cups
- Worcestershire sauce – 1 tbsp.
- Beef broth – 2 cups
- Tomatoes - 2 diced
- Spinach leaves – ½ bunch chopped
- Salt and pepper to taste
- Cheese to Serve

Directions:
1. Add beef broth in the instant pot. Let it boil for 2 minutes. Add onion, garlic, tomato sauce, Worcestershire sauce and tomatoes in it.
2. Add beef and let it cook for 15 minutes. Add spinach leaves with salt and pepper to it. Cook it for 2 more minutes. When ready, serve with sprinkling cheese over it!

Nutrition Information:
- **Calories: 155**
- **Fat: 10g**
- **Carbohydrates: 8g**
- **Protein: 40g**

Chili Mustard Beef With Beans

Prep time: 5 minutes
Cooking time: 10 minutes
Servings: 4
Ingredients:
- Beans – 2 cups
- Beef stock – 2 cups
- Grounded beef – 4 cups
- Yellow mustard – 2 cups
- Onion (minced) – 1
- Chili powder – ½ tbsp.
- Cumin powder – 1 tbsp.
- White vinegar – 1 tbsp.
- Salt and pepper to taste

Directions:
1. Add beef stock, yellow mustard, onion, chili powder and salt and pepper in the instant pot. Let it sauté.
2. Add grounded beef in it with beans and cumin powder. Mix well. Let it cook for 10 minutes.
3. When ready, serve and enjoy!

Nutrition Information:
- **Calories: 90**
- **Fat: 10g**
- **Carbohydrates: 11G; Protein: 55g**

Instant Pot Sesame Beef Steak

Prep time: 4 minutes
Cooking time: 15 minutes
Servings: 3
Ingredients:
- Soy sauce – ½ cup
- Wine vinegar – ¼ cup
- Sugar (brown) – ¼ cup

- Green onions (sliced) – ¼ cup
- Garlic (chopped) – 1 tbsp.
- Mustard powder – 1 tbsp.
- Beef Steak – 2 pounds
- Sesame seeds – 2 tbsp.

Directions:
1. Get a bowl and mix soy sauce, wine vinegar, sugar, mustard powder and sesame seeds in it. Mix well.
2. Add this mixture to the instant pot with beef steaks. Sprinkle the green onions with chopped garlic. Let it cook for 15 minutes.
3. When ready, serve!

Nutrition Information:
- **Calories: 100**
- **Fat: 20g**
- **Carbohydrates: 8g**
- **Protein: 50g**

Ginger Spicy Beef

Ready in: 0 h, 55 m
Prep 10 mins
Cook 45 mins
Servings: 4

Ingredients:
2-pounds boneless sirloin steaks – cut into strips
½ cup of baby carrots
8-ounces tomato sauce
2 garlic cloves
2 tsp. ground ginger
1 green or red bell pepper (your choice)
1 tsp. turmeric
1 tsp. salt
½ tsp. black pepper
1 tsp. cayenne pepper
½ tsp. ground cardamom

2 tbsp. olive oil
8-ounces water
½ tsp. paprika
½ tsp. cumin
1 sliced onion
1 sliced green bell pepper

Directions:
1. First, you will need to remove one tablespoon of tomato sauce from the can. This will be used later in the recipe. Then, blend the remaining ingredients, except for the oil, meat, cumin, and paprika. You should blend using a food processor, so that there are no chunks in the mixture.
2. Place the oil in your pressure cooker. Season the beef with salt and pepper. Brown all sides of the meat in the pressure cooker. This should only take a few minutes.
3. After browning the meat, add the water, the tablespoon of tomato sauce, paprika, and cumin.
4. Close the lid of the pressure cooker. After the cooker begins to hiss, cook for 10 minutes. Allow the pressure to drop naturally. Point the steam vent away from your face. Carefully open the lid.
5. Place all the ingredients together in the pressure cooker. Combine everything and stir thoroughly. Close the lid and simmer for 30 minutes or bring to high pressure and cook for 7 minutes.
6. If you bring the pressure back up, allow the pressure to reduce naturally. Check the ingredients. The vegetables and meat should be tender. Otherwise, continue cooking for a few more minutes. Serve and enjoy!

Nutrition Information:
Calories: 408
Total Fat: 16.5
Total Carbohydrate: 11.1
Dietary Fiber: 3.3
Protein: 52

England Pot Roast

Prep Time: 10 minutes
Cooking Time: 45 minutes
Servings: 6

Ingredients:
- 1 3-pound chuck roast
- 1 teaspoon salt
- 1/2 teaspoon black pepper
- 2 tablespoons olive oil
- 1 onion, chopped
- 2 carrots, sliced
- 2 stalks celery, sliced
- 1 can tomato paste
- 2 cups beef stock
- 2 thyme sprigs
- 2 bay leaves

Directions:

1. Season beef with salt and pepper. Heat olive oil in Instant Pot on Sauté mode. Brown beef on all sides. Remove to a plate.
2. Add onion, carrots, and celery to the pot and brown in the droppings. Stir in tomato paste and beef stock. Replace beef in the pot. Add thyme and bay leaf.
3. Close lid and set cooking time to 45 minutes on high pressure.
4. Discard bay leaf and thyme. Serve pot roast with mashed potatoes.

Nutritional Information:
Calories - 494
Fat - 24.08 g
Carbohydrates - 7.54 g
Fiber - 1.7 g
Protein - 62.98 g

Delicious Chicken Dumplings

Ready in: 30 m
Prep 10 mins
Cook 20 mins
Servings: 6-8

Ingredients:
4 peeled and diced carrots
1 diced onion
3 sliced celery stalks
2 pounds chicken breasts on bone (skin will be removed)
6-ounces water
½ tsp. dried thyme
1 tsp. salt
½ tsp. pepper
2 large eggs
2/3 cup of low-fat or non-fat milk
1 tbsp. baking powder
1 tsp. salt
2 cups of all-purpose flour
1 tbsp. chives

Directions:
1. First, combine the chicken, vegetables, water, herbs, salt, and pepper. Combine these ingredients in your pressure cooker. Close the lid and cook on low pressure for 15 minutes.
2. You should start with high heat and then reduce the heat to low to stabilize the pressure. After 15 minutes, use the quick release method to reduce pressure. Carefully open the lid, with the steam vent pointed away from your face.
3. Use tongs to remove the chicken. Place in a bowl and cover to keep the chicken warm.
4. You will now begin preparing the dumplings.
5. In a large mixing bowl, combine the eggs, milk, and salt. Whisk these ingredients until the mixture is frothy. Whisk in 1 cup of flour. Set aside the whisk. Stir in the remaining flour. Use a spoon for the last of the flour – instead of the whisk.

6. Bring the liquid in the pressure cooker to a boil. You will drop tablespoon-sized drops of dumpling dough into the boiling broth. After you've finished adding the dough to the broth, close the lid.

7. Bring to high pressure over high heat and then lower the heat to stabilize the pressure. Cook for 5 to 7 minutes.

8. While the dumplings are cooking, use forks to shred the chicken meat off the bones. When the timer for the dumplings goes off, use the quick release method to reduce pressure. Add the shredded chicken and stir gently.

9. Serve in bowls or scoop the chicken and dumplings onto plates and spoon the broth over the dumplings. Enjoy!

Nutrition Information:
Calories: 381.2
Total Fat: 5.2
Total Carbohydrate: 3g
Protein: 33.1

The Best Chop Suey

Ready in: 20 mins
Servings: 4

Ingredients:
1.5-pounds pork or beef cut into ½-inch chunks
Salt and pepper
Flour
3 cups of sliced celery
1 tbsp. shortening
1 diced large onion
3 tbsp. soy sauce
2 tbsp. molasses
1 cup of canned mushrooms – save the liquid
1 cup of sliced water chestnuts
Fresh or canned bean sprouts (optional)
White rice
Chow Mein noodles

Soy sauce

Directions:
1. First, slice some chicken breast. Slice it thinly and then stir fry it. It should be cooked before you begin the following steps. Though, you don't need to include chicken in this recipe if you don't want to.
2. Heat the shortening in the pressure cooker. Dust the meat with the seasoned flour and then brown the meat in batches. Next, add the onion, celery, soy, and molasses. Use the reserved liquid from the canned vegetables. Then, add about 1 cup of water.
3. Close the lid on your pressure cooker. Use 10-pounds of pressure and heat until the regulator is rocking steadily. Cook for 10 minutes. Allow the pressure to drop naturally. Remove from heat and allow to cool.
4. Stir in the vegetables and heat. Use the fresh bean sprouts and cook until they are done to your liking. Combine everything and stir. Serve over rice, along with Chow Mein noodles. A little soy sauce will round out this meal.

Nutrition Information:
Calories: 475
Total Fat: 18.3
Total Carbohydrate: 20.8
Dietary Fiber: 3.9
Protein: 51.4

Feta Cheese Tuna Noodles

Serves: 2
Time: About 20 minutes

Ingredients:

8 ounces of uncooked dry, wide egg noodles
1 ¼ cups water
1 can drained tuna

1 can diced tomatoes
1 jar drained (save the liquid!) marinated, chopped artichoke hearts
½ cup chopped red onion
1 tablespoon oil
Feta cheese
Dried parsley
Dried basil
Salt &Pepper

Directions:

1. Turn on your Instant Pot and hit "sauté."
2. Heat a little olive oil, then toss in the chopped red onion and cook, stirring, for 2 minutes.
4. Add water, noodles, tomatoes, and seasonings.
5. Hit "Soup" for 10 minutes.
6. When time is up, hit "Cancel" and quick-release the pressure.
7. Add the tuna, artichokes, and the saved liquid.
8. Hit "Sauté" and stir for 4 minutes.
9. Serve with feta cheese and parsley.

Nutritional Information:

Total calories - 547
Protein - 8
Carbs - 15
Fiber - 2
Fat - 10

Chicken Noodle Soup

Total Time: 20 minutes
Serves: 4 Servings

Ingredients:
- 2 cups chicken, cut into pieces
- 1 cup noodles, broken into pieces
- 1 garlic clove, chopped
- 1 medium onion, chopped
- 1 medium potato, chopped
- 1 cup celery, chopped
- 5 cups chicken broth
- 1 tsp. pepper

Directions:
1. Add all ingredients into the Instant Pot and stir well.
2. Seal pot with lid and cook on manual high pressure for 6 minutes.
3. Allow it to release pressure naturally then open the lid.
4. Stir well and serve.

Nutritional Information:
- **Calories 267**
- **Fat 4.8 g**
- **Carbohydrates 24.4 g**
- **Protein 29.8 g**

Onion Balsamic Beef

Prep time: 4 minutes
Cooking time: 20 minutes
Servings: 2

Ingredients:
- Balsamic Vinegar – ½ cup
- Soy sauce – ¼ cup
- Garlic (chopped) – 3 tbsp.
- Honey – 2 tbsp.
- Olive oil – 2 tbsp.
- Salt and pepper to taste
- Worcestershire sauce – 1 tsp.
- Onion powder – 1 tsp.

- Smoke flavor liquid – 1 tsp.
- Cayenne pepper – 1 pinch
- Beef Steaks – 2 (½ pound)

Directions:
1. Get a bowl and add balsamic vinegar, soy sauce, honey, salt and pepper, garlic, Worcestershire sauce, onion powder and cayenne powder. Stir well.
2. Add the beef steak to the instant pot and pour the mixture over it. Add olive oil and let it cook for 20 minutes.
3. When ready, take it out and serve!

Nutrition Information:
- **Calories: 100; Fat: 20G; Carbohydrates: 8G; Protein: 60g**

Italy Pepperoncini Beef Recipe

Prep Time: 15 minutes
Cooking Time: 45 minutes
Serving: 6

Ingredients
- 2 tablespoon of olive oil
- 2.5 to 3.5 pound beef roast
- 12 ounce jar of pepperoncini
- 2 tablespoon of minced garlic
- 2 cups of beef broth

Directions:
1. The first step is to prepare your instant pot by setting to Sauté mode
2. Toss in your roast and brown them, it should take about 4 minutes per side
3. Chop up the stems off your pepperoncini in the mean time
4. Once browned, turn off the pot and toss in the garlic, beef broth and just about half the liquid from the pepper jar
5. Close the pot and let it cook for about 45 minutes
6. Once the timer runs out, let the pressure flow out naturally
7. Unlock the lid and serve with cheddar cheese.
8. Bring out the juice from the pot and use it as a dip if you prefer it that way

Nutrition Information:

- **Calories: 331; Fat: 12.1G; Carbohydrates: 2.5G; Protein: 51g**

Sesame Mustard Mixed Beef

Prep time: 5 minutes
Cooking time: 15 minutes
Servings: 2

Ingredients:
- Soy sauce – ½ cup
- Maple syrup – ¼ cup
- Garlic (chopped) – 6 cloves
- Ginger (grated) – 1 tbsp.
- Mustard powder – 1 tsp.
- Sesame oil – 1 tsp.
- Hot pepper sauce – ¼ tsp.
- Beer – ½ cup
- Beef steak – 4 (10 ounce)

Directions:
1. Mix soy sauce, garlic, ginger, mustard powder, hot pepper sauce, maple syrup and beer together in a bowl.
2. Add sesame oil to the instant pot and place the beef steak on it. Pour the mixture and let it cook for 15 minutes.
3. Serve when ready!

Nutrition Information:
- **Calories: 155**
- **Fat: 7g**
- **Carbohydrates: 10g**
- **Protein: 40g**

Delicious Spanish Soup

Ready in: 1 h, 15 m
Prep 20 mins
Cook 55 mins
Servings: 6

Ingredients:
1 crushed garlic clove
½ finely diced onion
½ finely diced green capsicum
2 chopped tomatoes
2 tbsp. olive oil
1.1-pound rump steak – cut into cubes
5 large potatoes – cut into chunks
3 sliced carrots
½ a Japanese pumpkin – cut into chunks
2 tbsp. paprika
Salt and pepper
2 tsp. beef stock powder
56-ounces water
½ tsp. powdered saffron
1 bay leaf
2-ounces dry sherry

Directions:
1. Start by heating oil in your pressure cooker. Once the oil is heated, add the onion, garlic, capsicum, and tomato. Sauté these ingredients until they are soft and the onion is nearly translucent.
2. Add the beef and cook until browned. Next, add the sherry. Cook until the sherry begins to evaporate. Add water to cover the beef. Close the lid and cook on medium heat for 8 minutes. Release pressure and open the lid.
3. Next, add the rest of the ingredients and the water. Bring the mixture to a boil. Stir thoroughly. Lower the heat and close the lid. Stabilize on low heat with low pressure. Cook for 40 minutes. Release pressure and check the food. The potatoes should be soft and the soup should be thick.
4. You can continue cooking if the potatoes aren't soft enough or if the soup is too thin. This will help soften the potatoes and will thicken the sauce. You could also add a tablespoon of corn flour to help thicken the sauce.

5. Serve and enjoy!

Nutrition Information:
Calories: 516.5
Total Fat: 15.4g
Total Carbohydrate: 22.5g
Dietary Fiber: 9.3 g
Protein: 24.7 g

Vegetable Beef Shank Soup

Ready in: 1 h, 45 m
Prep 15 mins
Cook 1 hr. 30 mins
Servings: 4-6

Ingredients:
1-pound beef shank
Pinch of salt and fresh black pepper
2 minced garlic cloves
1 finely chopped onion
2 tbsp. olive oil
2 cloves
2 sprigs of fresh thyme
½ tsp. ground allspice
1 pinch of crushed red pepper flakes
2-ounces dry red wine
16-ounces chicken broth
16-ounces beef broth
16-ounces water
1 peeled and diced small potato
1 cup of peeled fava beans
4 tbsp. pearl barley
1 tbsp. tomato paste
1 cup of shredded cabbage

1 chopped green onion – for garnish

Directions:
1. Start by heating the oil over medium heat in your pressure cooker. Add the beef shank. Brown the beef on both sides. Season with salt and pepper. It should take about 10 minutes to brown. Set the beef aside.
2. Next, place the onion and garlic in the pot. Cook until softened. This should also take about 10 minutes. Just be careful to avoid burning the garlic.
3. Stir in the allspice, cloves, thyme, and the red pepper flakes. Next, add the wine and then deglaze the pan. This should take about 2 minutes.
4. Place the meat back in the cooker. Add the broths and the water. Close the lid and cook for about 45 minutes. Release pressure naturally.
5. Open the lid and add the barley and fava beans. Close the lid again and cook for 10 minutes on low heat. Release pressure naturally and uncover.
6. Add the potatoes, carrots, and cabbage. Again, close the lid. Cook for about 10 more minutes. The vegetables and meat should be tender and soft. You can adjust the seasoning with a bit of salt and pepper.
7. Garnish with green onions and serve.

Nutrition Information:
Calories: 396.5
Total Fat: 12.6g
Total Carbohydrate: 10.9g
Protein: 34.8g

Instant Pot White Fish With Beer

Serves: 6
Time: 40 minutes

Ingredients:
1 pound white fish (like cod or Pollock)
4 peeled and diced potatoes
1 cup beer
1 sliced red pepper
1 tablespoon sugar

1 tablespoon oil
1 tablespoon oyster sauce
1 teaspoon salt

Directions:
1. Put everything in the Instant Pot.
2. Secure the lid.
3. Push "Bean/Chili."
4. Cook for 40 minutes.
5. When time is up, quick-release.
6. Serve and enjoy!

Nutritional Information:
Total calories – 172; Fat – 2g; Protein – 16; Carbs – 22; Fiber - 2

Spicy Lemon Salmon

Serves: 4
Time: About 5 minutes
Ingredients:
3-4, 1-inch thick salmon fillets
1 cup water
1 juiced lemon
1 sliced lemon
1-2 tablespoons Nanami Togarashi
Sea salt
Pepper

Directions:

1. Season the salmon generously with lemon juice, spices, pepper, and salt.
2. Lower the steamer rack into the Instant Pot and pour in 1 cup of water.
3. Place the fillets in the rack, without overlapping.
4. Secure the Instant Pot lid.
5. Hit "Manual" and then "-" until you get to 5 minutes.
6. Seal the lid.
7. When ready, quick-release the pressure.

8. Serve!

Nutritional Information: Total calories – 118; Fat – 2; Carbs – 1; Protein – 24; Fiber - 0

Country-Style Delicious Ribs

Ready in: 55 m
Prep 15 mins
Cook 40 mins

Ingredients:

1 ½ tbsp. oil
3-pounds pork ribs
1 tsp. paprika
½ tsp. garlic powder
½ tsp. pepper
1 tsp. salt
2 chipotle chilies in adobo
3 garlic cloves
½ sweet onion – cut into large chunks
4-ounces dark beer
4 tbsp. cider vinegar
1 tbsp. Worcestershire sauce
8-ounces barbecue sauce

Directions:
1. Add oil to your pressure cooker and heat over medium heat. Rub the meat with the rib seasoning. Brown all sides of the meat in your pressure cooker.
2. Add the remaining ingredients to the pressure cooker. Stir thoroughly. Close the lid to your pressure cooker and bring to high pressure. Cook for 20 minutes.
3. Remove from heat and run the pot under cold water until the pressure drops. Remove the ribs.

4. Combine a ¼ cup of the cooking liquid with the barbeque sauce that you'll use. Grill the ribs on low heat, while basting with BBQ sauce. Continue cooking and basting until you have a good glaze on the ribs. Serve and enjoy!

Nutrition Information:
Calories: 554
Total Fat: 24g
Total Carbohydrate: 10.3 g
Protein: 47.6g

Garlic Soy Sauce Beef Steak

Prep time: 6 minutes
Cooking time: 16 minutes
Servings: 3
Ingredients:
- Oil – ½ cup
- Worcestershire sauce – ¼ cup
- Soy sauce – 6 tbsp.
- Garlic (chopped) – ¼ cup
- Onion (chopped) – 1
- Salt and pepper to taste
- Rosemary (dried) – 1 tbsp.
- Steak seasoning – 2 tbsp.
- Steak sauce – 2 tbsp.
- Delmonico beef steak – 4 (10 ounce)

Directions:
1. Add oil to the instant pot and place the beef steak on it. Add onion, garlic, and rosemary over it.
2. Get a bowl and mix Worcestershire sauce, soy sauce, steak seasoning, steak sauce with salt and pepper in it. Stir well. Pour the mixture into the pot and let it cook for 16 minutes.
3. When done, serve and enjoy!

Nutrition Information:
- **Calories: 90; Fat: 8G; Carbohydrates: 15G; Protein: 25g**

Weekend Treat Steak Roll Ups

Ready in: 0 h, 35 m
Prep 20 mins
Cook 15 mins
Servings: 8

Ingredients:
1 cup all-purpose flour
2 tsp. salt - divided
½ tsp. pepper
8-ounces of fresh breadcrumbs
2 ½ pounds round steaks (cut them 1/2 – inch thick)
10-ounces chopped onions
16-ounces finely chopped butternut squash
4 tbsp. chopped green pepper
4 tbsp. chopped celery
1 egg – beaten
2 tbsp. melted margarine
4 tbsp. margarine
8-ounces water

Directions:
1. Start by cutting the meat into 8 strips. Use a mallet to pound the steak until it is about ¼-inch thick.
2. In a shallow bowl, combine the flour, salt, and pepper. Coat the meat in the flour.
3. In a medium mixing bowl, combine the onion, squash, and green pepper, celery, and bread crumbs. Add a teaspoon of salt, 2 tablespoons of melted margarine, and the egg.
4. Spread this mixture evenly on top of each piece of meat. Roll the meat and fasten the rolls with toothpicks.

5. Add a ¼ cup of margarine to your pressure cooker. Heat the margarine. After the margarine melts, brown the meat rolls. Brown on all sides.

6. Remove the meat rolls from the cooker. Position the cooking rack or steamer basket in the pressure cooker and add 1 cup of water.

7. Place the meat rolls on the rack or basket and close the lid to the pressure cooker.

8. Cook the meat rolls for about 15-minutes. Cool the cooker and carefully remove the meat rolls. Place the rolls on a serving platter. You can continue heating the remaining juices while stirring to create a gravy for the meat rolls. Serve and enjoy!

Nutrition Information:
Calories: 494.9
Total Fat: 21.4g
Total Carbohydrate: 19.6 g
Dietary Fiber: 2.3 g
Protein: 34.3g

Instant Pot Shrimp Scampi With Rice

Serves: 4
Time: 10 minutes

Ingredients:

1 pound frozen wild-caught shrimp
1 cup jasmine rice
1 ½ cups water
4 minced garlic cloves
¼ cup chopped parsley
¼ cup butter
1 medium, juiced lemon
1 pinch saffron
Salt
Pepper

Red pepper flakes

Directions:

1. Mix everything in your pressure cooker, leaving the shells on the shrimp.
2. Close the lid and select "Manual," and 10 minutes on "high pressure."
3. When time is up, quick-release.
4. When you can touch the shrimp, peel off the shells.
5. Serve with parsley and grated cheese.

Nutritional Information:

Total calories - 225
Protein - 14
Carbs - 10
Fiber - 0
Fat - 12

Smoked Sausage Seafood Mixed

Serves: 6-8
Time: 75 minutes

Ingredients:

6 cups fish stock
1 pound crab meat
1 pound peeled and cleaned shrimp
24 shucked oysters
2 chopped smoked sausages
3 chopped celery stalks
2 chopped red bell peppers

1 chopped onion
½ cup flour
½ cup chopped green onions
½ cup veggie oil
¼ cup chopped parsley
2 tablespoons dried thyme
2 tablespoons minced garlic cloves
Salt and pepper to taste

Directions:
1. Turn on your Instant Pot to "sauté" and pour in 2 tablespoons of vegetable oil.
2. Add red pepper, celery, garlic, and onions.
3. When the veggies are browned, pour in the fish stock and add sausages, pepper, and thyme.
4. Close the Instant Pot lid and hit "Manual" and then 10 minutes.
5. When time is up, hit "Cancel." Quick-release.
6. In another skillet, heat up the rest of the oil and mix in the flour to make a roux.
7. Stir constantly until the flour becomes golden.
8. Take the skillet off the heat and mix in a bowl with some fish stock.
9. Pour into the Instant Pot and stir until the gumbo thickens.
10. Throw in the shrimp, oysters, and crab.
11. Lock the lid again and cook for just 1 minute on high pressure.
12. Quick-release.
13. Serve the gumbo with greens onions, parsley, and rice.

Nutritional Information

Total calories - 135
Protein - 13
Carbs - 5
Fiber - 0
Fat – 7

Healthy Chicken Potato Bake

Ready in: 50 mins
Prep 10 mins
Cook 40 mins
Servings: 4-6

Ingredients:
9-ounces frozen peas
18-ounces thinly sliced potatoes
1 tbsp. butter
2.2 pounds cooked chicken
Sliced carrots
Sliced broccoli
Sweetcorn
Sliced zucchini
Sliced sweet red pepper
Finely sliced leek

Directions:

1. Start by heating the pan of your pressure cooker. Add the peas and chicken mix. Add the remaining vegetables. The potatoes should be added last.
2. Close the lid on your cooker and cook for 30 to 40 minutes. If you bake this in your oven, you should place the ingredients in a greased 13x9-inch baking pan.

Nutrition Information:
Calories: 587
Total Fat: 19.8
Total Carbohydrate: 30.4
Dietary Fiber: 5.4
Protein: 68.3

Not another Instant Pot Meatloaf

Total Time: 30 minutes
Serves: 6 Servings

Ingredients:
- 1 egg
- 1 lb. ground beef
- 1/2 cup breadcrumbs
- 2 carrots, shredded
- 1/2 onion, shredded
- 1/4 tsp. pepper
- 1/4 cup milk
- 1/2 tsp. salt

Directions:
1. Add all ingredients in mixing bowl and mix well until combined.
2. Shape the mixture into a loaf about 6 inches thick to fit on steamer rack.
3. Pour 2 cups water into the Instant Pot and place trivet in the pot.
4. Place prepared loaf steamer rack on the trivet.
5. Seal pot with lid and select manual high pressure for 25 minutes.
6. Allow releasing pressure naturally then open the lid.
7. Remove steamer rack and spread ketchup over the top of the loaf.
8. Cut into the slices and serve.

Nutritional Information:
- **Calories 204**
- **Fat 10 g**
- **Carbohydrates 6 g**
- **Protein 25 g**

Heavy Cream Scallop Chowder

Serves: 4-6
Time: 10 minutes

Ingredients:

2 pounds cut Yukon Gold
1 ½ pounds bay scallops
3 thin bacon slices
2 chopped celery stalks
1 chopped yellow onion
2 cups chicken broth
1 cup heavy cream
1 cup clam juice
½ cup dry white wine
¼ cup chopped parsley
2 bay leaves
2 tablespoons butter
2 tablespoons minced chives
1 tablespoon fresh thyme leaves

Directions:

1. Fry the bacon in your Instant Pot on the "Sauté" setting.
2. Move to a plate.
3. Add butter to the pot and melt.
4. Toss in celery and onion. Cook until soft.
5. Pour in clam juice, broth, and wine.
6. Deglaze.
7. Add potatoes, thyme, and bay leaves.
8. Secure and lock the lid.
9. Hit "Manual," and select "high pressure" for 7 minutes.
10. When time is up, hit "Cancel" and quick-release.
11. Open the lid.
12. Stir and turn to the "Sauté" setting.
13. Crumble in the bacon and add scallops, cream, chives, and parsley.
14. Cook for 2 minutes while stirring the whole time.
15. Pick out bay leaves.
16. Serve!

Nutritional Information:

Total calories: 396
Protein: 26.7
Carbs: 26.1
Fat: 13.1

Classic Beef Stroganoff with Pasta

Ready in: 30 mins
Prep 10 mins
Cook 20 mins
Servings: 3

Ingredients:
2 tbsp. olive oil
1 finely chopped small onion
14 ounces beef rump (trim and cut into sticks)
1 tbsp. plain flour
12-ounces beef stock
3 tbsp. sour cream
1 tbsp. Dijon mustard
1 tbsp. tomato puree
½ tsp. black pepper
14-ounces Fusilli twists or spirals

Directions:
1. Heat the olive oil in your pressure cooker pan. Sear the beef in batches. You just want to brown the meat on both sides. Don't burn the outside. Remove the meat and set aside.
2. Next, add the onion and sauté for about 2-minute. Sauté until the onion is almost translucent.
3. Stir the flour into the onion for 60-seconds and then add the stock. Allow the stock to bubble for about 5-minutes or until it has thickened.
4. Next, add the mustard, cream, puree, and black pepper. Stir these ingredients together and then place the meat back in the pan.

5. Close the lid on your pressure cooker and bring to pressure. Lower the heat to low once the pressure is reached. Continue to cook for 15-minutes and then naturally release the pressure.

6. Cook the pasta according to the directions on the package. Drain the water and serve with the stroganoff from your pressure cooker.

Nutrition Information:
Calories: 629.2
Total Fat: 13.9 g
Total Carbohydrate: 10.5 g
Dietary Fiber: 5.1
Protein: 19.6

Wonderful Milk-Braised Pork Loin

Prep Time: 10 minutes
Cooking Time: 1 hour
Servings: 4

Ingredients:
- 1 2-pound pork loin roast
- 1 teaspoon salt
- 1/2 teaspoon black pepper
- 2 tablespoons olive oil
- 2 tablespoons butter
- 3 cups whole milk
- 1 onion, sliced
- 3 cloves garlic, peeled

Directions:
1. Season the pork with salt and pepper. Heat the oil and butter in the Instant Pot on Sauté mode. Brown the pork on all sides.

2. Pour in milk, plus more to cover if necessary. Arrange onions and garlic around the pork. Close lid and set cooking time for 60 minutes on high pressure. Use quick release to remove the steam.
3. Transfer pork to a serving dish. Pour sauce into a blender and blend until smooth. Pour back into Instant Pot and set to Sauté mode. Reduce to your desired consistency and season to taste with salt and pepper.
4. Serve sauce over pork.

Nutritional Information: Calories - 663; Fat - 28.52 g; Carbohydrates - 9.95 g; Fiber - 0.2 g; Protein - 56.02 g

Light n' Delicious Shrimp Corn Stew

Serves: 4
Time: 10 minutes

Ingredients:

1 pound peeled and cleaned shrimp, cut in half
2 cups chicken broth
1 cup corn kernels
2 chopped bacon slices
1 chopped yellow onion
1 stemmed, cored, and chopped yellow bell pepper
½ cup heavy cream
2 tablespoons butter
1 tablespoon minced oregano leaves
2 teaspoons lemon zest
½ teaspoon celery seeds

Directions:

1. Turn your Instant Pot to "Sauté" and melt the butter.
2. Cook the bacon for about 3 minutes, until crispy.
3. Add bell pepper and onion. Cook until softened.
4. Toss in the lemon zest, oregano, and celery seeds, and cook for about 30 seconds.

5. Pour in the broth.
6. Stir before locking the lid.
7. Select "Manual," and then 5 minutes on "high pressure."
8. When time is up, hit "Cancel" and quick-release.
9. Open the cooker.
10. Turn the pot back to "Sauté."
11. Stir in the corn, cream, and shrimp.
12. Keep stirring as the shrimp cooks, which should take about 3 minutes, or until the shrimp becomes firm and pink.
13. Serve!

Nutritional Information:
Total calories: 258
Protein: 19
Carbs: 12
Fiber: 1
Fat: 15

Delicious Soy Sauce Broccoli Beef

Ready in: 3h
Prep 2 hrs.
Cook 1 hr.
Servings: 8

Ingredients:
6 cups of steamed rice
2-pounds frozen broccoli
15-ounces canned ears of corn – drained
2 ½ pounds stew meat (would suggest you to use partially frozen meat because it's easier to cut up)
8-ounces canned sliced water chestnuts – drained
4 diced garlic cloves
1 diced large sweet onion
4 to 6 tbsp. brown sugar

4 tbsp. soy sauce
4 tbsp. ground ginger
1 tbsp. granulated garlic
1 tbsp. Tabasco sauce
2 tsp. sesame seed oil
Freshly ground pepper

Directions:
1. First, cut the beef stew meat into smaller pieces. You should be able to cut it into 3 or 4 pieces. Place the beef in a gallon-sized freezer bag.
2. In a mixing bowl, combine the brown sugar, garlic, ginger, soy sauce, tabasco, and sesame seed oil. Whisk these ingredients together until smooth.
3. Pour this mixture into the bag with the beef. Close the bag and squish the mixture around in order to completely coat the beef. Squeeze the air out of the bag and set on your counter. Allow the meat to sit for about an hour. You should flip the bag several times during this period.
4. When you're ready to prepare the meal, chop the onion and garlic. Drain and rinse the corn and water chestnuts. Have these ingredients prepared and ready for use in the cooker. Also, keep a medium mixing bowl ready for storing the cooked beef.
5. Set your pressure cooker to "Brown" and add a ½ tablespoon of oil. Brown the beef in small groups. Squeeze the extra liquid as you remove the meat. Place the browned meat in the bowl.
6. After you've finished browning the meat, add a drizzle of oil to the pot. Toss the onions with a little salt. Toss the diced garlic and then add the browned beef. Stir everything together and then add the rest of the marinade from the freezer bag.
7. Turn on the rice steamer. Close the lid on your pressure cooker and steam for 10 minutes.
8. Allow the steam to naturally release and then add the water chestnuts, corn, and frozen broccoli. Stir the ingredients and set for "Low Pressure" for 2-minutes.
9. Give the ingredients one final stir and then serve while still hot. Make sure that you store leftovers as soon as the meal has cooled.

Nutrition Information:
Calories: 520; Total Fat: 9.1; Carbohydrate: 42; Dietary Fiber: 6.6
Protein: 41.9

Hearty Beef in Light Sauce

Ready in: 0 h, 55 m
Prep 15 mins
Cook 40 mins
Servings: 4

Ingredients:
1 tsp. sea salt
1 tsp. black pepper
1-pound beef schnitzel
2 tbsp. flour (millet)
2 tbsp. olive oil
2 tbsp. butter
1 cup of pancetta – cut into cubes
3 chopped garlic cloves
2 thickly sliced carrots
1 chopped onion
1 sliced leek
2 sprigs of rosemary
3 tsp. dried marjoram
10-ounces water
12-ounces red wine
2 bay leaves
1 tbsp. tomato paste
15-ounces tomato puree
1 tbsp. chopped parsley

Directions:
1. Start by combining the flour with the salt and pepper in a medium mixing bowl. Coat the steaks in the flour mixture. Make sure that both sides of the steak are covered. Shake the steaks to remove excess flour.

2. Sauté the beef schnitzels in hot oil and the butter. You can do this in the bottom of your pressure cooker pot. It should take about 3-minutes to sear each side. Remove the beef from the pot and set aside.
3. Sauté the pancetta in the same pot. Sauté for about 2 minutes and then add the onion and garlic. Sauté for about 30-seconds and then add the rosemary sprigs and marjoram.
4. Next, add the leeks and carrots. Stir the ingredients together and simmer for 2 to 3-minutes. Stir in the red wine, water, and bay leaves.
5. Add the tomato paste and tomato puree. Season with a bit of salt and pepper. Stir to combine the ingredients.
6. Place the schnitzels back in the pan and bring to a boil. Close the lid on your pressure cooker and cook on low heat for about 40-minutes.
7. Release pressure and serve on large plates. Sprinkle with chopped parsley and a side dish of pasta.

Nutrition Information:
Calories: 291; Total Fat: 17.3; Total Carbohydrate: 10.3; Dietary Fiber: 3.8; Protein: 20.9g

Flavorful Applesauce Pork Chops

Prep Time: 10 minutes
Cooking Time: 8 minutes
Servings: 4

Ingredients:
- 4 bone-in pork chops
- 1/2 teaspoon salt
- 1/2 teaspoon black pepper
- 1 apple, grated or cut into small pieces
- 1 onion, sliced
- 1 cup apple cider

Directions:
1. Season the pork chops with salt and pepper. Place in Instant Pot and cover with apple, onion, and cider.
2. Close lid and set cooking time to 8 minutes on high pressure. Use quick release to remove steam.

3. Transfer pork chops to a serving plate. Set Instant Pot to Sauté. Mash the apples, reduce sauce to desired consistency, and season to taste.
4. Serve applesauce over pork.

Nutritional Information: Calories - 377; Fat - 17.5 g; Carbohydrates - 12.49 g; Fiber - 1.1 g; Protein - 40.45 g

Cheesy Lobster Casserole

Serves: 4
Time: 10 minutes

Ingredients:
6 cups water
Three, 6-ounce lobster tails
8-ounces dried ziti
1 cup half-and-half
¾ cup Gruyere cheese
½ cup dry white wine
1 tablespoon chopped tarragon leaves
1 tablespoon Worcestershire sauce
1 tablespoon flour
½ teaspoon black pepper

Directions:
1. Pour 6 cups of water into the Instant Pot.
2. Add lobster tails and pasta.
3. Lock the lid.
4. Select "Manual," and then cook for 8 minutes on "high pressure."
5. When time is up, hit "Cancel" and quick-release.
6. Drain the pasta and lobster in a colander in the sink.
7. Cool.
8. Take out the meat from their shells, chop, and put back into the pasta.
9. Turn the Instant Pot to "Sauté."
10. Pour in wine, half-and-half, Worcestershire, tarragon, flour, and pepper.
11. Let the liquid simmer while stirring, so the flour dissolves.
12. Add pasta and lobster back into pot, stirring for 30 seconds.

13. Sprinkle on the cheese and stir until melted.
14. Hit "Cancel" and cover halfway with the lid, so the casserole thickens.
15. Serve hot!

Nutritional Information:

Total calories: 441
Protein: 28
Carbs: 44
Fiber: 0
Fat: 15

Garlicky Carrot Shrimp Rice

Total Time: 25 minutes
Serves: 3 Servings

Ingredients:
- 1 egg
- 6 oz. frozen shrimp, peeled
- 1 cup rice, rinsed and drained
- 2 tbsp. soy sauce
- 3/4 cup frozen carrots and peas
- 2 garlic cloves, minced
- 1/4 tsp. ground ginger
- 1/8 tsp. cayenne pepper
- 2 cups water
- 1 small onion, chopped
- 1 1/2 tbsp. olive oil
- Pepper
- Salt

Directions:
1. Heat 1 tbsp. olive oil in Instant Pot.

2. Once oil is hot, add eggs and scramble them.
3. Transfer scramble egg from pot and set aside.
4. Add remaining oil with garlic and onion and sauté for 2 minutes.
5. Add carrots, peas, shrimp, rice, water, ginger, soy sauce, pepper and salt. Mix well.
6. Seal pot with lid and select high for 5 minutes.
7. Release pressure using quick release method then open the lid.
8. Add scramble egg and mix well.
9. Serve and enjoy.

Nutritional Information:
- **Calories 392**
- **Fat 11.4 g**
- **Carbohydrates 52.7 g**
- **Sugar 1.3 g**
- **Protein 19.5 g**

Ketchup Garlic Honey Chicken

Prep time: 4 minutes
Cooking time: 14 minutes
Servings: 3

Ingredients:
- Chicken thighs (boneless) – 2 lb.
- Garlic (minced) – 2 cloves
- Garlic sauce – 2 tbsp.
- Ketchup – 2 tbsp.
- Honey – 1 tbsp.
- Cornstarch – 1 tbsp.
- Chopped basil for garnishing

Directions:
1. Add garlic with chicken thighs in the instant pot. Let it cook for 4 minutes.

2. Add garlic sauce, ketchup, honey and cornstarch in a bowl. Stir well. Pour the mixture in the instant pot. Let it cook for 10 minutes.
3. When ready, garnish it with basil and enjoy!

Nutrition:
- **Calories: 100**
- **Fat: 6g**
- **Carbohydrates: 10g**
- **Protein: 20g**

Buttery Chicken Wings

Total Time: 15 minutes
Serves: 12 Servings
Ingredients:
- 3 lbs. chicken wings, frozen
- 8 tbsp. butter
- 1/2 cup water
- 1 cup hot sauce
- 1 oz. ranch seasoning

Directions:
1. In a bowl, combine together hot sauce, butter, and ranch seasoning.
2. Add chicken wings into the Instant Pot.
3. Pour water and hot sauce mixture over the top of chicken wings.
4. Seal pot with lid and cook on manual high pressure for 12 minutes.
5. Release pressure using quick release method then open lid carefully.
6. Remove chicken wings from pot and place on baking tray.
7. Place in broiler and broil for 2 minutes.
8. Serve hot and enjoy.

Nutritional Information:
- **Calories 285**
- **Fat 16.1 g**
- **Carbohydrates 0.4 g**
- **Protein 33.0 g**

Instant Pot Pork Carnitas

Prep Time: 5 minutes
Cooking Time: 30 minutes
Servings: 6

Ingredients:

- 2 pounds pork shoulder
- 1 teaspoon salt
- 1 teaspoon cumin
- 1 teaspoon dried oregano
- 1/2 teaspoon black pepper
- 1 onion, chopped
- 2 garlic cloves, minced
- 1 bay leaf
- 2 cups chicken stock
- Juice of 1 orange
- Juice of 2 limes

Directions:

1. Rub pork with salt, cumin, oregano, and pepper. Place in Instant Pot with onion, garlic, bay leaf, chicken stock, and fruit juice.
2. Close lid and set cooking time for 30 minutes on high pressure.
3. Transfer pork to a serving dish, leaving the juice in the pot. Shred into strands using 2 forks.
4. Serve in tacos or burritos with limes for squeezing.

Nutritional Values (Per Serving):

Calories - 784

Fat - 35.58 g

Carbohydrates - 6.43 g

Fiber - 1.1 g

Protein - 103.36 g

Instant Pot Barbecue Pork Ribs

Prep Time: 5 minutes
Cooking Time: 25 minutes
Servings: 4

Ingredients:

- 1 rack baby back ribs
- 1 teaspoon salt
- 1 teaspoon black pepper
- 1 cup water
- 1/2 cup barbecue sauce

Directions:
1. Season ribs with salt and pepper. Place in Instant Pot with 1 cup water. Close lid and set cooking time for 20 minutes.
2. When ribs are finished, lay on a foil-lined baking sheet and brush with barbecue sauce. Place under broiler 5 minutes or until sauce bubbles and begins to brown.

Nutritional Information:
Calories - 569
Fat - 25.07 g
Carbohydrates - 13.32 g

Protein - 37.9 g

Tender Soy Sauce Pork Belly

Prep Time: 5 minutes
Cooking Time: 35 minutes
Servings: 6

Ingredients:
- 2 pounds pork belly, cut into 2-inch cubes
- 2 cups water
- 1 tablespoon sugar
- 1/4 cup rice wine or dry sherry
- 1/4 cup soy sauce
- 1-star anise
- 2 garlic cloves, peeled,
- 2 slices ginger, peeled

Directions:
1. Combine all ingredients in the Instant Pot. Close lid and set cooking time for 35 minutes.
2. Discard anise and ginger and serve with white rice.

Nutritional Information: Calories - 809; Fat - 80.38 g; Carbohydrates - 3.33 g; Fiber - 0.1 g; Protein - 15.1 g

Sweet and Sour Chicken

Total Time: 20 minutes
Serves: 4 Servings

Ingredients:

- 16 oz. chicken breast, skinless and boneless, cut into small pieces
- 4 tbsp. water
- 2 tbsp. cornstarch
- 1/2 tsp. ground ginger
- 2 garlic cloves, minced
- 1 tbsp. apple cider vinegar
- 2 tbsp. ketchup
- 1/3 cup soy sauce
- 4 tbsp. brown sugar
- 1/2 cup orange juice
- 1/4 cup water

Directions:

1. In a small bowl, combine together 1/4 cup water, orange juice, brown sugar, soy sauce, ketchup, apple cider vinegar, garlic, and ginger.
2. Place chicken into the Instant Pot.
3. Pour bowl mixture over the top of chicken.
4. Seal pot with lid and cook on manual high pressure for 5 minutes.
5. Release pressure using quick release method then open lid carefully.
6. Select sauté mode of Instant Pot.
7. In a small bowl, combine together cornstarch and 4 tbsp. water and pour into the Instant Pot. Stir well.
8. Cook chicken on sauté mode for 2 minutes or until sauce thickens.
9. Serve hot and enjoy.

Nutritional Information:
- **Calories 554**
- **Fat 20.5 g**
- **Carbohydrates 12.9 g**
- **Protein 80.8 g**

CHAPTER 4 INSTANT POT DINNER RECIPES

Ginger Mixed Meat Recipes

Prep time: 4 minutes
Cooking time: 20 minutes
Servings: 2
Ingredients:
- Onion (chopped) – 1
- Beef (grounded) – 2/3 pound
- Pork (grounded) – 1/3 pound
- Salt and pepper to taste
- Nutmeg – ¼ tsp.
- Ginger powder – ¼ tsp.
- Beef Broth – 2 cups
- Sour cream – ½ cup

Directions:
1. Add beef broth to the instant pot and let it cook for 3 minutes.
2. Add ginger, nutmeg, salt and pepper and onion in it.
3. Add beef and pork; let it cook for 20 minutes. When done, serve with cream or any of your favorite dishes!

Nutrition Information:
- **Calories: 110; Fat: 10G; Carbohydrates: 6G; Protein: 25g**

Bell Pepper Carrot Beef Mixed

Prep time: 5 minutes
Cooking time: 19 minutes
Servings: 3
Ingredients:
- Beef (grounded) – 2 pounds
- Eggs – 2
- Bread crumbs – 1 cup
- Onion (chopped) – ½ cup

- Ginger powder – ½ tsp.
- Salt and pepper to taste
- Sugar – 2 tsp.
- Vinegar – 3 tbsp.
- Soy sauce – 1 tbsp.
- Ginger powder – ½ tsp.
- Carrot – 1 large
- Green bell pepper – 1 large

Directions:
1. Get a bowl and add soy sauce, vinegar, ginger powder, salt and pepper and ginger powder in it. Mix well.
2. Now add the grounded beef in it and make small balls out of it. Dip them in whisked eggs and roll in the breadcrumbs.
3. Place the balls in the instant pot with adding carrots and green bell pepper with it. Let it cook for 19 minutes. When ready, serve and enjoy!

Nutrition Info: Calories: 155; Fat: 7G; Carbohydrates: 10G; Protein: 40g

Buttery Ground Meat Mixed Veal

Prep time: 5 minutes
Cooking time: 10 minutes
Servings: 2

Ingredients:
- Grounded Beef – 1 pound
- Veal (grounded) – ½ pound
- Pork (grounded) – ½ pound
- Salt and pepper to taste
- Eggs – 2
- Onion (chopped) – 1/3 cup
- Bread crumbs – 1 cup
- Butter – 1 cup
- Flour (all-purpose) – ¼ cup
- Sour cream – 2 cups
- Fresh Dill – ¼ cup

Directions:
1. Get a bowl and add fresh dill, flour, butter, cream, onion, pork, veal and grounded beef in it.

2. Add butter to the instant pot and let it sauté. Make small balls out of the mixture you made in step 1. Dip them in whisked eggs and roll in the breadcrumbs. Place each ball in the instant pot and let them cook for 10 minutes.
3. When ready, serve with sour cream and enjoy!

Nutrition Info: Calories: 90; Fat: 10G; Carbohydrates: 21g; Protein: 95g

Cabbage Jalapeno Cod Fillets

Prep time: 5 minutes
Cooking time: 15 minutes
Servings: 3

Ingredients:

- Flour - all-purpose, 1 cup
- Cornstarch - 1/2 tbsp.
- Baking powder - 1/2 tsp.
- Salt to taste
- Lemon Juice - 1
- Jalapeno - 1
- Oregano - 1/2 tsp.
- Cumin powder - 1/2 tsp.
- Cayenne pepper - 1/2 tsp.
- Oil – 2 tbsp.
- Cod fillets (2-3)
- Cabbage – 2 cups

Directions:

1. Get a bowl and add flour, cornstarch, salt, baking powder and lemon juice in it. Mix well. If you need to add water, it can be added accordingly as well.
2. Now mix cayenne powder, cumin powder, and oregano in the mixture made in step 1. Stir well.

3. Add oil to the instant pot and let it sauté. Add the cod fillets, jalapeno, and cabbage over it. Pour the mixture and let it cook for 15 minutes.
4. When done, enjoy the delicious meal!

Nutrition Information:
- **Calories: 109**
- **Fat: 20g**
- **Carbohydrates: 8g**
- **Protein: 60g**

Ginger Ketchup Honey Shrimp

Prep time: 6 minutes
Cooking time: 13 minutes
Servings: 2
Ingredients:
- Ketchup - 2 tbsp.
- Soy sauce - 1 tbsp.
- Cornstarch - 2 tbsp.
- Honey - 1 tsp.
- Red pepper - 1/2 tsp.
- Ginger powder - 1/2 tsp.
- Vegetable oil - 1/4 tsp.
- Onions – 2
- Garlic cloves – 2
- Shrimps (tails removed) – 1 lb.

Directions:
1. Get a bowl and mix honey, red pepper, cornstarch, soy sauce, ketchup, ginger powder and garlic cloves in it.
2. Add vegetable oil in the instant pot and pour the mixture. Let it cook for 3 minutes.
3. Add shrimps to it and mix well. Cook for another 10 minutes.
4. When ready, serve and enjoy!

Nutrition: Calories: 150g Fat: 15g Carbohydrates: 8g Protein: 55g

Dark Beer Sauce Chicken

Prep Time: 5 minutes
Cooking Time: 8 minutes
Serving: 4

Ingredients
- 2 pieces of chicken breast cut into fine pieces
- 1 cup of beef broth
- ½ a cup of dark beer
- 1 tablespoon of garlic powder
- 1 tablespoon of black pepper

Directions:
1. The first step of this simple recipe is to open up you're the lid of your instant pot and toss in all of the ingredients in your inner pot
2. Set your pressure to high and let it cook for about 8 minutes
3. Once done, wait for 10 minutes and let the pressure release naturally
4. Take it out and place it on a platter and serve with a side of bread or salad

Nutrition Information:
- **Calories: 264**
- **Fat: 12.1g**
- **Carbohydrates: 7.4g**
- **Protein: 37.6**

Pork Carnitas With White Pepper

Prep Time: 5 minutes
Cooking Time: 45 minutes
Serving: 6

Ingredients
- 4 pound of pork roast
- 2 tablespoon of olive oil
- 1 head butter lettuce
- 2 grated carrot

- 2 wedge cut limes
- Water

For the spice mixture
- 1 tablespoon of cocoa powder
- 1 tablespoon of salt
- 1 tablespoon of red pepper flakes
- 2 teaspoon oregano
- 1 teaspoon of white pepper
- 1 teaspoon of garlic powder
- 1 teaspoon of cumin
- 1/8 teaspoon of coriander
- 1/8 teaspoon of cayenne pepper
- 1 large finely chopped up onion

Directions:
1. Preparation of this dish should begin one day before cooking. The first step is to combine all of the ingredients listed under the spice mix and season the roast in the mixture properly
2. Let the seasoned roast freeze over night
3. In your instant pot, pour down the olive oil and brown your meat accordingly
4. Add enough water to submerge the meat
5. Turn the lid down and let the it cook at high pressure for about 50-60 minutes
6. Once done, let the pressure release naturally
7. Take out the meat and place it on a platter, gently pull out the flesh from the bones
8. Reduce the liquid in the cooker by simmering it
9. Shred the pork meat properly and fry it until lightly browned
10. Toss in some extra spice and olive oil before serving
11. If you are want to go creative, then take some lettuce and make prepare them into cups. Fill up the cup with carrots and fried pork and serve

Nutrition Information
- **Calories: 294**
- **Fat: 9.9g**
- **Carbohydrates: 7.3g**
- **Protein: 41.7g**

Maple Soy Sauce Salmon

Prep time: 4 minutes
Cooking time: 10 minutes
Servings: 3
Ingredients:
- Maple syrup - 1/2 cup
- Soy sauce - 2 tbsp.
- Garlic powder – 1 tbsp.
- Salt and pepper to taste
- Salmon - 1-2

Directions:
1. Add maple syrup, soy sauce, salt and pepper and garlic powder to a bowl.
2. Dip salmon in it and place it in the instant pot. Let it cook for 10 minutes.
3. When done, serve and enjoy!

Nutrition Information:
- **Calories: 90**
- **Fat: 8g**
- **Carbohydrates: 10g**
- **Protein: 25g**

Garlic Linguine Cheesy Shrimp

Prep time: 4 minutes
Cooking time: 14 minutes
Servings: 2
Ingredients:
- Linguine - 1 pound
- Butter – 1 tbsp.
- White wine – ½ cup
- Cheese (shredded) – 1 cup
- Garlic cloves (minced) – 2

- Parsley – 1 cup
- Salt and pepper to taste
- Shrimps (cleaned) – 1 lb.

Directions:
1. Add butter to the instant pot and let it sauté.
2. Add linguine, white wine, cheese, garlic cloves and parsley in it. Let it cook for 4 minutes.
3. Add shrimps to it and then cook for 10 more minutes.
4. When done, serve and enjoy!

Nutrition Information:
- **Calories: 109**
- **Fat: 6g**
- **Carbohydrates: 10g**
- **Protein: 27g**

Instant Pot Soy Sauce Red Meat Rice Dish

Prep time: 4 minutes
Cooking time: 20 minutes
Servings: 3

Ingredients:
- Eggs - 1-2
- Vegetable oil - 1 Tablespoon
- Finely Chopped Onion - 1
- Cold Cooked White Rice - 2 Cups
- Soy Sauce - 2 Tablespoons
- Black Pepper, Ground - 1 Teaspoon
- Red Meat Chopped and Cooked - 1 Cup

Directions:
1. Whisk eggs in a bowl and keep aside.
2. Add onion, white rice, soy sauce, pepper and vegetable oil to the instant pot. Let it cook for 10 minutes. Add the red meat and then pour the eggs.
3. Let it cook for another 10 minutes.
4. When ready, serve and enjoy!

Nutrition Information:
- **Calories: 185**

- **Fat: 8g**
- **Carbohydrates: 20g**
- **Protein: 35g**

Chili Ground Beef

Prep time: 6 minutes
Cooking time: 15 minutes
Servings: 2
Ingredients:
- Garlic Cloves - 3
- Cheddar Cheese, Mature - 50g
- Grounded beef – 2 lb.
- Dried Oregano - 2 Teaspoons
- Olive Oil - 2 Tablespoons
- Dried Chili Flakes - 1 Pinch
- Chopped Tomatoes – 2

Directions:
1. Get a bowl and mix garlic cloves, dried oregano, chili flakes, and chopped tomatoes with grounded beef.
2. Make small balls out of it. Add olive oil to the instant pot and place the balls. Let it cook for 10 minutes. Add cheese on all the balls and then cook for 5 more minutes.
3. When ready, take it out and enjoy eating!

Nutrition Information:
- **Calories: 295**
- **Fat: 20g**
- **Carbohydrates: 8g**
- **Protein: 70g**

Apple Juicy Pork Tenderloins

Prep Time: 5 minutes
Cooking Time: 30 minutes
Serving: 4

Ingredients:
- 2 tablespoon of unsalted butter
- 3 pound of boneless pork loin roast
- 1 large red onion halved and thinly sliced
- 2 medium sized tart green apple
- 4 fresh thyme sprigs
- 2 bay leaves
- ½ a cup of moderately sweet white wine
- ¼ cup of chicken broth
- ½ teaspoon of salt
- ½ teaspoon of ground black pepper

Directions:
1. The first step here is to set your pot to sauté mode
2. Toss in just pork tenderloin pieces and let them brown nicely for 8 minutes
3. Transfer it to another plate and repeat for the rest of the pieces (if any)
4. Toss in the onions to your pot and let it cook for 3 minutes
5. Stir in your thyme, apple, and bay leaves and pour in the wine and scrape off any browned bits
6. Pour in your broth, stir in your pepper and salt
7. Nestle in the pork loin alongside the apple mixture and pour the juice from the plate to your pot
8. Lock up the lid and let it cook for about 30 minutes at high pressure
9. Release pressure quickly
10. Unlock and discard the bay leaves
11. Transfer the pork to cutting board and let it stand for 5 minutes while you dish out the sauce into different serving bowls
12. Slice up your loin into ½ inch thick rounds and lay it all over the sauce

Nutrition Information:
- **Calories: 230**
- **Fat: 25g**
- **Carbohydrates: 13g**
- **Protein: 51g**

Parsley Celery Salmon

Prep time: 5 minutes
Cooking time: 5 minutes
Servings: 3
Ingredients:
- Salmon (cooked) – mashed 1 lb.
- Eggs - 2
- Onion – 2
- Celery – 2
- Parsley – 1 cup chopped
- Oil – 1 tbsp.
- Salt and pepper to taste

Directions:
1. Get a bowl and mix salmon, onion, celery, parsley and salt and pepper.
2. Add oil in the instant pot and let it sauté.
3. On the other hand, make patties out of the mixture and dip it in the whisked eggs. Place each patty in the pot and when all are made, let it cook for 5 minutes.
4. When ready, enjoy the delicious fish patties.

Nutrition Information:
- **Calories: 155**
- **Fat: 7g**
- **Carbohydrates: 4g**
- **Protein: 40g**

Red Pepper Butter Shrimp

Prep time: 6 minutes
Cooking time: 7 minutes
Servings: 2
Ingredients:
- Shrimps - 1 lb.

- Garlic cloves – 2
- Oil – 2 tbsp.
- Butter – 1 tbsp.
- Red pepper as needed
- Salt and pepper to taste
- Parsley (chopped) – 1 cup

Directions:
1. Add shrimps to the instant pot and let it cook for 2 minutes.
2. Add garlic cloves, oil, butter, red pepper and salt, and pepper. Let it cook for another 5 minutes.
3. When ready, take it out and garnish with parsley. Enjoy!

Nutrition Information:
- **Calories: 205**
- **Fat: 15g**
- **Carbohydrates: 8g**
- **Protein: 55g**

Hot Sauce Mushroom Beef

Prep time: 6 minutes
Cooking time: 15 minutes
Servings: 2

Ingredients:
- Oil – ¼ cup
- Flour (all-purpose) - ¼ cup
- Bell pepper – 1
- Onion (chopped) - 1
- Beef (chopped, breast) – 2 cups
- Mushrooms- 4.5 ounce
- Tomatoes – diced, 4.5 ounce
- Sauce (any) – 2 tsp.
- Garlic cloves – 3
- Soy sauce – 1 tsp.
- Sugar (white) - 1 tsp.

- Salt and pepper to taste
- Hot sauce – 3 drops

Directions:
1. Get a bowl and add flour, any sauce, soy sauce, sugar, salt and pepper with hot sauce. Mix well.
2. Add oil in the instant pot and place the beef in it. Sprinkle the bell pepper, onion, tomatoes, mushrooms and garlic on it. Pour the mixture and let it cook for 15 minutes.
3. When the pot beeps, take it out and serve!

Nutrition Information:
- **Calories: 355**
- **Fat: 16g**
- **Carbohydrates: 10g**
- **Protein: 55g**

Onion Buttery Scallops

Prep time: 4 minutes
Cooking time: 20 minutes
Servings: 2

Ingredients:
- Scallops – 1 lb.
- Onions (chopped) – 2
- Butter – 1 tbsp.
- Mushrooms – 1 cup
- Salt and pepper to taste
- Lemon juice – 1 tbsp.

Directions:

1. Add onions, butter, mushrooms, salt and pepper, lemon juice and scallops in the instant pot.
2. Let it cook for 20 minutes.
3. When ready, it beeps so take it out and serve!

Nutrition Information:
- **Calories: 350**
- **Fat: 12g**
- **Carbohydrates: 20g**
- **Protein: 55g**

Mayonnaise Cheesy Crab Meat

Prep time: 5 minutes
Cooking time: 10 minutes
Servings: 3

Ingredients:
- Crab meat – 1 lb.
- Cream cheese - 1/2 cup
- Mayonnaise - 2 tbsp.
- Sauce if needed
- Salt and pepper to taste
- Lemon juice – 1 tbsp.
- Cheese (shredded) – 1 cup

Directions:
1. Get a bowl and mix mayonnaise, cream cheese, sauce if you want to, salt and pepper along with lemon juice.
2. Add crab meat to it and make small balls. Place the balls in the instant pot and let it cook for 10 minutes.
3. When done, sprinkle the cheese over it and serve!

Nutrition Information:
- **Calories: 400**
- **Fat: 13g**
- **Carbohydrates: 10g**

- **Protein: 60g**

Ginger Maple Cooked Red Pork

Prep Time: 5 minutes
Cooking Time: 25 minutes
Serving: 4

Ingredients:
- 2 pound of fatty pork belly
- 2 tablespoon of maple syrup
- 3 tablespoon of sherry
- 1 tablespoon of blackstrap molasses
- 2 tablespoon of coconut aminos
- 1 teaspoon of salt
- 1/3 cup of water
- 1 piece of peeled and smashed ginger of 2.5cm length
- Just a few sprigs of cilantro leaves of coriander for a fine garnish

Directions:
1. Pour in a generous amount of water in your pot after tossing the pork cubes to make sure that they are fully submerged
2. Heat up the water to a boil
3. Boil the cubes for about 3 minutes and rinse and drain out any impurities
4. Once done, pick up the cubes and set them aside to drain
5. Pour down the maple syrup and put the pot in sauté mode.
6. Toss in the cube and cook them in the heated maple syrup for about 1-minutes until brown
7. After 10 minutes, toss in the rest of the ingredients into the mixture and bring to a boil
8. Close up the lid and let them cook for about 25 minutes
9. Let the pressure release naturally
10. Open up the lid and set in sauté mode
11. Let the contents shimmer for a while until they are sufficiently reduced and enough thick to coat the cubes
12. Serve the dish up with some cilantro and coriander leaves as garnish

Nutrition Information
- **Calories: 623**
- **Fat: 30.2g**
- **Carbohydrates: 16.5g**
- **Protein: 80**

Creamy Broccoli Chicken Rice Casserole

Prep Time: 5 minutes
Cooking Time: 10 minutes
Servings: 4

Ingredients:
- 1 pound boneless chicken, cubed
- 1/2 teaspoon salt
- 1/2 teaspoon black pepper
- 1 can cream of chicken soup
- 1 cup water
- 1 onion, finely chopped
- 1 teaspoon dried thyme
- 3/4 cup uncooked rice
- 2 cups broccoli florets, chopped small
- 1/2 cup shredded Cheddar cheese

Directions:
1. Season the chicken with salt and pepper. Place in instant pot with soup, water, onion, thyme, rice, broccoli, and cheese.
2. Close lid and set cooking time for 10 minutes. Allow steam to release naturally. Serve.

Nutritional Information: Calories - 362; Fat - 17.14 g; Carbohydrates - 25.21 g; Fiber - 5.7 g; Protein - 33.26 g

Yummy Chicken Taco Salad

Prep Time: 5 minutes
Cooking Time: 10 minutes
Serving: 4

Ingredients
- 2 pound of skinless and boneless chicken breast
- 1 teaspoon of chili powder
- ½ a teaspoon of kosher salt
- 1 cup of roasted tomato Salsa
- Grain free pieces of tortillas

Directions:
1. The first step here is to gently arrange the chicken pieces in your instant pot in a single layer
2. Sprinkle them both with some seasoning, covering both sides
3. Pour down the salsa finely over all of the chicken pieces
4. Cover up the lid and let them cook for about 10 minutes under high pressure.
5. Once done, release the pressure quickly and remove the lid
6. Transfer the chicken, and using forks, finely shred up the chicken and season them with pepper and salt if needed
7. Pour down the liquid of the pot into the shredded chicken making sure that it is evenly coated
8. Serve the mixture on by pouring it on top of grain free tortillas and eat up!

Nutrition Info: Calories: 91; Fat: 2.2G; Carbohydrates: 4.8G; Protein: 13.3g

Buttery onion Broccoli Beef

Prep Time: 10 minutes
Cooking Time: 15 minutes
Serving: 3

Ingredients

- 1 pound of ground beef

- 2 cups of cubed up potatoes
- 2 cups of shredded up pepper jack cheese
- 2 cups of tomato sauce
- 2 cups of beef broth
- 2 tablespoon of butter
- 1 chopped up yellow onion
- 5 pieces of broccoli florets

Directions:

1. The first step here is to set up your instant pot to its sauté mode and toss in the onion with the butter tossed prior
2. Toss in the beef in your instant pot and set it to high pressure and let it cook for 5 minutes
3. Release the pressure naturally and stir it finely
4. Toss in the potatoes, broccoli alongside the beef broth
5. Set the instant pot to high heat and pressure to low and cook it for 5 minutes
6. Once done, release the pressure naturally and stir in the tomato sauce and spices
7. Finally top it up wish some cheese
8. Once done, serve hot

Nutrition Information:
- **Calories: 266**
- **Fat: 10g**
- **Carbohydrates: 9g**
- **Protein: 14g**

Garlic Mushroom Chicken Marsala

Prep Time: 5 minutes
Cooking Time: 15 minutes
Servings: 4

Ingredients:

- 4 chicken thighs
- 1/2 teaspoon salt
- 1/2 teaspoon black pepper
- 1 tablespoon olive oil
- 1 tablespoon butter
- 1 onion, finely chopped
- 1 garlic clove, minced
- 1 cup mushrooms, sliced
- 1 teaspoon thyme
- 1/2 teaspoon rosemary
- 2 tablespoons flour
- 2 cups chicken stock
- 1/2 cup Marsala wine

Directions:

1. Season chicken thighs with salt and pepper. Set Instant Pot to Sauté and add olive oil. Brown chicken on both sides, then removes to a plate.
2. Add butter to pot. When melted, add onion and garlic. When the onion is translucent, add mushrooms and cook until tender. Add thyme and rosemary and cook 30 seconds.
3. Stir flour into the pot and cook about 1 minute or until the flour begins to take on color. Add wine, stirring constantly, and deglaze the pot. Stir in chicken stock and wine. Replace chicken in the pot.
4. Close the lid and set cooking time for 10 minutes on high.
5. Serve with pasta or crusty bread.

Nutritional Information

Calories - 534
Fat - 28.17 g
Carbohydrates - 11.18 g
Fiber - 1 g
Protein – g

Chili Black Bean Pork

Prep Time: 5 minutes
Cooking Time: 18 minutes
Serving: 6

Ingredients
- 1 tablespoon of olive oil
- 1 small sized red onion
- 3 medium sized cubanelle peppers
- 3 tablespoon of chili powder
- 1 tablespoon of ground cumin
- 1 piece of 2 pound boneless pork sirloin roast diced up
- 1 piece of 15 ounce can black beans all drained up and rinsed
- 1 piece of 14 ounce of can diced up tomatoes
- ½ a cup of chicken broth
- 2 tablespoon of Worcestershire sauce

Directions:

1. Set your Pot to Sauté mode and pour in some oil
2. Toss in your pepper and onions and let it cook for 4 minutes
3. Stir in the cumin, chili powder and cook for 1 minutes
4. Stir in the pork and stir it to coat finely with spices
5. Pour in the tomatoes, beans, broth and Worcestershire sauce
6. Lock up and let it cook at high pressure for 18 minutes
7. Quick release the pressure
8. Unlock the pot and stir well before serving

Nutrition Information
- **Calories: 543**
- **Fat: 12g**
- **Carbohydrates: 25g**
- **Protein: 43g**

Macaroni Mixed Beef Casserole

Prep Time: 4 minutes
Cooking Time: 8 minutes
Serving: 4

Ingredients
- 1 tablespoon of olive oil
- 1 medium sized chopped up onion
- 1 medium sized green bell pepper, deseeded and chopped up
- 1 tablespoon of minced garlic
- 1 pound of lean ground beef
- 28 ounce can of diced tomatoes
- 2 cups of fresh corn kernels
- 15 ounce of kidney beans
- 12 ounce of bottle dark beer
- 2 tablespoon of sweet paprika
- 1 teaspoon of dried oregano
- 1 teaspoon of ground cumin
- ½ a teaspoon of pure Chile powder
- ½ teaspoon of salt
- 8 ounce of pasta shells (medium)

Directions

1. Heat up your cooker in sauté mode and pour some oil
2. Toss in the onion, garlic, bell pepper and cook for 4 minutes
3. Crumble your ground beef and toss them in as well, and let it cook for another 4 minutes
4. Toss In the corn, tomatoes, beer, beans, paprika, oregano, cumin, Chile powder alongside the salt and keep stirring it until the beer foam diminishes down
5. Then stir in the pasta
6. Lock up the lid and let it cook at high pressure for 9 minutes

7. Quick release the pressure
8. Unlock, stir and serve

Nutrition Information
- **Calories: 687**
- **Fat: 22g**
- **Carbohydrates: 32g**
- **Protein: 55g**

Asian Style Garlic Broccoli Pork Chop

Prep Time: 10 minutes
Cooking Time: 15 minutes
Serving: 4

Ingredients
- 1 and a ½ tablespoon of toasted sesame oil
- 4 pieces of ½ inch thick bone-in pork loin
- 6 medium sized thinly sliced scallions
- 1 teaspoon of minced up garlic
- ½ cup of chicken broth
- ¼ cup of soy sauce
- 2 tablespoon of packed dark brown sugar
- 1 tablespoon of rice vinegar
- 4 cups of small broccoli florets

Directions:
1. The first step here is to set your pot to sauté mode and melt in 1 tablespoon of butter
2. Toss your chops into your pot and cook for 4 minutes
3. Transfer the chops to a plate and repeat to cook and brown the rest
4. Once done, into your pot toss in the scallions, garlic and cook for 1 minutes until fragrance comes

5. Stir in your broth, brown sugar, soy sauce vinegar and keep stirring it until the vinegar begins to bubble
6. Toss the chops to your cooker alongside any juice
7. Lock up the lid and let it cook for about 10 minutes at high pressure
8. Quick release the pressure
9. Open up the lid and sprinkle broccoli florets over the chops
10. Lock up again and steam for 5 minutes
11. Unlock and serve the chops with the broccoli in a pan with some sauce poured on top

Nutrition Information:
- **Calories: 630**
- **Fat: 28g**
- **Carbohydrates: 18g**
- **Protein: 57g**

Summer Italian Chicken

Prep Time: 10 minutes
Cooking Time: 15 minutes
Serving: 4

Ingredients
- 8 pieces of boneless chicken thighs
- Kosher salt
- 1 tablespoon of ghee
- 1 coarsely chopped up small onion
- 2 coarsely chopped up medium sized carrots
- ½ a pound of cremini mushrooms
- 3 pieces of peeled and smashed garlic cloves
- 2 cups of 400g cherry tomatoes
- ½ a cup of 60g pitted green olives
- ¼ teaspoon of freshly cracked black pepper

- ½ a cup of thinly sliced basil leaves
- ¼ a cup of coarsely chopped Italian parsley

Directions:
1. The first step is to grab the chicken thighs and season them with about ¾ teaspoon of kosher salt. It is wise to keep them in the fridge for about 2 days with the seasoning prior to cooking
2. Pour in the ghee and melt them in your Instant Pot using the sauté mode
3. Once the ghee is in shimmering stage, toss in the carrots, mushrooms, onions and about ½ a teaspoon of salt
4. Sauté the vegetable until it has been softened, it should take no more than 3 or 5 minutes
5. Drop in the tomato paste and garlic and cook for another 30 seconds
6. Toss in the seasoned chicken alongside the olives and cherry tomatoes
7. Give everything a nice stir
8. Lock up the lid let everything cook under high pressure for 7-10 minutes
9. Once done, release the pressure valve for a quick release of the steam
10. Stir in some fresh herbs and serve hot with pasta if desired

Nutrition Information:
- **Calories: 313**
- **Fat: 6.5g**
- **Carbohydrates: 7.1g**
- **Protein: 51.6g**

Hot and Sour Pork Stew

Prep Time: 20 minutes;
Cook Time: 6 hours
Servings: 4

Ingredients:

- 4 large banana chili for garnish
- 2 bird's eye chili, minced

- 2 pounds pork belly, sliced into 2-inch thick pieces
- 2 cups Homemade Buttery Mushroom Broth, Unsalted
- 2 cups tomatoes, quartered, deseeded
- 2 cups white onions, peeled, quartered
- 2 cups water
- 1 cup daikon (Japanese radish), peeled, diagonally sliced into ¼-inch thick disks
- 1 cup taro, peeled, cubed
- 1 cup young taro leaves (tops), rinsed well, drained
- ½ cup yard long beans, ends and strings removed, sliced into 2 inch-long slivers
- ½ cup winged beans, ends and strings removed, sliced into 2 inch-long slivers
- ¼ cup tamarind paste
- 1 Tbsp. brown sugar
- 1 Tbsp. fish sauce, add more later if needed
- 1 Tbsp. freshly cracked black peppercorns

Directions:

1) Except for banana chili, tamarind paste, taro leaves, winged beans and yardlong beans, place ingredients into crockpot.
2) Press: SLOW COOKER and HIGH. Set timer to 6 hours. Secure lid.
3) After cooking cycle, stir in remaining ingredients.
4) Press: SAUTÉ and HIGH. Secure lid once more. Cook veggies for 10 minutes or until crisp tender.
5) Turn off machine. Taste. Adjust seasoning if needed.
6) Ladle stew into bowls. Garnish bowls with banana chili. Serve.

Nutritional info per cup: 299 calories, 33 g. protein, 22 g. carbohydrates, 9 g. fat, 113 mg. sodium

Lima Beans Lamb Chops

Prep Time: 15 minutes;

Cook Time: 6½ hours
Servings: 6

Ingredients:

- 6 large lamb shoulder blades or arm chops, bone-in, sliced into inch-thick pieces, rinsed, and drained
- 4 large garlic cloves, peeled, smashed with flat side of knife
- 2 large leeks, roots trimmed, minced
- 2 cups shallots, quartered
- 1 cup water
- ½ cup white wine
- 1 10 oz. pack frozen cream baby lima beans, thawed well, drained
- 1 tsp. butter
- 1 tsp. dried rosemary, crumbled
- 1 tsp. sea salt, add more later if needed
- ¼ tsp. saffron powder
- ¼ tsp. white pepper

Directions:

1) Except for butter and lima beans, place ingredients into crockpot.
2) Press: SLOW COOKER and LOW. Set timer to 6 hours. Secure lid.
3) After cooking cycle, stir in butter and lima beans.
4) Press: SAUTÉ and HIGH. Cook until Lima beans are fork-tender, which should take about 30 minutes. Taste. Adjust seasoning if needed.
5) Place a lamb chop on each plate, with beans on the side. Serve.

Nutritional information:
383 calories,
38 g. protein,
28 g. carbohydrates,
13 g. fat,

Arrowroot Lemon Garlic Chicken

Prep Time: 10 minutes
Cooking Time: 39 minutes
Serving: 4

Ingredients

- 1 -2 pounds of chicken breast
- 1 teaspoon of sea salt
- 1 diced onion
- 1 tablespoon of ghee
- 5 minced garlic cloves
- ½ a cup of organic chicken broth
- 1 teaspoon of dried parsley
- 1 large lemon juice
- 3-4 teaspoon of arrowroot flour

Directions:
1. The first step if to turn on your Instant Pot and put it in Sauté mode. Toss in the diced onion and cooking fat
2. Let the onion cook for about 5-10 minutes
3. Toss in the remaining ingredients with the exception of the arrowroot flour and close the lid firmly
4. Then, choose the poultry setting and close the valve
5. Let it cook until the timer runs out
6. If you want to thicken the sauce, just remove ¼ cup of sauce form the pot and pour down the arrowroot flour
7. Then pour down the removed sauce again
8. Keep stirring it and serve

Nutrition Information
- **Calories: 205.3**
- **Fat: 5.8g**
- **Carbohydrates: 1.1g**
- **Protein: 35.1g**

Pork Tenderloin Coconut Rice

Prep Time: 5 minutes
Cooking Time: 1 minutes
Serving: 4

Ingredients
- 2 tablespoon of peanut oil
- 1 pound of pork tenderloin cut into 4 pieces
- 1 small sized leek with all of its white and pale green parts taken out, halved lengthwise, washed up and thinly slice
- 4 and a ½ ounce of chopped up mild green chiles
- 1 teaspoon of dried thyme
- 1 teaspoon of ground cumin
- ½ teaspoon of ground coriander
- ¼ teaspoon of salt
- ¼ teaspoon of salt
- ¼ teaspoon of ground black pepper
- 1 piece of 15 ounce black beans, all drained up and rinsed
- 1 cup of chicken broth
- 1 cup of regular canned coconut milk
- 1 cup of white long-grain rice
- 2 tablespoon of packed up light brown sugar

Directions:
1. The first step here is to set your pot to sauté mode
2. Toss in just pork tenderloin pieces and let them brown nicely for 6 minutes
3. Transfer it to another plate and repeat for the rest of the pieces (if any)
4. Toss in the leek, chiles and cook for 2 minutes
5. Stir in the cumin, thyme, coriander, pepper and salt and further cook until aromatic

6. Stir in the broth, coconut milk, beans, rice and brown sugar and stir until the sugar dissolves
7. Nestle in the pieces of pork and submerge the meat and rice in the liquid, pour any excess juice in the cooker as well
8. Lock up the lid and let it cook for about 15 minutes at high pressure
9. Release pressure quickly
10. Set it aside for 10 minutes to let the rice steam
11. Unlock the cooker door and transfer the pieces and spoon the rice and beans around them

Nutrition Information:
- **Calories: 563**
- **Fat: 12g**
- **Carbohydrates: 34g**
- **Protein: 32g**

Marina Sauce Meatballs

Total: 40 minutes
Servings: 4

Ingredients:

- 2 tablespoons olive oil
- 1 onion, diced
- 2 teaspoons garlic, minced
- ¼ cup red pepper flakes
- 2 teaspoons oregano
- 2 cans (14.5 oz. each) tomatoes, crushed
- ½ cup breadcrumbs
- ¼ cup milk
- ½ pound each lean ground beef and ground pork, mixed together
- 3 tablespoons parsley, minced
- 1 large egg
- ½ cup Parmesan cheese, grated
- Salt and pepper to taste

- Fresh basil, chopped, for garnish

Directions:

- Heat oil in Instant Pot®; sauté onion for 5 minutes.
- Add garlic, red pepper flakes, and oregano; sauté for an additional 30 seconds.
- Add crushed tomatoes; reduce heat and simmer for 10 minutes.
- Mix breadcrumbs and milk in medium bowl.
- Mix in meat, parsley, egg, cheese, salt and pepper; form into balls.
- Add to pressure cooker. Secure lid; set at high pressure and cook for 5 minutes.
- Carefully use quick release; garnish with basil.

Nutrition Information:
Calories: 550,
Protein: 38g,
Fat: 24g,
Total Carbs: 25g,
Fiber: 15g

Barbecue Gravy Classic Meatloaf

Prep Time: 4 minutes
Cooking Time: 30 minutes
Serving: 6
Ingredients
- 1 cup of canned up crushed tomatoes
- ¾ cup of chicken broth
- 1 small sized sweet potato
- 2 tablespoon of packed dark brown sugar
- 1 tablespoon of white wine vinegar
- 2 teaspoon of paprika

- 1 teaspoon of chili powder
- ½ a teaspoon of ground cloves
- ½ teaspoon of celery seeds
- ½ teaspoon of salt
- 2 pound of lean ground beef
- ½ cup of Italian seasoned dry breadcrumbs
- 1 large sized egg
- ¼ cup of loosely packed fresh parsley
- 1 tablespoon of Worcestershire sauce
- 2 teaspoon of minced up garlic
- 2 teaspoon of dried thyme

Directions:

1. Here, start off by pouring in your broth followed by sweet potato, vinegar, brown sugar, paprika, chili powder, celery seeds, cloves and about ¼ teaspoon of salt and keep stirring it until the sugar dissolves
2. Mix in the ground beef, egg, parsley, bread crumbs, Worcestershire sauce, thyme, garlic, and ¼ teaspoon of salt in a large sized bowl until the crumbs and herbs are distributed even throughout the mixture
3. Ball up the mixture in a dome shaped sphere and cut in half
4. Spoon in and smear some tomato sauce and set in the cooker mixture
5. Lock up the lid and let it cook for about 30 minutes at high pressure
6. Release the pressure naturally
7. Open up the lid and let it cool for about 5 minutes
8. Take it out and using a sharp knife, cut the meat loaf in ½ inch slices and serve in a plate
9. Dress it up with a bit of sauce and serve

Nutrition information
- **Calories: 231**
- **Fat: 16g**
- **Carbohydrates: 6g**
- **Protein: 15g**

Delicious Corned Up Beef and Cabbage

Prep Time: 5 minutes
Cooking Time: 120 minutes
Serving: 4

Ingredients
- 1 piece of corned beef brisket
- 4 cups of water
- 1 small sized peeled and quartered onion
- 3 cloves of peeled and smashed garlic clove
- 2 pieces of bay leaves
- 3 whole sized black peppercorns
- ½ a teaspoon of allspice berries
- 1 teaspoon of dried thyme
- 5 medium sized carrots
- 1 head of a cabbage cut into wedges

Directions
1. First step is to toss in the corned beef, onion, water, garlic cloves, allspice, peppercorn and thymes into your instant pot and close down the lid and set the timer to 90 minutes
2. Once the cooking is complete, turn off your device and allow the pressure to be excreted naturally
3. Gently take out the meat and place them in a plate, only to cover them up with a tin foil and let it sit for just 15 minutes
4. Toss in the carrots and cabbage to the pot and lock up the lid, letting it cook for 10 minutes
5. Once the cooking is done, release the pressure quickly and take out the prepared vegetables and serve them alongside the corned beef

Nutrition Information
- **Calories: 478**
- **Fat: 25**
- **Carbohydrates: 3.8g**
- **Protein: 34.2g**

Yummy Creole Cod

Total: 20 minutes
Servings: 8

Ingredients:

- ¼ cup olive oil
- 1 cup celery, chopped
- 1 green pepper, chopped
- 2 cups white onion, chopped
- 1 teaspoon minced garlic
- 1 can (28-oz) tomatoes
- ¼ cup white wine
- 2 pounds frozen cod fillets
- 2 bay leaves
- 1 tablespoon paprika
- ½ teaspoon cayenne pepper
- Sea salt to taste

Directions:

- Heat oil in Instant Pot®; sauté celery, green pepper, onion, and garlic.
- Remove veggies and place on plate.
- Drain juice from a can of tomatoes.
- Pour the tomato juice and wine into the Instant Pot®.
- Place fish in a steamer basket in a crisscross fashion.
- Put into the Instant Pot®. Secure lid, set at high pressure and cook for 5 minutes. Use quick release.
- Remove fish; add veggies, tomatoes, bay leaves, paprika, cayenne pepper and salt to liquid in pot.
- Place fish back into pot, secure lid and cook at high pressure for 10 more minutes.

- Release heat using quick release.

Nutrition Information:
Calories: 350,
Protein: 52g,
Fat: 11g,
Carbs: 6g,
Fiber: 0g

Healthy Turkey Veggie Soup

Servings: 8

Broth Ingredients:

- Turkey bones with meat on them
- 1 stalk celery, chopped
- 2 bay leaves
- 1 carrot, sliced
- 1 onion, diced
- ½ teaspoon salt
- 3 quarts water

Soup Ingredients:

- 1 tablespoon butter
- 1 minced shallot
- 1 teaspoon fresh thyme
- 2 quarts turkey stock
- 2 cups shredded turkey
- 2 cups frozen mixed veggies
- 1 ½ cups egg noodles
- Salt and pepper to taste

Directions:

- To make the broth: place turkey bones, celery, bay leaves, carrot, onion, and salt in pressure cooker.
- Pour in water, secure lid, set at high pressure and cook for 50 minutes.
- Let pressure release naturally.
- Remove solids. Use 2 quarts of this stock for soup:
- Melt some butter in Instant Pot®. Sauté the shallot with thyme until browned.
- Add in 2 quarts of turkey stock. Bring to a boil.
- Add in the turkey meat and mixed veggies along with noodles.
- Salt and pepper to taste. Simmer for 10 minutes or until heated through.

Nutrition Information:
Calories: 273,
Protein: 34g,
Fat: 103g,
Carbs: 8.3g,
Fiber: .6

Jasmine Rice Congee Chicken

Prep Time: 5 minutes
Cooking Time: 40 minutes
Serving: 6

Ingredients
- 1 cup of jasmine rice
- 7 cups of water
- 5-6 pieces of chicken drumstick
- 1 tablespoon of sliced up ginger strips
- Green onions
- Salt as needed

Directions:
1. Start off by rinsing your rice under cold water to clean it up until clean water runs through
2. into your pot, toss in the ginger, chicken drumsticks alongside 7 cups of water

3. Close the lid and let it cook for 30 minutes at high pressure
4. Naturally release the pressure later on
5. Open up the lid
6. Set the pot to sauté mode and keep stirring until your desired consistency is achieved
7. Season with a good amount of salt
8. Take a fork and tong to separate the chicken meat from the bones and remove the bones alongside the skin
9. Remove the congee from the pot and serve with garnish of onions

Nutrition Information
- **Calories: 620**
- **Fat: 28g**
- **Carbohydrates: 38g**
- **Protein: 76g**

Tasty Mongolian Beef

Total: 25 minutes
Servings: 6
Ingredients:
- 2 pounds flank steak
- Salt and pepper to taste
- 1 tablespoon olive oil
- 1 teaspoon garlic, minced
- ½ cup soy sauce, low-sodium
- ½ cup water
- ½ teaspoon minced ginger
- 2/3 cup dark brown sugar
- 2 tablespoons cornstarch
- 3 tablespoons water
- 3 green onions, sliced into 1-inch pieces

Directions:
- Season beef with salt and pepper. Heat olive oil in Instant Pot® and brown the meat.
- Remove meat once browned.
- Add garlic to pot and sauté.
- Add soy sauce, half cup of water, ginger, and brown sugar to pot.

- Add beef back to pot. Secure lid, set at high pressure and cook for 12 minutes. Use quick release.
- Mix cornstarch and 3 tablespoons of water in a bowl; add to pot and bring to boil. Mix in the green onions; serve with rice and veggies.

Nutrition: Calories: 359, Protein: 30g, Fat: 13g, Carbs: 23g

Garlic Artichoke Pork Chops

Prep Time: 5 minutes
Cooking Time: 24 minutes
Serving: 4

Ingredients
- 2 tablespoon of unsalted butter
- 2 pieces of 2 inch thick bone-in pork loin or rib chops
- 3 ounce of pancetta diced of chunks
- 2 teaspoon of ground black pepper
- 1 medium sized minced up shallots
- 4 pieces of 2 inch lemon zest strips
- 1 teaspoon of dried rosemary
- 2 teaspoon of minced garlic
- 1 piece of 9 ounce box of frozen artichoke heart quarters
- ½ a cup of moderately dry white wine
- ¼ cup of chicken broth

Directions:
1. The first step here is to set your pot to sauté mode
2. Add in the pancetta and cook for 5 minutes
3. Transfer the browned pancetta to plate
4. Season your chops with pepper
5. Toss your chops into your pot and cook for 4 minutes
6. Transfer the chops to a plate and repeat to cook and brown the rest
7. Add in the shallots to your cooker and stir for 1 minutes
8. Pour in the lemon zest, rosemary and garlic and keep stirring it until aromatic
9. after a while, stir in the wine, broth and artichokes
10. Return the pancetta back to the cooker
11. Return the chops to your pot

12. Lock up the lid and let it cook for about 24 minutes at high pressure
13. Release pressure quickly
14. Unlock and transfer the chops to a carving board
15. Slice up the eye of your meat off the bone and slice the meat into strips
16. Divide in serving bowls and sauce ladled up

Nutrition Information
- **Calories: 245**
- **Fat: 45g**
- **Carbohydrates: 12g**
- **Protein: 48g**

Cinnamon Ginger Pork Chops With Cherry Sauce

Prep Time: 5 minutes
Cooking Time: 24 minutes
Serving: 4

Ingredients
- ½ a teaspoon of ground cinnamon
- ¼ teaspoon f ground cardamom
- ¼ teaspoon of ground coriander
- ¼ teaspoon of ground ginger
- ½ teaspoon of salt
- 2 pieces of 2 inch t hick bone-in pork loin or rib chops
- 1 tablespoon of unsalted butter
- 2 tablespoon of olive oil
- 1 cup of fresh pearl onions
- ½ cup of cherry jam
- ¼ cup of medium level red wine

Directions:
1. The first step here is to set your pot to sauté mode
2. In a small sized bowl toss in the cinnamon, coriander, cardamom, ginger and salt and mix them well
3. Massage the chops with that mix

4. Melt butter over your inner pot
5. Toss in just one chop and let it brown nicely for 3 minutes
6. Transfer it to another plate and repeat for the rest of the chops
7. Toss in the onions to your cooker and stir until browned for 4 minutes
8. Stir in the jam and wine until they melt, making sure to scrap up the browned bits in the bottom of your pot
9. Return the chops to your pot
10. Lock up the lid and let it cook for about 24 minutes at high pressure
11. Release pressure quickly
12. Unlock and transfer the chops to a carving board
13. Slice up the eye of your meat off the bone and slice the meat into strips
14. Divide in serving bowls and sauce ladled up

Nutrition Information
- **Calories: 431**
- **Fat: 12g**
- **Carbohydrates: 43g**
- **Protein: 23g**

Mozzarella Lime-Salsa Chicken

Total: 32 minutes
Servings: 4

Ingredients:
- 4 chicken breasts, skinless, boneless
- 1 cup tomato sauce
- 1 cup salsa
- Juice of 2 limes
- ½ teaspoon salt
- ¼ teaspoon pepper
- 1 cup grated Mozzarella cheese

Directions:

- Add chicken to Instant Pot® along with sauce, salsa, lime juice, salt and pepper. Secure lid, set at high pressure and cook for 12 minutes.
- Use quick release. Remove chicken and place in oven-proof dish.
- Cook sauce a little longer in pot, then spoon over chicken and top with cheese.
- Place under broiler for 5 minutes; serve with Mexican rice or veggies.

Nutrition Information: Calories: 294, Protein: 34g, Fat: 5g, Carbs: 9g, Fiber: 0g

Corn Starch Thai Peanut Butter Chicken

Total: 20 minutes
Servings: 4-6

Ingredients:

- 1 tablespoon olive oil
- 8 chicken thighs, skinless, boneless
- ½ cup chicken broth, low-sodium
- 1 tablespoon dried cilantro
- ¼ cup soy sauce
- ¼ cup natural peanut butter
- 1 teaspoon red pepper flakes
- 1 tablespoon ground ginger
- 2 tablespoons lime juice
- 1 tablespoon cornstarch
- 2 tablespoons water
- ¼ cup unsalted peanuts, chopped
- 3 chopped green onions, for garnish
- Salt and pepper to taste

Directions:

- Heat olive oil in Instant Pot® using 'browning' setting.

- Brown chicken; set aside on plate.
- Mix broth, cilantro, soy sauce, peanut butter, red pepper flakes, ginger and lime juice in pot.
- Add chicken back to the pot. Secure lid, set at high pressure and cook for 12 minutes.
- Use quick release. Whisk cornstarch and water in a bowl, add to cooker, mix well and serve.
- Garnish with peanuts and green onions.

Nutrition Information:

Calories: 365,
Protein: 35.2g,
Fat: 20.1g,
Carbs: 7.5g,
Fiber: 2.1g

Tender Gravy Cornish Hens

Prep Time: 5 minutes
Cooking Time: 25 minutes
Servings: 2

Ingredients:
- 2 small Cornish hens
- 1 teaspoon salt
- 1/2 teaspoon black pepper
- 1 teaspoon thyme
- 1/2 teaspoon rosemary
- 1 cup chicken stock
- 2 tablespoons flour
- 2 tablespoons water

Directions:

1. Rub the Cornish hens with salt, pepper, thyme, and rosemary. Place into Instant Pot and add the stock.
2. Close lid and set cooking time for 20 minutes. Use quick release to remove steam. Open the lid and transfer hen to a serving dish.
3. Set Instant Pot to Sauté and bring the stock to a boil. Stir together flour and water in a small bowl. Pour into boiling stock, stirring constantly, and cook until thickened. Serve with gravy

Nutritional Information: Calories - 316; Fat - 8.34 g; Carbohydrates - 7.12 g; Fiber - 0.5 g; Protein - 49.6 g

Ketchup Ghee Garlic Chicken

Prep Time: 5 minutes
Cooking Time: 40 minutes
Serving: 5

Ingredients

- 2 pound of fresh boneless chicken thigh
- 3 tablespoon of homemade ketchup
- 1 and a ½ teaspoon of salt
- 2 teaspoon of garlic powder
- ¼ cup of ghee
- ½ teaspoon of finely ground black pepper
- 3 tablespoon of gluten free organic tamari
- ¼ cup of honey

Directions:

1. The first step here is to place all the ingredients in your pot
2. Stir everything evenly to make sure that the chicken are coated
3. Close down the lid and let it cook for about 18 minutes
4. Once done, release the pressure quickly and open up the lid
5. Transfer the chicken and use forks to shred it up
6. Put the Instant Pot in Sauté mode and reduce the remaining juice for 5 minutes

7. Pour the sauce over the Yum chicken and serve it with vegetable of your preference

Nutrition Information:
- **Calories: 179**
- **Fat: 11.1g**
- **Carbohydrates: 5.1g**
- **Protein: 13g**

Shredded Flank Pepper Steak

Total: 30 minutes
Servings: 4

Ingredients:

- 2 pounds flank steak
- Dash of sea salt
- 1 cup chicken broth, low-sodium
- 2 teaspoons minced garlic
- 1 large onion, quartered
- Black pepper to taste

Directions:

- Season steak with salt. Add steak, broth, garlic and onion to Instant Pot
- Set at medium-high heat and bring to boil.
- Once boiling secure the lid, set at high pressure and cook for 20 minutes. Use quick release.
- Remove steak; shred and season with favorite seasonings.

Nutrition Information: Calories: 448, Protein: 56g, Fat: 22g, Carbs: 2g, Fiber: 0g

Lemon Creamy Shrimp Chowder

Prep Time: 10 minutes
Cooking Time: 5 minutes
Serving: 6

Ingredients
- 3 large russet potatoes peeled up into ½ inch cubes
- 1 large sized onion chopped up
- 2 medium sized chopped up shallot
- 2 chopped up celery ribs
- 3 strips of lemon zest
- 1 piece of bay leaf
- 3 cups of shrimp stock
- 2 cups of whole milk
- 1 cup of organic heavy cream
- 2 tablespoon of flour
- 2 tablespoon of soft unsalted butter
- 1 and a ½ pound of medium shrimp
- 2 tablespoon of finely chopped fresh basil
- Salt as needed
- Ground black pepper as needed
- White pepper as needed
- Oyster crackers

Directions:
1. Toss in your potatoes, onions, bell pepper, shallots and celery
2. Tuck in the strips of zest and bay leaf as well
3. Pour in the broth then
4. Close down the lid and let it cook at high pressure for 30 minutes
5. One done, let the pressure release naturally
6. Discard the bay leaf and zest strips
7. Mash the potatoes using a fork to gain a chunky texture
8. Pour in the milk and cream and let it heat over low heat
9. Whisk in the butter and simmer for 5 minutes until the flour has completely dissolved and the soup is thick
10. Then add in the shrimp and basil, making sure to stir it a few times
11. Let it cook for 2-3 minutes and wait until the shrimps turn pink and curl up

12. Serve hot with lots oyster crackers

Nutrition Information:
- **Calories: 625**
- **Fat: 22g**
- **Carbohydrates: 37g**
- **Protein: 46g**

Yummy Barbecue Pulled Chicken

Prep Time: 5 minutes
Cooking Time: 15 minutes
Servings: 4

Ingredients:
- 2 pounds bone-in chicken breasts
- 1 onion, diced
- 1 can cola
- 1 teaspoon chili powder
- 1/2 teaspoon garlic powder
- 1/2 teaspoon salt
- 1/2 teaspoon black pepper
- 1 cup barbecue sauce

Directions:
1. Place chicken, onion, cola, chili powder, garlic powder, salt, and pepper in the Instant Pot.
2. Close lid and set cooking time to 15 minutes on high pressure. Use quick release to remove the steam. Open lid and transfer chicken to a dish, leaving the liquid in the pot.
3. Remove the bones from the chicken. Use 2 forks to shred the flesh into strands.
4. Pour barbecue sauce over chicken and toss to coat. Serve on bread.

Nutritional Information: Calories - 562; Fat - 21.59 g; Carbohydrates - 41.38 g; Fiber - 1.5 g; Protein - 48.44 g

Butternut Squash and Ginger Soup

Total: 35 minutes
Servings: 4
Ingredients
- 1 tablespoon olive oil
- 1 onion, chopped
- 1 sprig sage
- Salt and pepper to taste
- 4 pounds butternut squash, seeded, peeled and cubed
- 2-inch piece fresh ginger, peeled, sliced
- 4 cups vegetable stock
- ¼ teaspoon nutmeg

Directions:
- Place oil in Instant Pot® and sauté onions and sage seasoned with salt and pepper.
- Once onions are softened, add enough squash to cover the bottom of the pot; stir and brown for 10 minutes.
- Add in remainder of squash, ginger, stock and nutmeg. Secure the lid, set at high pressure and cook for 15 minutes.
- Use quick release; remove sage stem.
- Blend into a soup with immersion blender. (If using regular blender, be very careful with hot liquids!) Serve and enjoy!

Nutrition Information: Calories: 396, Protein: 17g, Fat: 7g, Carbs: 6g, Fiber: 2g

Almond Rosemary Meatloaf

Prep Time: 10 minutes
Cooking Time: 40 minutes
Serving: 2
Ingredients
- 2 pound of ground beef
- 2 pieces of eggs
- 1 cup of almond flour
- 1 teaspoon of thyme

- 1 teaspoon of rosemary
- 1 teaspoon of garlic powder
- 3 tablespoon of olive oil

Directions:
1. The first step here is to take a bowl and toss in your eggs, beef, and flour alongside the seasoning in a large sized mixing bowl
2. Take a wooden spoon and mix them very gently
3. Open up the lid of your instant pot and grease up the inner pot with olive oil
4. Gently place the meatloaf mixture in your grease up instant pot and firmly pack it up with your hand to make sure it's even
5. Set the Instant Pot to normal pressure setting and choose meat mode
6. Let it cook for about 40 minutes
7. Once done, wait for about 10 minutes and manually release the pressure of your instant pot
8. Open it up and serve the meal with salad and mashed potatoes

Nutrition: Calories: 363; Fat: 14G; Carbohydrates: 5G; Protein: 29g

Mushroom Gravy Chicken

Prep Time: 10 minutes
Cooking Time: 25 minutes
Servings: 4

Ingredients:

- 4 chicken thighs
- 1/2 teaspoon salt
- 1/2 teaspoon pepper
- 1/2 teaspoon thyme
- 1 tablespoon olive oil
- 1 tablespoon butter
- 1/2 onion, finely chopped
- 1 cup mushrooms, sliced
- 1 sprig fresh rosemary
- 1 bay leaf
- 2 cups chicken stock
- 2 tablespoons flour
- 2 tablespoons water

Directions:

1. Season chicken with salt, pepper, and thyme. Heat olive oil in the Instant Pot on Sauté mode. Add chicken and brown on both sides. Remove to a plate.
2. Melt butter in the pot. Add onion and cook until translucent, then add mushrooms and cook until tender. Replace chicken in the pot. Add rosemary, bay leaf, and stock.
3. Close lid and set cooking time for 20 minutes. Use quick release to remove steam. Open lid and place chicken on a serving plate. Discard bay leaf and rosemary.
4. Bring stock to a boil on Sauté mode. Whisk together flour and water in a small bowl. Pour into stock, stirring constantly, and cook until gravy is thickened. Serve over chicken.

Nutritional Information

Calories - 519
Fat - 18.66 g
Carbohydrates - 7.74 g
Fiber - 0.6 g
Protein - 33.61 g

Peppercorn Lamb Curry

Total: 75 minutes
Servings: 4

Ingredients:
- 4 pounds lamb chops, cut into 2-inch cubes
- ¾ teaspoon ground pepper
- ½ cup soy sauce
- 1 cup water

- 2 bay leaves
- 2 teaspoons peppercorns
- ½ cup vinegar
- 1 teaspoon minced garlic

Directions:
- Combine all ingredients with lamb and marinate in refrigerator overnight.
- Place lamb and marinade in Instant Pot®, set at 'meat' setting and cook for 50 minutes. Release pressure naturally.
- Serve and enjoy.

Nutrition Information: Calories: 486, Protein: 5 8.3g, Total Fat: 1 3.2g, Total Carbs: 10.5g,

Creamy Cabbage Beef &Chicken

Total: 70 minutes
Servings: 8
Ingredients:
- 2 tablespoons tomato puree
- 2 pounds ground beef, cooked and browned
- ¼ teaspoon black pepper
- 1 tablespoon Worcestershire sauce
- Salt to taste
- ¼ cup water
- 1/8 teaspoon paprika
- 2 pounds chicken breast, skinless, boneless, cut into small pieces
- 1 red bell pepper, chopped
- ¼ cup cream cheese
- ¼ cabbage, chopped

Directions:
- Mix tomato puree with ground beef, black pepper, Worcestershire sauce, salt, water and paprika in Instant Pot. Secure lid, set at 'meat' setting and cook for 30 minutes.
- Use quick release; add remaining ingredients and mix well. Secure lid, set at 'poultry' setting and cook for additional 25 minutes.

- Allow pressure to release naturally. Serve with side dish of cauliflower rice.

Nutrition Info: Calories: 810, Protein: 74.1g, Total Fat: 25.7g, Total Carbs: 18.9g,

Amazing Chipotle-Chocolate Chicken Chili

Serves: 6
Time: 45 minutes

Ingredients:

1 pound ground chicken
1 cup chicken broth
1 chopped onion
1 chopped red bell pepper
2-3 minced garlic cloves
Two, 14.5-ounce cans of crushed tomatoes
15-ounces rinsed and drained dark red kidney beans
2 chipotle chilies
2 tablespoons of adobo sauce (from the can of chipotle chilis)
2 tablespoons brown sugar
2 tablespoons unsweetened cocoa powder
2 tablespoons chili powder
2 teaspoons olive oil
1 teaspoon apple cider vinegar
1 teaspoon ground cumin
¼ teaspoon salt

Directions:

1. Pour olive oil into the Instant Pot and click "sauté."
2. When the oil is shiny and hot, add the onion, garlic, bell pepper, and meat.
3. Cook and stir frequently, until the veggies are soft and the meat is brown.
4. Add everything else except the vinegar and chopped chocolate bits.
5. Hit "Cancel" and close the pressure cooker lid.
6. Select "Manual" and then 10 minutes at "high pressure."

7. When the beep sounds, quick-release the pressure.
8. Open the lid and stir in chocolate and vinegar.
9. Time to eat!

Nutritional Information

Total calories - 436
Protein - 42
Carbs - 39
Fiber - 12
Fat - 14

Buttery French Onion Chicken

Serves: 4-6
Time: 30 minutes

Ingredients:

8 bone-in chicken thighs
3 big, thinly-sliced yellow onions
1 cup grated Gruyere cheese
½ cup beef broth
½ cup dry white wine
1 tablespoon olive oil
1 tablespoon butter
2 teaspoons fresh thyme
½ teaspoon sugar
½ teaspoon black pepper
½ teaspoon salt

Directions:

1. Turn your Instant Pot to "Sauté" and melt the butter.
2. When shiny, add the chicken and brown on all sides, for a total of 6 minutes.
3. Move to a bowl.

4. Toss in the salt, sugar, and onions.
5. Cook for about 20 minutes.
6. Pour in the wine and deglaze the pot.
7. Add thyme, pepper, and broth.
8. Return the meat to the pot and stir everything together.
9. Secure the lid.
10. Hit "Manual," and then 18 minutes at "high pressure."
11. Hit "Cancel" and let the pressure decrease naturally.
12. Open the lid.
13. Sprinkle on cheese.
14. Close the lid so the cheese can melt, using the leftover heat.
15. Serve the chicken with sauce.

Nutritional Information:

Total calories: 483
Protein: 57
Carbs: 8
Fiber: 0
Fat: 23

Hot Sauce Sesame Beef

Total: 70 minutes
Servings: 4

Ingredients:
- 2-3 pounds beef, cut into thin strips
- ¼ teaspoon hot sauce
- ¼ cup packed light brown sugar
- 1 teaspoon minced garlic
- 1 teaspoon lemon juice
- ⅛ teaspoon cayenne pepper
- ½ cup soy sauce, low-sodium
- 8 ounces tomato sauce

- Salt and pepper to taste
- ¼ cup heavy cream
- 1 red bell pepper, finely sliced
- 1 tablespoon toasted sesame seeds

Directions:

- Place first 11 ingredients in Instant Pot; secure lid, set at 'meat' and cook for 50 minutes.
- Release pressure naturally. Garnish with sesame seeds.

Nutrition Info: Calories: 651, Protein: 65.7g, Total Fat: 15.9g, Total Carbs: 29.7g,

Tasty BBQ-Flavored Pork

Total: 50 minutes
Release: Naturally
Servings: 4

Ingredients:

- 3 pounds roasted pork shoulder
- 2 tablespoons balsamic vinegar
- 1 tablespoon bacon grease
- ½ teaspoon paprika
- ½ teaspoon chipotle powder
- 1 teaspoon hot sauce
- 1 tablespoon prepared yellow mustard
- ½ teaspoon onion powder
- Pinch ground ginger
- Dash coriander
- 3 tablespoons apple butter
- 1 teaspoon minced garlic
- Pinch allspice

Directions:

- Cut roasted pork into bite-size pieces, set aside.
- In a mixing bowl, combine remaining ingredients to make BBQ sauce.

- Dip pork pieces into sauce, coating evenly; place pork into Instant Pot
- Pour remaining sauce into pot. Secure lid, set at 'meat' and cook for 30 minutes.
- Release pressure naturally.

Nutrition Information:
Calories: 520
Protein: 62 .3g,
Fat: 24.6g,
Carbs: 28.8g,

Buttery Mushrooms Chicken Cubes

Total: 45 minutes
Servings: 3-4

Ingredients:

- 2 tablespoons butter
- 2 tablespoons chopped onions
- 16 Portobello mushrooms, chopped
- 4 chicken breasts, skinless, boneless, cut into cubes
- 1½ cups cheddar cheese, shredded
- 1 tablespoon chopped fresh parsley

Directions:

- Place butter, onion and mushrooms in Instant Pot® and sauté for 3 minutes.
- Add in the chicken, cheese and parsley; stir to combine. Secure lid, set at 'poultry' and cook for 30 minutes.
- Use quick release.

Nutrition Information: Calories: 496, Protein: 42.8g, Total Fat: 19.3g, Total Carbs: 4.3g,

Walnut Dates Lamb Stew

Serves: 4
Time: 50 minutes

Ingredients:

2 ½ pounds boneless leg of lamb
1 thinly-sliced red onion
1 cup pitted dried dates, cut in half
½ cup chicken broth
½ cup walnuts
½ cup unsweetened apple juice
2 tablespoons olive oil
½ tablespoon ground cinnamon
1 teaspoon ground ginger
½ teaspoon salt
¼ teaspoon grated nutmeg
¼ teaspoon allspice

Directions:

1. Mix ginger, cinnamon, allspice, nutmeg, and salt in a bowl.
2. Coat the lamb in the spices.
3. Turn your Instant Pot to "Sauté" and heat the olive oil.
4. When shiny, add the onion and soften for 5 minutes.
5. Add the meat into the pot and brown.
6. Toss in the dates, walnuts, apple juice, and broth, and deglaze.
7. Close and lock the lid.
8. Press "Manual," and then 38 minutes on "high pressure."
9. When the timer goes off, hit "Cancel" and let the pressure go down naturally.
10. Open the lid and stir.
11. Serve!

Nutritional Information

Total calories: 597
Protein: 76
Carbs: 23
Fiber: 1
Fat: 22

Garlic Stingy Sword Fish

Prep Time: 10 minutes
Cooking Time: 180 minutes
Serving: 3
Ingredients
- 5 sword fish fillets
- ½ a cup of melted butter
- 6 chopped up garlic cloves
- 1 tablespoon of black pepper

Directions:
1. Take a mixing bowl and toss in all of your garlic, black pepper alongside the melted butter
2. Take a parchment paper and place your cod fillet in that paper
3. Cover it up with the butter mixture and wrap up the fish
4. Repeat the process until all of your fish are wrapped up
5. Let it cook for 2 and a half hours and release the pressure naturally
6. Serve

Nutrition Information:
- **Calories: 379**
- **Fat: 15g**
- **Carbohydrates: 1g**
- **Protein: 34g**

Instant Pot Coconut Turkey Curry

Serves: 6
Time: About 45-50 minutes

Ingredients:

6 peeled and halved shallots
4 whole cloves
4 little dried red chilies
3 green cardamom pods
¾ cup grated, unsweetened coconut
1-inch cinnamon stick
2 teaspoons black peppercorns
2 teaspoons fennel seeds
2 teaspoons coriander seeds
1 teaspoon cumin seeds
1 teaspoon brown mustard seeds
1 teaspoon turmeric powder

3 pounds boneless turkey thighs (cut into pieces)
1 tablespoon coconut oil
2 minced garlic cloves
2 sliced tomatoes
2 sliced yellow onions
1 inch minced ginger
1 tablespoon vinegar
3 teaspoons salt

Directions:

1. We'll tackle the first ingredient list right away. Turn on the Instant Pot to "Sauté."
2. Throw in the chiles and shallots, and roast until parts have blackened.
3. Carefully take them out with tongs and put them in a food processor bowl. Do not blend yet.

4. Add the shredded coconut and whole spices to the Instant Pot and stir for 1 minute. The coconut should be a pale brown, and the spices fragrant and toasty.
5. Add the turmeric and stir for a few more seconds before moving everything to the food processor.
6. Pulse with 4-6 tablespoons of water until you get a paste.
7. Keep the paste in the bowl for now.
8. Return to the pressure cooker and add oil.
9. When shiny and hot, add the ginger, onions, and garlic.
10. Cook for 10-15 minutes until onions have softened and browned.
11. Add the coconut paste and cook for 1 minute.
12. Throw in the tomatoes and cook for 5 minutes.
13. Lastly, add the vinegar, salt, and turkey
14. Stir everything before locking the pressure cooker lid.
15. Hit "Manual," and then adjust to 10 minutes on "high pressure."
16. When time is up, hit "Cancel" and wait for the pressure to come down.
17. Serve with plain yogurt and rice.

Nutritional Information:

Total calories - 320
Protein - 47
Carbs - 5
Fiber - 4
Fat - 9

Coriander Bacon Cheese Beef

Total: 65 minutes
Servings: 4

Ingredients:

- 1 large onion, sliced

- 1 teaspoon minced garlic
- 1 tablespoon bacon grease
- 1 pounds ground beef
- 2 tablespoons Worcestershire sauce
- ¼ teaspoon black pepper
- 3 ounces shredded mozzarella cheese
- 2 ounces heavy cream
- 2 tablespoons lemon juice
- ¼ teaspoon ground coriander
- Salt and pepper to taste
- 1 teaspoon ginger powder
- 1 tablespoon prepared yellow mustard
- Dash hot sauce

Directions:

- Sauté onion, minced garlic and bacon grease in Instant Pot® for 3 minutes.
- Add ground beef and sauté for 5 minutes.
- In a mixing bowl, blend remaining ingredients and add to pot. Secure lid, set at 'meat' and cook for 50 minutes.
- Use quick release.

Nutrition Information:
Calories: 545
Protein: 50.6g,
Fat: 1 9.5g,
Carbs: 21.0g,

Delicious Multi-Meat Blend

Total: 70 minutes
Servings: 6-8

Ingredients:

- 4 tablespoons butter
- 1 teaspoon minced garlic
- 2 teaspoons minced ginger
- 1 onion, sliced
- ½ pound ground beef
- ½ pound chicken, minced
- ½ pound ground lamb
- ½ pound ground pork
- 1 red bell pepper, chopped
- 2 cups chicken broth, low-sodium
- 2 tablespoons tomato puree
- Salt and pepper to taste
- 4 eggs
- 2 cups heavy cream
- 1 teaspoon allspice

Directions:

- Place butter, garlic, ginger, and onion into Instant Pot® and sauté for 3 minutes.
- In a mixing bowl, add remaining ingredients and blend well.
- Pour mixture into pot. Secure lid, set at 'meat' and cook for 50 minutes.
- Use quick release.

Nutrition Information:

Calories: 650,
Protein: 98.4g,
Fat: 25.5g
Carbs: 36.9g

Crab Black Bean Soup

Prep Time: 10 minutes
Cooking Time: 30 minutes
Serving: 6

Ingredients:

- 2 tablespoon of olive oil
- 1 large white onion roughly chopped up
- 1 clove of garlic that is peeled off and smashed
- ½ of a red bell pepper, chopped up and seeded
- 1 celery rib diced up
- 1 teaspoon of smoked paprika
- 2 cups of dried black beans
- 2 cups of dried black beans
- 8 cups of chicken broth
- Salt as needed
- 1 and a ½ cup of crab meat
- ¼ cup of chopped up fresh cilantro
- 2 tablespoon of minced fresh chives
- Lime wedges for serving

Directions:
1. Pour in the oil in your instant pot and heat it until hot
2. Toss in the red pepper, celery, garlic and onions and Sauté them nicely for 3 minutes
3. Add in the Chile powder and paprika then followed by the beans and broth
4. Stir to mix completely and place tomato paste on top
5. Close down the lid and let it cook at high pressure for 30 minutes
6. One done, let the pressure release naturally
7. Puree the soup in an immersion blender until nicely smooth
8. Season it with some salt and chipotle powder
9. Place a heaping quarter cup of crab meat in the bottom of each soup bowl
10. Ladle the soup and sprinkle some cilantro
11. Serve with lime wedges

Nutrition Information

- **Calories: 572**
- **Fat: 18g**
- **Carbohydrates: 15g**
- **Protein: 52g**

Healthy Continental Chicken

Total: 45 minutes
Servings: 4

Ingredients:
- 4 chicken breasts, boneless, skinless
- 1 teaspoon minced garlic
- 2 teaspoons olive oil
- ½ teaspoon ground ginger
- ½ teaspoon cinnamon
- ½ teaspoon black pepper
- 1 teaspoon cumin
- 1 green onion, chopped, for garnish

Directions:

- Mix all ingredients in mixing bowl; place in refrigerator overnight to marinate.
- Add ingredients to Instant Pot®. Secure lid, set at 'poultry' and cook for 25 minutes.
- Use natural release. Garnish with green onion and serve.

Nutrition Information: Calories: 98, Protein: 0.7g, Total Fat: 9.9g, Total Carbs: 3.2g,

Tasty Ginger Duck

Total: 60 minutes
Servings: 8

Ingredients:

- 1 duck, properly processed
- 2 carrots, diced
- 1 cucumber, cut into small pieces
- 2 cups water
- 2 tablespoons cooking wine
- 1 inch ginger, chopped
- Salt and pepper to taste

Directions:

- Add duck to Instant Pot® and pour all the other ingredients over it.
- Secure lid, set at 'poultry' and cook for 40 minutes.
- Release pressure naturally.

Nutrition Information: Calories: 564, Protein: 54.9g, Total Fat: 25.1g, Total Carbs: 23.8g,

Delicious Pork Fried Rice

Serves: 4
Time: 40 minutes

Ingredients:

3 cups + 2 tablespoons water
2 cups white rice
8-ounces thin pork loin, cut into ½-inch slices
1 beaten egg
½ cup frozen peas
1 chopped onion

1 peeled and chopped carrot
3 tablespoons olive oil
3 tablespoons soy sauce
Salt + pepper

Directions:

1. Turn your Instant Pot to "Sauté."
2. Pour in 1 tablespoon of oil and cook the carrot and onion for 2 minutes.
3. Season the pork.
4. Cook in the pot for 5 minutes.
5. Hit "Cancel" and take out the onion, carrot, and pork.
6. Deglaze with the water.
7. Add rice and a bit of salt.
8. Lock the lid.
9. Hit "Rice" and cook for the default time.
10. When time is up, hit "Cancel" and wait 10 minutes.
11. Release any leftover steam.
12. Stir the rice, making a hollow in the middle so you can see the bottom of the pot.
13. Hit "Sauté" and add 2 tablespoons of oil.
14. Add the egg in the hollow and whisk it around to scramble it while it cooks.
15. When cooked, pour in peas, onion, carrot, and pork.
16. Stir until everything has warmed together.
17. Stir in soy sauce, hit "Cancel," and serve.

Nutritional Information

Total calories - 547
Protein - 42
Carbs - 11
Fiber - 3
Fat - 10

Mouth-Watering Hawaiian Pork

Serves: 8
Time: 2 hours

Ingredients:

5 pounds bone-in pork roast
6 minced garlic cloves
1 cup water
1 quartered onion
1 ½ tablespoons red Hawaiian coarse salt
Black pepper

Directions:

1. Cut the meat into 3 pieces.
2. Put in the Instant Pot.
3. Add in garlic, onion, and salt.
4. Season with black pepper.
5. Pour in the water and lock the lid.
6. Hit "Manual," and cook for 1 ½ hours on "high pressure."
7. When time is done, hit "Cancel," and wait for the pressure to decrease naturally.
8. Before serving, shred the pork with two forks.

Nutritional Information:

Total calories - 536
Protein - 51
Carbs - 2
Fiber - 0
Fat - 13

Cashews Thai Chicken

Total: 45 minutes
Servings: 6

Ingredients:

- 3 chicken breasts, boneless, skinless, cut into small pieces
- 1 cup coconut milk
- 1 cup cauliflower florets
- 1 package frozen mixed veggies
- 4 ounces Thai curry paste
- 4 tablespoons butter
- ½ cup chopped cashews

Directions:

- Place all ingredients into Instant Pot®; secure lid, set at 'poultry' and cook for 30 minutes.
- Use quick release.

Nutrition Information: Calories: 624, Protein: 81.9g, Total Fat: 19.8g, Total Carbs: 20.3g,

Cumin Zucchini Curry Chicken

Total: 65 minutes
Servings: 8

Ingredients:

- 1 teaspoon coconut oil
- ½ cup diced white onion
- 1 teaspoon minced garlic
- 4 chicken breasts, boneless, skinless, chopped into chunks
- 4 zucchini, finely chopped
- 1 teaspoon garam masala
- ¼ teaspoon cayenne pepper
- ¼ cup chopped, fresh cilantro

- ½ teaspoon cumin
- 1 tablespoon curry powder
- 1 cup coconut milk

Directions:

- Add coconut oil to Instant Pot® along with onion and garlic; sauté for 3 minutes.
- Add remaining ingredients; secure lid, set at 'poultry' and cook for 40 minutes.
- Use quick release and enjoy!

Nutrition Information: Calories: 610, Protein: 59, Total Fat: 24.4g, Total Carbs: 30.4g,

Chili Beef

Prep Time: 10 minutes
Cooking Time: 35 minutes
Serving: 6

Ingredients:

- 1 pound of grass fed organic feed
- 1 sliced and seeded green bell pepper
- 1 large sized onion
- 4 large pieces of chopped up small carrot
- ½ a teaspoon of ground black pepper
- 1 teaspoon of sea salt
- 1 teaspoon of onion powder
- 1 tablespoon of chopped up fresh parsley
- 1 tablespoon of Worcestershire sauce
- 4 teaspoon of chili powder
- 1 teaspoon of paprika
- 1 teaspoon of garlic powder
- Just a pinch of cumin

Directions:

1. The first step here is to press the Sauté button on your Instant Pot
2. Toss in the ground beef and let it cook until it is brown
3. Toss in the rest of the ingredients and gently mix them properly
4. Close up the lid and press the warm button, after which press the meat/stew button
5. Let them cook for about 35 minutes keeping the steam valve closed
6. Once the timer runs out, naturally let the pressure out and serve

Nutrition Information
- **Calories: 320**
- **Fat: 6.8g**
- **Carbohydrates: 2.1g**
- **Protein: 18g**

Easy Salsa Verde Chicken

Serves: 6
Time: 25 minutes

Ingredients:
2 ½ pounds of boneless chicken breasts
16-ounces of salsa Verde
1 teaspoon smoked paprika
1 teaspoon cumin
1 teaspoon salt

Directions:
1. Throw everything into your Instant Pot pressure cooker.
2. Select "Manual," and then 25 minutes at "high pressure."
3. When the timer goes off, quick-release the pressure.

4. Carefully open the cooker and shred the chicken.
5. Eat and enjoy!
Nutritional Information:
Total calories - 340
Protein - 59
Carbs - 6
Fiber - 0
Fat - 7

CHAPTER 5 INSTANT POT DESSERT RECIPES

Popular Pumpkin Pie

Prep Time: 10 minutes
Cooking Time: 35 minutes
Servings: 4

Ingredients:
- 1 prepared graham cracker pie crust in aluminum pan
- 1 can pumpkin
- 1/2 cup milk
- 1 egg
- 1/2 cup brown sugar
- 1 teaspoon cinnamon
- 1/2 teaspoon nutmeg

Directions:
1. Blend together pumpkin, milk, egg, sugar, cinnamon, and nutmeg. Pour into prepared graham cracker crust.
2. Place the trivet in the pot and pour in enough water to reach just the top of the trivet. Place the pie over the trivet.
3. Close the lid and set cooking time for 35 minutes on high pressure. Chill pie before serving.

Nutritional Info: Calories – 413; Fat - 13.85 g; Carbohydrates - 12.5 g; Fiber - 4.8 g; Protein - 28 g

Instant Pot Crème Brule

Serves: 6
Time: 2 hours chill,
16 minutes cook time

Ingredients:

8 egg yolks
2 cups heavy cream
6 tablespoons superfine sugar
⅓ Cup white sugar
1 ½ teaspoons vanilla
Pinch of salt

Directions:

1. Pour 1 ½ cups of water into your Instant Pot and lower in the trivet.
2. In a bowl, mix the egg yolks, white sugar, and a pinch of salt.
3. Add in the cream and vanilla, whisking until smooth and blended.
4. Strain this into a pitcher, and then pour into six custard cups.
5. Wrap tightly in foil and put on the trivet. You'll need a second trivet to go on top of that first layer so you can put the rest of the cups in the cooker.
6. Close the lid.
7. Hit "manual," then cook on high pressure for 6 minutes.
8. When time is up, hit "cancel" and wait for the pressure to reduce for 10 minutes.
9. Quick-release the leftover pressure.
10. Take out the cups and unwrap so they can cool.
11. Once cool, cover with plastic wrap and chill for at least 2 hours.
12. When you're ready to serve, sprinkle the superfine sugar on top.
13. Use a torch, holding it about 2 inches from the sugar, and caramelize.

Nutritional Information:
Total calories: 210
Protein: 13
Fat: 10
Carbs: 15
Fiber: 3

Orange Marble Cheesecake

Serves: 8

Time: 4 hours, 47 minutes (12 minutes active time, 35 minutes cook time, 4 hours chill time)

Ingredients:

For crust

12 crushed Oreos

2 tablespoons melted butter

For filling

16-ounces room-temperature cream cheese

½ cup melted and cooled orange candy melts

½ cup sugar

2 tablespoons sour cream

2 room-temperature eggs

1 tablespoon orange zest

1 teaspoon vanilla extract

Directions:

1. Grease a 7-inch springform pan.
2. In a bowl, mix the melted butter and cookie crumbs together.
3. Pour into the springform pan to make the crust, pressing down on the crumbs, with it going up 1-inch on the pan's sides.
4. Refrigerate for 10 minutes to set.
5. Put 8-ounces of cream cheese in a bowl along with ¼ cup sugar.
6. Beat until smooth.
7. Add sour cream and vanilla.
8. Mix in one egg until the ingredients are just incorporated.
9. In another bowl, put the rest of the cream cheese with the rest of the sugar and mix.
10. Add the melted candy and blend.
11. Add eggs until blended, and then the orange zest.
12. Take out the springform pan, and spoon in the plain vanilla batter and orange batter.
13. With a skewer or chopstick, swirl the batters together to get the marbled look.
14. Pour 1 cup of water into your Instant Pot and lower in the trivet.
15. Put the springform pan on the trivet. You don't need to wrap it.
16. Close the lid, select "manual," and then high pressure for 25 minutes.
17. When time is up, hit "cancel" and wait 10 minutes before quick-releasing leftover pressure.

18. The cheesecake should be set, but a little wiggly, like Jell-O.
19. Soak up excess water with the corner of a paper towel.
20. Take out the pan to cool before covering with plastic wrap, and chilling in the fridge for at least 4 hours. Serve and enjoy

Nutritional Information
Total calories: 383
Protein: 8
Fat: 20
Carbs: 29.5
Fiber: 1

Yummy Coffee Espresso Pudding

Prep Time: 5 minutes
Cooking Time: 15 minutes
Serving: 6

Ingredients
- 1 cup of heavy cream
- 1 cup of half and half
- 1 tablespoon of instant espresso powder
- ½ a cup of sugar
- 1 large egg
- 4 egg yolks

Directions:
1. Start off by taking a large sized bowl and toss in your half and half, cream, espresso powder and keep whisking it until the powder has fully dissolved
2. Pour in the mixture over your white chocolate and whisk in the egg yolks, sugar, zest and lemon extract
3. Pour in the mixture in six ½ cup heat safe ramekins, covering them up with aluminum foil
4. Place them in your pressure cooker and pour in just 2 cups of water
5. Lock up the lid and let it cook at high pressure for 15 minutes
6. Release the pressure naturally
7. Unlock the cooker and take out the hot ramekins to a cooling rack
8. Serve hot or let it refrigerate for a while if you prefer something cold

Nutrition: Calories: 310; Fat: 20G; Carbohydrates: 25G; Protein: 14g

Beautiful Carved Out Of Cherry

Prep Time: 5 minutes
Cooking Time: 18 minutes
Serving: 6

Ingredients
- 2 cups of pitted sour cherries
- ¾ cups of regular cream
- 4 large pieces of egg yolk
- 1/3 cup of honey
- 1/ cup of whole milk
- 1 tablespoon of vanilla extract
- ½ teaspoon of salt
- ½ a cup of all-purpose flour

Directions:
1. Take a nice 2 quart soufflé dish and toss in your butter and pour 2 cups of water
2. Place the cherries in the bottom of your baking dish
3. Take a bowl and whisk in the sour cream, egg yolks, honey, and milk, vanilla and salt until it is nicely smooth and creamy
4. Whisk in your flour until fully dissolved
5. Pour the batter over your baking dish containing the cherry
6. Make aluminum foil sling and set the baking dish on top of it, then use the sling to place the baking dish in your cooker
7. Lock up the lid and let it cook for 18 minutes at high pressure
8. Release the pressure naturally
9. Unlock the lid and take out the baking dish out of your pot and place it on a cooking rack
10. Let it cool for 10 minutes and serve

Nutrition Information
- **Calories: 155**
- **Fat: 5g**
- **Carbohydrates: 6g**
- **Protein: 23g**

Raisin Bread Pudding

Prep Time: 15 minutes
Cooking Time: 25 minutes
Servings: 4

Ingredients:

- 6 slices day-old bread
- 1/4 cup butter, melted
- 3 eggs
- 3 cups milk
- 1/2 cup white sugar
- 1/2 cup brown sugar
- 1 teaspoon vanilla
- 1 teaspoon cinnamon
- 1/2 cup raisins

Directions:

1. Toss the bread with the butter. Sprinkle in raisins. Arrange the bread in a baking pan that fits in the Instant Pot.
2. Whisk together eggs, milk, sugars, vanilla, and cinnamon. Pour over the bread. Press down to help the bread absorb the liquid.
3. Place a trivet in the Instant Pot. Pour enough water into the Instant Pot to just reach the top of the trivet. Place the pan on the trivet.
4. Close the lid and set the cooking time for 25 minutes on high pressure. Serve warm or chilled.

Nutritional Information:

Calories - 547

Fat - 20.65 g

Carbohydrates - 46.51 g

Fiber - 1.2 g

Protein - 12.75 g

Coconut Samoa Cheesecake

Serves: 6
Time: 4 hours, 55 minutes (10 minutes active time, 45 minutes cook time, 4 hours chill time)

Ingredients:

For the crust
½ cup crushed chocolate graham crackers
2 tablespoons melted butter

For the filling
12-ounces room-temperature cream cheese
2 room-temperature eggs
1 room-temperature egg yolk
½ cup sugar
¼ cup sour cream
¼ cup heavy cream
1 tablespoon all-purpose

For the topping
12 unwrapped chewy caramels
1 ½ cups shredded coconut

¼ cup chopped semisweet chocolate
3 tablespoons heavy cream

Directions:

1. Grease a 7-inch springform pan.
2. In a bowl, mix the cracker crumbs and melted butter.
3. Pour into the pan and press down evenly, covering the bottom and up the sides by about 1-inch.
4. Stick in the fridge for 10 minutes to set.
5. In another bowl, mix sugar and cream cheese.
6. Add and mix heavy cream, vanilla, flour, and sour cream.
7. Add eggs until just incorporated.
8. Pour into the pan and cover with foil.
9. Pour 1 cup of water into the Instant Pot and lower in the trivet.
10. Put the pan on top and close the lid.
11. Select "manual," then cook on high pressure for 35 minutes.
12. When time is up, hit "cancel" and let the pressure decrease naturally for 10 minutes.
13. Carefully take out the cheesecake and look beneath the foil. If the cheesecake looks set and jiggles a little, it's ready. If not, cover, and put back in the pressure cooker to cook on high for 5 more minutes. Quick-release this time.
14. Take out the pan to cool without the foil.
15. When cool, cover with plastic wrap and chill for at least 4 hours.
16. To make the topping when you're ready to serve the cheesecake, preheat the oven to 300-degrees.
17. Spread the coconut evenly on a baking sheet lined with parchment, and toast for 20 minutes, stirring every 5 minutes to prevent burning.
18. Cool.
19. Microwave the cream and caramels for 1-2 minutes, stopping to stir every 20 seconds.
20. When totally smooth, add the coconut.
21. Spread on top of cheesecake.
22. Melt the chocolate in a microwave.
23. Pour into a Ziploc bag and use like a pastry bag, with a corner snipped off, and drizzle on top of the caramel.

Nutritional Information:
Total calories: 461
Protein: 30

Fat: 19
Carbs: 21
Fiber: 0

Cherry Topping Almond Pudding Cake

Prep Time: 5 minutes
Cooking Time: 25 minutes
Serving: 6

Ingredients
- 1 cup of cherry jam
- 8 tablespoon of unsalted butter
- ¼ cup of dark brown sugar
- ¼ cup of granulated white sugar
- 2 large eggs
- 3 tablespoon of almond liquor
- 1 tablespoon of vanilla extract
- ¾ cup of finely ground almonds
- ½ a cup of all-purpose flour
- ¼ teaspoon of salt

Directions:
1. Take a nice 2 quart soufflé dish and toss in your butter and pour 2 cups of water in your pot
2. Spread jam across the bottom of your baking dish and place it in your pot
3. Take an electric mixer and beat your butter and sugars in a bowl until it is finely creamy and pale yellow for about 5 minutes, making sure to scrap down the inside of the bowl from time to time
4. Beat in the eggs one at a time, while making sure to mix it after each egg drop.
5. Toss in the almonds, flour, salt then and keep beating it at low speed again
6. Pour in the batter into your prepared baking dish and butter one side of a 12 inch foil before sealing up the dish nicely

7. Make aluminum foil sling and set the baking dish on top of it, then use the sling to place the baking dish in your cooker
8. Lock up the lid and let it cook for 35 minutes at high pressure
9. Release the pressure naturally
10. Unlock the lid and take out the baking dish out of your pot and place it on a cooking rack
11. After it is cooled, invert the dish to drop down the cake
12. Serve warm

Nutrition Information
- **Calories: 290**
- **Fat: 12g**
- **Carbohydrates: 4g**
- **Protein: 12g**

Fudgy Brownies

Prep Time: 10 minutes
Cooking Time: 20 minutes
Servings: 4

Ingredients:
- 1/2 cup butter
- 1 cup sugar
- 2 eggs
- 1 teaspoon vanilla
- 2/3 cup flour
- 1/3 cup cocoa powder
- 1/2 teaspoon baking powder
- 1/2 teaspoon salt

Directions:
1. Cream butter and sugar, then beat in eggs one at a time. Add vanilla last. In a separate bowl, whisk together flour, cocoa, baking powder, and salt. Fold dry

ingredients into wet ingredients. Pour batter into a baking pan that fits into the Instant Pot.
2. Place a trivet in the Instant Pot. Add enough water to just reach the top of the trivet. Place the baking pan over the trivet.
3. Close the lid and set the cooking time to 20 minutes. Serve brownies warm or room temperature.
Nutritional information:
Calories - 324; Fat - 10.25 g; Carbohydrates - 12.72 g; Fiber - 2.7 g; Protein - 6.45 g

Chocolate Mix Lemon Pudding

Prep Time: 5 minutes
Cooking Time: 15 minutes
Serving: 6

Ingredients

- 6 ounce of chopped up white chocolate
- 1 cup of heavy cream
- 1 cup of half and half
- 4 large pieces of egg yolk
- 1 tablespoon of sugar
- 1 tablespoon of finely grated lemon zest
- ¼ teaspoon of extracted lemon

Directions:

1. Start off by taking a large sized bowl and toss in your whiter chocolate
2. Mix the cream and half and half in a small sized sauce pan and warm it over low heat until the bubble starts to fizz around the edges
3. Pour in the mixture over your white chocolate and whisk in the egg yolks, sugar, zest and lemon extract
4. Pour in the mixture in six ½ cup heat safe ramekins, covering them up with aluminum foil
5. Place them in your pressure cooker and pour in just 2 cups of water

6. Lock up the lid and let it cook at high pressure for 15 minutes
7. Release the pressure naturally
8. Unlock the cooker and take out the hot ramekins to a cooling rack
9. Serve hot or let it refrigerate for a while if you prefer something cold

Nutrition Information
- **Calories: 280**
- **Fat: 20g**
- **Carbohydrates: 40g**
- **Protein: 7g**

Mango Cake

Serves: 8
Time: 45 minutes (5 minutes active time, 40 minutes cook time)

Ingredients:

1 ¼ cups flour
¾ cup milk
½ cup sugar
¼ cup coconut oil
1 tablespoon lemon juice
1 teaspoon mango syrup
1 teaspoon baking powder
¼ teaspoon baking soda
⅛ Teaspoon salt

Directions:

1. Grease a baking pan that will fit in your Instant Pot.
2. Mix the sugar, oil, and milk in a bowl until the sugar has melted.

3. Pour in mango syrup and mix again.
4. Pour all the dry ingredients through a sieve into the wet.
5. Add lemon juice and mix well.
6. Pour into the baking pan.
7. Pour 1 cup of water into the Instant Pot and lower in a trivet.
8. Lower the baking pan into the cooker and close the lid.
9. Select "manual," and cook on high pressure for 35 minutes.
10. When time is up, hit "cancel" and wait for the pressure to come down naturally.
11. Check the cake for doneness before cooling for 10 minutes.
12. Serve!

Nutritional Information:

Total calories: 230
Protein: 2
Fat: 7
Carbs: 19
Fiber: 0

Creamy Chocolate Cheesecake

Serves: 6-8
Time: 4 hours, 40 minutes (10 minutes active time, 30 minutes cook time, 4 hours chill time)

Ingredients:

For the crust
1 ½ cups chocolate cookie crumbs
4 tablespoons butter

For the batter
1 pound room-temperature cream cheese

5 ounces sifted, packed brown sugar
2 room temperature eggs
6-ounces melted and cooled bittersweet chocolate
2-ounces sour cream
2 tablespoons cocoa powder
1 ½ teaspoons instant coffee (dissolved in 1 ½ teaspoons water)
1 teaspoon vanilla extract
¼ teaspoon fine sea salt

Directions:

1. Grease a 6x3 springform pan and cut a piece of parchment paper, so you get a round that will go on top of the pan when you close up the cooker.
2. In a bowl, mix the cookie crumbs and melted butter.
3. Press the crust down evenly into the bottom of the pan and 1-inch up the sides. Store in the fridge until it's time to pour in the batter.
4. To make the batter, begin by creaming the cream cheese in a low mixer until smooth.
5. Add the salt, vanilla, and sugar and continue to beat on low until combined.
6. Add 1 egg and mix completely.
7. Add the second egg and mix.
8. Add the instant coffee/water mixture.
9. In a separate bowl, whisk the cocoa and sour cream together until you get a whipped-cream like consistency.
10. Add the mixer and slowly incorporate.
11. Pour in the melted (and cooled) chocolate and mix until just combined.
12. Pour into the pan. Wrap completely in foil, including the bottom and sides.
13. Pour 2 cups of water into the Instant Pot and lower in the trivet.
14. Close the lid.
15. Select "manual," and cook on high pressure for 25 minutes.
16. When time is up, hit "cancel" and wait 10 minutes for the pressure to come down on its own.
17. Chill the cheesecake for at least four hours before serving.

Nutritional Information:
Total calories: 498
Protein: 8.5
Fat: 21

Carbs: 29
Fiber: 2

California Cheesecake

Prep Time: 10 minutes
Cooking Time: 25 minutes
Servings: 4

Ingredients:

- 1 prepared graham cracker crust in aluminum pan
- 1 package cream cheese, softened
- 1/2 cup sour cream
- 2 eggs
- 2/3 cup sugar
- 2 tablespoons cornstarch
- 2 teaspoons vanilla

Directions:

1. Beat together cream cheese, sour cream, eggs, sugar, cornstarch, and vanilla. Pour into pie crust.
2. Place a trivet in the Instant Pot. Add enough water to reach the top of the trivet. Place the pie pan on the trivet.
3. Close lid and set cooking time for 25 minutes on high pressure. Chill before serving.

Nutritional Information

Calories - 523
Fat - 23.78 g
Carbohydrates - 49.89 g
Fiber - 0.9 g

Protein - 7.37 g

Delicious Oreo Cheesecake

Prep Time: 15 minutes
Cooking Time: 45 minutes
Serving: 6

Ingredients
For Crust
- 12 whole Oreo cookies completely crushed
- 2 tablespoon of salted butter

For Cheesecake
- 16 ounce of cream cheese
- ½ cup of granulated sugar
- 2 large pieces of eggs
- 1 tablespoon of all-purpose flour
- 2 teaspoon of pure vanilla extract
- 8 whole Oreo cookies chopped up

For Topping
- 1 cup of whipped cream
- 8 whole Oreo cookies
- Chocolate sauce

Directions:
1. Start off by taking a spring form pan (7 inch) and wrap the bottom of it using a foil
2. Grease the inside with cooking spray
3. Take a small sized bowl and toss in 12 crushed cookies and melt the butter
4. Press the crumbs into the bottom of your previously readied pan
5. Place the pan in a freezer and let it chill for 15 minutes

6. Take a bowl and pour in your cream cheese and mix it using a blender until smooth, toss in the eggs then making sure to keep blending from time to time
7. Toss in the flour, heavy cream vanilla and blend until smooth
8. Fold in 8 chopped up Oreo chipped up cookies and pour them in the batter
9. Cover it up with a piece of foil
10. Make aluminum foil sling and set the baking dish on top of it, then use the sling to place the baking dish in your cooker
11. Lock up the lid and let it cook at high pressure for 40 minutes
12. Allow the pressure to release naturally
13. Take it out using the sling and let it cool down to room temperature
14. Once the cheesecake has been cooled, let it cool over night
15. Serve cool with whipped cream and Oreo toppings

Nutrition Information
- **Calories: 247**
- **Fat: 16g**
- **Carbohydrates: 24g**
- **Protein: 23g**

Mouth-Watering Apple Crisp

Prep Time: 10 minutes
Cooking Time: 8 minutes
Servings: 4

Ingredients:

- 5 apples, peeled and chopped
- 1/2 cup apple cider
- 2 tablespoons maple syrup
- 1 teaspoon cinnamon
- 1/2 teaspoon nutmeg
- 3/4 cup rolled oats
- 1/4 cup flour

- 1/4 brown sugar
- 1/4 cup butter, melted

Directions:

1. Place apples in the Instant Pot. Pour apple cider and maple syrup over the apples. Sprinkle with cinnamon and nutmeg.
2. In a bowl, whisk together oats, flour, and sugar. Stir in melted butter. Drop spoonfuls of topping over the apples.
3. Close lid and set cooking time to 8 minutes on high pressure. Serve warm with ice cream.

Nutritional Information:

Calories - 335

Fat - 13.36 g

Carbohydrates - 29.88 g

Fiber - 8.8 g

Protein - 14.66 g

Apple Blast Cheese Cake

Prep Time: 5 minutes
Cooking Time: 10 minutes
Serving: 4
Ingredients
- ½ a cup of applesauce
- 4 cups of cream cheese

- 3 pieces of whole egg
- 1 teaspoon of vanilla extract

Directions:
1. The first step here is to grease up your pie pan container with butter
2. In that container, pour in your apple sauce, cream cheese, eggs alongside the vanilla
3. Place the pan in the inner pot of your instant pot
4. Gently set the pressure of your pot to high and let it cook for about 10 minutes
5. Once done, release the pressure naturally
6. Take it out and let it cool for a while and serve it with a topping of either cherries or apple

Nutrition Information: Calories: 350; Fat: 15G; Carbohydrates: 13G; Protein: 11g

Yummy Red-Wine Baked Apples

Serves: 6
Time: 30-40 minutes

Ingredients:
6 cored apples
1 cup red wine
½ cup sugar
¼ cup raisins
1 teaspoon cinnamon

Directions:
1. Set the apples inside the Instant Pot.
2. Pour in wine and add the sugar, cinnamon, and raisins.
3. Secure the lid.
4. Select "Manual" and cook for 10 minutes on "high pressure."
5. When the timer beeps, hit "cancel" and wait 20-30 minutes for the pressure to come down.
6. Serve the apples in a bowl with the cooking liquid spooned over.

Nutritional Info:

Total calories - 188.7; Protein – 0; Carbs - 1.9; Fiber - 3.8; Fat - 0

Crumble Cinnamon Stuffed Peaches

Serves: 5
Time: About 15 minutes

Ingredients:

5 medium-sized peaches
¼ cup brown sugar
¼ cup flour
2 tablespoons butter
½ teaspoon ground cinnamon
1/2 teaspoon pure almond extract + ¼ teaspoon almond extract
Pinch of sea salt

Directions:

1. Carefully slice about ¼ inch off the top of your peaches.
2. With a sharp knife, cut into the top and take out the pits, so the peaches have a little hollow.
3. In a bowl, mix the flour, sugar, cinnamon, and salt.
4. Melt the butter and add, along with the ½ teaspoon of almond extract.
5. Mix until crumbly.
6. Fill peaches.
7. Pour 1 cup of water into the Instant Pot and add ¼ teaspoon of almond extract right into the water.
8. Lower in the steamer basket and arrange the peaches inside.
9. Secure the lid.
10. Press "Manual" and decrease the time to 3 minutes.
11. When the timer sounds, press "Cancel" and unplug.
12. Quick-release the pressure.
13. Remove the peaches with tongs and cool for 10 minutes.
14. Serve with vanilla ice cream or devour as is!

Nutritional Information:

Total calories - 162
Protein - 2
Carbs - 10
Fiber - 2.3
Fat - 5

Instant Pot Berry Cobbler

Prep Time: 10 minutes
Cooking Time: 25 minutes
Servings: 6

Ingredients:

Filling:
- 2 cups frozen blueberries
- 1 teaspoon vanilla
- Juice of 1/2 lemon
- 1 cup sugar
- 1 teaspoon cornstarch

Topping:
- 2 cups flour
- 1 tablespoon baking powder
- 1/2 cup sugar
- 1/4 cup butter, melted
- 1 cup milk

Directions:

1. Pour blueberries into pot and top with vanilla, lemon juice, sugar, and cornstarch. Stir.
2. In a bowl, whisk together flour, baking powder, sugar, butter, and milk. Drop onto blueberries in clumps.
3. Close lid and set cooking time for 25 minutes on high pressure. Serve warm with ice cream.

Nutritional Information

Calories - 408

Fat - 9.79 g

Carbohydrates - 15.42 g

Fiber - 2.6 g

Protein - 10.91 g

Mini Lava Cake

Prep Time: 5 minutes
Cooking Time: 10 minutes
Serving: 2
Ingredients
- 1 piece of whole egg
- 2 tablespoon of extra virgin olive oil
- 4 tablespoon of sugar
- 4 tablespoon of milk
- 4 tablespoon of all-purpose organic unbleached
- 1 tablespoon of Cacao powder
- Just a pinch of salt

Directions:

1. The first step here is to take a ramekin and grease it up with a bit of butter
2. Pour in about 1 cup of water in your instant pot and place a trivet in your inner pot
3. Take a medium sized bowl and toss in all of the ingredients, only to mix them up nicely until finely blended
4. Pour in the mixture in you ramekins
5. Place the ramekins inside your instant pot and close up the lid
6. Set the timer to 6 minutes and let it cook
7. Once done, let the pressure release naturally and take out the cake
8. Sprinkle a bit of powdered sugar for added taste and serve

Nutrition Info: Calories: 231; Fat: 14G; Carbohydrates: 10G; Protein: 3g

Maple Syrup Crème Caramel

Prep Time: 5 minutes
Cooking Time: 9 minutes
Servings: 4

Ingredients:
- 1/2 cup maple syrup
- 3 eggs
- 1 can condensed milk
- 1 can evaporate milk
- 2 teaspoons vanilla

Directions:

1. Whisk together eggs, milk, and vanilla.
2. Pour maple syrup into the bottom of a pan that fits into the Instant Pot. Slowly pour the egg mixture over the syrup.
3. Place a trivet into the Instant Pot. Add enough water to reach the top of the trivet. Place the pot on top of the trivet.
4. Close the lid and set the cooking time for 9 minutes on high pressure.
5. Chill completely before inverting onto a plate.

Nutritional Values (Per Serving):

Calories - 401; Fat - 10.07 g; Carbohydrates - 23.04 g; Fiber - 0 g; Protein - 19.88 g

Honey Cranberries Pear Cake

5 servings
Total Time Taken: 5 minutes

Ingredients
8 ounce chopped pear
4 ounce chopped cranberries
6-ounce whole wheat pastry flour
½ teaspoon baking soda
½ teaspoon baking powder
0.5-ounce ground flax seeds
1/8 teaspoon salt
½ teaspoon ground cardamom
2-ounce honey
2 tablespoons melted coconut oil
4 fluid ounce almond milk
12 fluid ounce water

Directions
1. In a mixing bowl stir together flour, baking soda, baking powder, salt, and cardamom until combined.
2. In another mixing bowl whisk together flax seeds, coconut oil, honey and flax seeds until combined and then stir in flour mixture, 2-3 tablespoons at a time, until incorporated.
3. Fold in berries and pears.
4. Grease a 7-inch Bundt pan with oil, then spoon cake mixture in it and cover the pan with aluminum foil.
5. Into a 6-quarts instant pot, pour in water, then insert a trivet and place cake pan on it.
6. Secure pot with lid, then position pressure indicator, select manual option and adjust cooking time on timer pad to 35 minutes and let cook. Instant pot will take 10 minutes to build pressure before cooking timer starts.

7. When the timer beeps, switch off the instant pot and let pressure release naturally for 10 minutes and then do quick pressure release.
8. Then uncover the pot, carefully remove the cake pan and uncover.
9. Let cake cool on the wire rack before taking out to serve.

Nutritional Information:
244 Cal,
8.3 g total fat;
Carb. 2.1 g
3.1 g protein.

Delicious Tapioca Pudding

Yield: 5 servings
Total Time Taken: 30 minutes
Ingredients
1/3 cup tapioca pearls, rinsed
4-ounce brown sugar
Half of a lemon, zested
10 fluid ounce coconut milk
4 fluid ounce water
Directions
1. Take a big heatproof bowl enough to fit into the pot and add tapioca pearls, sugar, lemon zest, coconut milk and water and mix well until sugar dissolves completely.
2. Into a 6-quarts instant pot pour in 1 cup water, then insert a trivet and place pudding bowl in it.
3. Secure pot with lid, then position pressure indicator, select manual option and adjust cooking time on timer pad to 8 minutes and let cook. Instant pot will take 10 minutes to build pressure before cooking timer starts.
4. When the timer beeps, switch off the instant pot and let pressure release naturally for 10 minutes and then do quick pressure release.
5. Then uncover the pot and carefully pull out the bowl and immediately stir with a fork.

6. Cover bowl tightly with plastic wrap and let cool in the refrigerator for 2-3 hours or more until chilled, before serving.

Nutritional Information: 122 Cal, 2 g total fat ;15 g carb., 0 g fiber, 5 g protein.

Delicious Orange-Glazed Poached Pears

Serves: 4
Time: 17 minutes (5 minutes prep time, 12 minutes cook time)

Ingredients:

4 ripe pears
1 cup orange juice
⅓ Cup sugar
1 cinnamon stick
2 teaspoons cinnamon
1 teaspoon nutmeg
1 teaspoon ginger
1 teaspoon ground clove

Directions:

1. Peel the pears, leaving the stem alone.
2. Pour 1 cup of orange juice into your cooker and add spices.
3. Arrange pears in the steamer basket and lower in the cooker.
4. Close and seal the lid.
5. Click "manual" and adjust time to 7 minutes on high pressure.
6. When time is up, press "cancel" and wait 5 minutes before quick-releasing.
7. Carefully remove trivet and pears.
8. Pick out the cinnamon stick.
9. Turn your pot to sauté and add sugar.
10. Stir until the liquid has reduced to a sauce.
11. Serve pears with sauce poured on top.

Nutritional Information:
Total calories: 188

Protein: 1
Carbs: 14g
Fiber: 6g
Fat: 0g

Coconut Cashew-Lemon Cheesecake

Serves: 8
Time: About 4 hours total (2 hours soak time, 5 minutes prep time, 20 minutes cook time, 20 minutes natural release, 1 hour 30 minutes chill time)

Ingredients:
1 cup oats
½ cup chopped dates (soaked in ¼ cup water for 15-30 minutes)
½ cup walnuts
1 cup soaked cashews (2-4 hours of soak time)
½ cup coconut flour
½ cup sugar
½ cup vanilla almond milk
½ cup fresh raspberries
2 tablespoons lemon juice
1 tablespoon arrowroot powder
1 teaspoon vanilla extract
1-2 teaspoons lemon zest

Directions:
1. Drain your dates, but keep the liquid.
2. Pour 1 ½ cups of fresh water into your Instant Pot and add steamer basket.
3. To make the crust, mix ingredients in the first list in a food processor.
4. If it is too dry and crumbly, add 1 tablespoon of date-liquid until it's right.
5. Your dough should be firm, but not too moist so it's gooey.

6. Press down into a springform pan on the bottom and about an inch up the sides.
7. For the filling, drain the cashews, and keep the water.
8. Add half of this water and cashews into a food processor and pulse until smooth.
9. Add flour, sugar, zest, lemon juice, vanilla, and milk.
10. Blend, add arrowroot, and then blend for one last time.
11. Pour into the pan, using a spatula to smooth the top.
12. Wrap the pan with foil, so the top is covered.
13. Lower into the steamer basket.
14. Close and seal lid.
15. Hit "manual," and adjust time to 20 minutes on high pressure.
16. When time is up, hit "cancel" and wait for the pressure to come down naturally.
17. Carefully remove pan and cool for a little while.
18. Arrange raspberries on the cheesecake and then cool for at least 30 minutes before chilling in the fridge for at least 1 hour.

Nutritional Information:
Total calories: 346
Protein: 10 g
Carbs: 28 g
Fiber: 2.6g
Fat: 14g

CHAPTER 6 INSTANT POT VEGAN RECIPES

Vegan Strawberries + Cream Oats

Serves: 2
Time: 13 minutes
Ingredients:

6 large strawberries
2 cups of water
1 cup steel-cut oats
1 cup full-fat coconut milk
½ vanilla bean

Directions:
1. Scrape the vanilla bean so you get the seeds out.
2. Add everything (except the strawberries) to your Instant Pot, including the vanilla bean pod.
3. Select "Manual" on your pot and decrease the time to 3 minutes at "high pressure."
4. When time is up, unplug the cooker and wait 10 minutes.
5. Cut up the strawberries and serve.
6. To sweeten, use a vegan-friendly option like maple syrup or agave.

Nutritional Info: Total calories – 264; Protein – 5g; Carbs – 31g; Fiber - 10 g; Fat – 13g

Rice Milk Buckwheat Porridge

Serves: 3-4
Time: 26 minutes

Ingredients:
3 cups rice milk
1 cup raw buckwheat groats

¼ cup raisins
1 sliced banana
1 teaspoon ground cinnamon
½ teaspoon vanilla

Directions:
1. Rinse the buckwheat and put in the Instant Pot.
2. Pour in rice milk, and add raisins, bananas, vanilla, and cinnamon.
3. Lock the lid.
4. Select "Manual," and then "high pressure" for 6 minutes.
5. When time is up, hit "Cancel" and wait for the pressure to come down naturally.
6. Open the lid and stir.
7. Serve with a little more rice milk and any desired toppings.

Nutritional Information:
Total calories – 297; Protein – g 6; Carbs – 36g; Fiber – 4g; Fat – 3g

Healthy Vegan Yogurt

Makes: 2 pints
Time: 12+ hours

Ingredients:
1 quart room-temperature organic plain soy milk
1 packet Cultures for Health vegan yogurt starter

Directions:
1. Pour the soy milk into a pitcher and stir in yogurt starter.
2. Pour into two clean pint jars.
3. Put jars into the Instant Pot.
4. Lock the lid.
5. Hit "Yogurt" and set for 12 hours.
6. When time is up, hit "Cancel" and let the pressure come down on its own for 20 minutes. Carefully quick-release the rest of the pressure.
7. Chill in the fridge overnight before serving.

Nutritional Information:
Total calories - 50
Protein – 4g
Carbs – 4g
Fiber - .5 g
Fat – 2g

Yummy Veggies Rice Dish

Servings: 4
Preparation time: 10 minutes
Cooking time: 15 minutes

Ingredients:
- 2 cups long grain rice
- 1 red bell pepper, thinly sliced
- 1 tablespoon extra-virgin olive oil
- 1 yellow onion, finely chopped
- 1 carrot, grated
- Salt and black pepper to the taste
- 4 cups water
- ½ cup peas

Directions:
1. Heat up a pan with the oil over medium high heat, add the onions, stir and cook for 4 minutes.
2. Transfer this mix to your instant pot, add rice, water, bell pepper, carrot, peas, salt and pepper, stir and cook on High for 10 minutes.
3. Release pressure naturally, divide rice mix amongst plates and serve. Enjoy!

Nutritional Info: calories 270, fat 2.6g, fiber 2.4g, carbs 1.2, protein 5.5 g

Tasty Asparagus Millet Veggies

Servings: 4
Preparation time: 10 minutes
Cooking time: 25 minutes

Ingredients:
- ½ cup oyster mushrooms, thinly sliced
- 1 cup millet, soaked and drained
- 1 cup leeks, finely chopped
- 2 garlic cloves, minced
- 1 teaspoon vegetable oil
- ½ cup green lentils, rinsed
- ½ cup bok choy, sliced
- 2 and ¼ cups veggie stock
- 1 cup asparagus, cut in medium pieces
- 1 cup snow peas, sliced
- ¼ cup mixed chives and parsley, finely chopped
- A drizzle of lemon juice
- Salt and black pepper to the taste

Directions:
1. Heat up a pan with the vegetable oil over medium high heat, add mushrooms, leeks and garlic, stir and cook for 2-3 minutes
2. Add lentils and millet, stir, cook for 3-4 minutes and transfer to your instant pot.
3. Add bok choy, asparagus, snow peas and veggie stock, cover and cook on High for 10 minutes.
4. Release pressure naturally, add salt and pepper to the taste, stir and divide amongst serving bowls.
5. Drizzle lemon juice on top of each bowl, add chives and parsley and serve.

Enjoy!

Nutritional Information:
Calories: 170,
Fat 7g

Carbs 12g
Fiber 9g
Protein 14g

Instant Pot Garlic Lentils And Rice Risotto

Servings: 6
Preparation time: 10 minutes
Cooking time: 15 minutes
Ingredients:
- 1 tablespoon extra virgin olive oil
- 1 cup arborico rice
- 1 cup lentils, soaked overnight
- 1 yellow onion, finely chopped
- 1 celery stalk, finely chopped
- Salt and black pepper to the taste
- 1 tablespoon parsley, finely chopped
- 3 and ¼ cup veggie stock
- 2 garlic cloves, crushed

Directions:
1. Heat up a pan with the oil over medium high heat, add onions, stir and sauté them for 3-4 minutes.
2. Add celery and parsley, stir, cook for 1 minute and then transfer everything to your instant pot.
3. Add garlic, rice, stock and lentils, cover and cook on High for 10 minutes.
4. Release pressure naturally, divide amongst bowls and serve.
Enjoy!

Nutritional value: calories 190, fat 2.5g, carbs 25g, fiber 3.7g, protein 5.7g

Mushroom Curry Lentils Burgers

Servings: 10
Preparation time: 15 minutes
Cooking time: 40 minutes

Ingredients:
- 2 teaspoons ginger, grated
- 1 cup mushrooms, minced
- 1 cup yellow onion, minced
- 1 cup red lentils, rinsed
- 2 and ½ cups veggie stock
- 1 and ½ sweet potatoes, chopped
- Vegetable cooking spray
- ¼ cup parsley, finely chopped
- ¼ cup hemp seeds
- ¼ cup cilantro, finely chopped
- 1 tablespoon curry powder
- 1 cup quick oats
- 4 tablespoons brown rice flour
- Salt and pepper to the taste

Directions:
1. Set your instant pot on Sautee more, add onion, mushroom and ginger, stir and cook for 3 minutes.
2. Add stock, sweet potatoes and lentils, cover pot and cook on High for 6 minutes.
3. Release pressure naturally, transfer lentils mix to a bowl and leave aside for 15 minutes.
4. Mash lentils mix, add parsley, curry powder, salt and pepper, hemp seeds and cilantro and stir well.
5. Add oats and rice flour and stir again well.
6. Shape 10 burgers with your wet hands, arrange them on a baking sheet after you've sprayed it with some vegetable cooking oil, introduce them in the oven at 375 degrees F and bake for 10 minutes.
7. Flip burgers, bake them for 10 more minutes, take them out of the oven, leave to cool down a bit and serve.

Enjoy!

Nutritional Information:
Calories 140,
Fat 8g
Carbs 15g
Fiber 4.7g
Protein 11 g

Red Cabbage Black Bean Burgers

Servings: 5
Preparation time: 15 minutes
Cooking time: 35 minutes

Ingredients:
- 1 cup black beans, soaked for 3 hours
- 1 tablespoon flaxseed+1 tablespoon water
- 1 red onion, chopped
- 3 tablespoon vegetable oil
- ½ cup quick oats
- ½ teaspoon cumin
- 2 teaspoons chipotle powder
- Salt to the taste
- 2 garlic cloves, minced
- 2 teaspoons lemon zest, grated
- Burger buns for serving
- Red cabbage, thinly sliced for serving

Directions:
1. Drain beans, place them in your instant pot, and add water to cover them, cook on High for 20 minutes, release pressure quick, drain the beans again, put them in a bowl, crush them with a fork and leave aside for now.
2. Heat up a pan with 1 tablespoon oil over medium high heat, add onion, stir and cook for 3 minutes.
3. Add garlic, stir and cook for 3 more minute.

4. Take this mix off heat, leave aside to cool down and add to the bowl with the beans.
5. Add flaxseed mixed with 1 tablespoon water, oats, cumin, chipotle powder, salt to the taste and lemon zest and stir everything well.
6. Shape 5 burgers with your wet hands and place them on a working surface.
7. Heat up a pan with the rest of the oil over medium high heat, add burgers, cook for 3 minutes, flip, cook them for 3 more minutes, transfer them to paper towels and drain grease.
8. Divide on burger buns, add red cabbage and serve.
Enjoy!

Nutritional Information:
Calories 251g
Fat 9.3g
Carbs 32g
Fiber 7.3g
Protein 10.5g

Healthy Dairy-free Mashed Potatoes

Serves: 8
Time: About 20 minutes
Ingredients:
4 pounds of peeled and rinsed red + yellow potatoes
1 ½ cups water + ½ cup water
2 tablespoons olive oil Earth Balance
⅛ Cup pine nuts
1 teaspoon salt
Soy milk

Directions:
1. Pour 1 ½ cups of water into your Instant Pot, lower in the trivet, and add the potatoes.

2. Press "Steam" and then 15 minutes on "high pressure."
3. As the potatoes cook, puree ½ cup water and pine nuts.
4. When the pot timer goes off, quick-release the cooker.
5. Take out the potatoes and roughly chop in a bowl.
6. Add the pine nut mixture, Earth balance, ¼ cup soy milk, and salt to the bowl.
7. Mash till smooth, adding soy milk as needed.

Nutritional Information:
Total calories – 213; Protein – 5g; Carbs – 31g; Fiber – 3g; Fat – 5g

Nutritious Soup

Serves: 4-6
Time: 18 minutes

Ingredients:
28-ounce can of tomatoes
3 minced garlic cloves
4 cups veggie broth
2 cups cooked white beans
2 diced celery stalks
½ cup fresh spinach, torn
1 bay leaf
1 diced onion
1 diced carrot
1 cup elbow pasta
2 tablespoons olive oil
1 teaspoon dried basil
1 teaspoon dried oregano
Salt + pepper

Directions:

1. Turn your Instant Pot to "Sauté."
2. Add in the olive oil, carrot, celery, garlic, and onion.
3. When softened, add in basil, oregano, pepper, and salt.
4. Pulse the can of tomatoes (along with its liquid) in a processor to break them down.
5. Pour into the pot, along with broth, spinach, pasta, and the bay leaf.
6. Secure the Instant Pot lid and press "Manual," and then 6 minutes on "high pressure."
7. When the timer beeps, hit "Cancel" and wait 2 minutes.
8. Quick-release.
9. Add in the beans and stir.
10. Serve!

Nutritional Information:

Total calories - 82
Protein - 4.3g
Carbs – 11g
Fiber – 1g
Fat - 2.5 g

Mild Chili Beans Mixed

Serves: 6-8
Time: About 26-30 minutes
Like they've been simmering for ages.

Ingredients:

3 ½ cups vegetable broth
2 cups chopped onion
1 ½ cups of cooked black beans
1 ½ cups cooked red beans
1 ½ cups cooked pinto beans
¾ cup chopped carrots
¼ cup chopped celery

14.5-ounces of diced tomatoes
14.5-ounces of tomato sauce
1 chopped red bell pepper
2 tablespoons mild chili powder
1 tablespoon minced garlic
1 ½ teaspoons dried oregano
1 ½ teaspoons cumin
1 teaspoon cumin seeds
1 teaspoon smoked paprika
½ teaspoon coriander

Directions:

1. Drain and rinse the beans.
2. In your Instant Pot, select "sauté" and cook the cumin seeds, onion, and minced garlic for 5 minutes. Pour in vegetable broth to avoid burning the spices.
3. Once fragrant, add in everything except the tomatoes and tomato sauce.
4. Stir before securing the lid.
5. Select "Manual" and choose 6 minutes on "high pressure."
6. When time is up, unplug the cooker (or press "cancel") and wait 10 minutes for the pressure to decrease naturally.
7. Open the lid and stir in the tomatoes and tomato sauce.
8. Let the chili rest and thicken, leaving the lid off.
9. When it reaches your desired texture, serve with toppings like green onions, parsley, vegan cheese, and so on.

Nutritional Information

Total calories - 456
Protein - 27.6 g
Carbs – 55g
Fiber – 24g
Fat – 4g

Tomato Cilantro Mushrooms Beans

Servings: 3

Preparation time: 10 minutes
Cooking time: 30 minutes

Ingredients:
- 2 tablespoons barley
- ½ cup faro
- 1 cup navy beans, dried
- 3 cups mushrooms, chopped
- 1 tablespoon red curry paste
- 1 jalapeno pepper, seeded and chopped
- 1 tablespoon shallot powder
- 2 tablespoons onion powder
- Salt and pepper to the taste
- 9 garlic cloves, minced
- 2 tomatoes, diced
- Some chopped cilantro for serving
- Some chopped scallions for serving

Directions:
1. Put beans, faro and barley in your instant pot.
2. Add mushrooms, garlic, jalapeno, curry paste, shallot and onion powder, salt, pepper to the taste and water to cover all the ingredients.
3. Cook in your instant pot on High for 30 minutes.
4. Release pressure naturally, add tomatoes, stir and divide amongst plates.
5. Sprinkle cilantro and scallions at the end and serve.

Enjoy!

Nutritional Information:
Calories 240,
Fat 6.6g
Carbs 40g
Fiber 1.4g
Protein 11g

Tasty Chili Onion Vegan Polenta

Servings: 3
Preparation time: 15 minutes
Cooking time: 10 minutes

Ingredients:
- 2 cups very hot water
- 1 bunch green onion, thinly sliced
- 2 cups veggie stock
- 2 teaspoon garlic, minced
- 1 tablespoon chili powder
- 1 cup corn meal
- ¼ cup cilantro, finely chopped
- Salt and black pepper to the taste
- 1 teaspoon cumin
- 1 teaspoon oregano
- A pinch of cayenne pepper
- ½ teaspoon smoked paprika

Directions:
1. Heat up a pan over medium heat; add a splash of water, the green onion and garlic, stir and sauté for 2 minutes.
2. Transfer this to your instant pot, add stock, hot water, corn meal, cilantro, salt, pepper, chili powder, cumin, oregano, paprika and a pinch of cayenne pepper, close the pot and cook on High for 10 minutes.
3. Release pressure naturally for 10 minutes, divide amongst plates and serve.

Enjoy!

Nutritional value: calories 200, fat 4.5, carbs 13, fiber 7.8, proteins 14

Apple Cider Vinegar Spicy Braised Cabbage

Serves: 4
Time: About 10 minutes

Ingredients:

1 ¼ cups of water + 2 teaspoons of water
3 pounds of cabbage, divided into 8 wedges

¾ cup grated carrots
¼ cup apple cider vinegar
1 tablespoon sesame oil
2 teaspoons cornstarch
1 teaspoon raw demerara sugar (Bob's Red Mill is a good brand)
½ teaspoon red pepper flakes
½ teaspoon cayenne powder

Directions:
1. Turn on the Instant Pot to the "sauté" function.
2. Pour in sesame oil and lay down the cabbage wedges to brown for 3 minutes on one side.
3. Remove the wedges.
4. Pour in 1 ¼ cups of water, sugar, cayenne, pepper flakes, and vinegar.
5. Return the cabbage wedges to the pot along with the grated carrot.
6. Secure the lid and select the "Manual" setting. Choose "high pressure" and cook for 5 minutes.
7. Quick-release the pressure.
8. Remove the cabbage wedges.
9. Turn the cooker back on to "sauté" and bring the cooking liquid to a bowl.
10. In a bowl, mix 2 teaspoons of cold water with the cornstarch.
11. Pour into the Instant Pot.
12. Keep boiling, allowing the liquid to thicken.
13. Pour over the cabbage wedges before serving.

Nutritional Information:

Total calories - 127
Protein – 4g
Carbs – 22g
Fiber – 6g
Fat - 4 g

Yummy Buckwheat Beans Porridge

Servings: 12
Preparation time: 10 minutes
Cooking time: 40 minutes
Ingredients:
- 3 tablespoons pearl barley

- 3 tablespoons pot barley
- 3 tablespoons buckwheat
- 3 tablespoons rice
- 3 tablespoons black rice
- 3 tablespoons brown rice
- 3 tablespoons red beans
- 3 tablespoons black eye beans
- 3 tablespoons Romano beans
- 1 purple potato, chopped
- A pinch of baking soda

Directions:
1. Put potato pieces in your instant pot.
2. Add pearl barley, pot barley, all types of rice and beans and stir.
3. Add baking soda, close pot and cook for 45 minutes.
4. Release pressure naturally, leave aside for 10 minutes, pour into bowls and serve right away.

Enjoy!

Nutritional Information:
Calories 120, fat 1g, carbs 18g, fiber 4g, protein 4g

Instant Pot Quinoa Almond Pilaf

Servings: 4
Preparation time: 10 minutes
Cooking time: 15 minutes

Ingredients:
- ½ cup yellow onion, finely chopped
- 1 and ½ cups quinoa, washed and drained
- 1 tablespoon vegan butter
- 14 ounces canned veggie stock
- 1 celery stalk, finely chopped
- Salt to the taste
- ¼ cup water
- 2 tablespoons parsley leaves, chopped

- ½ cup almonds, sliced and toasted

Directions:
1. Heat up a pan with the vegan butter over medium heat, add onions and celery, stir, cook for 5 minutes and transfer them to your instant pot.
2. Add stock, water, quinoa and salt, stir, cover and cook on High for 3 minutes.
3. Release pressure naturally for 10 minutes, fluff quinoa with a fork, divide amongst plates, add parsley, more salt if needed and almonds, stir gently and serve.

Nutritional value: calories 160, fat 5.7g, carbs 15g, fiber 3.2g, protein 7g

Amazing One-Pot Artichokes Rice

Servings: 4
Preparation time: 10 minutes
Cooking time: 15 minutes

Ingredients:
- 6 ounces graham crackers, crumbled
- 6 ounces arborico rice
- 16 ounces vegan cream cheese, soft
- 14 ounces artichoke hearts, chopped
- 1 and ½ tablespoons vegan cheese, grated
- 8 ounces veggie stock
- 8 ounces water
- 2 tablespoons white wine
- Salt and black pepper to the taste
- 1 tablespoon vegetable oil
- 2 garlic cloves, minced
- 1 and ½ tablespoon thyme, finely chopped

Directions:

1. Heat up a pan with the oil over medium high heat, add rice and garlic, stir and cook for 3 minutes.
2. Transfer everything to your instant pot, add stock, wine, water, cover and cook on High for 10 minutes.
3. Release pressure naturally for 5 minutes, crackers, add artichokes, vegan cheese, vegan cream cheese, salt, pepper and thyme, stir well, divide into bowls and serve right away.

Enjoy!

Nutritional Information:
Calories 240,
Fat 7.1g,
Carbs 23g,
Fiber 5.1g,
Protein 6g

Nutritious Chipotle-Pumpkin Apple Soup

Serves: 6
Time: 18 minutes

Ingredients:
2 cups veggie broth
2 cups water
2 cups diced red potatoes
2 cups diced green apples
15-ounce can of pumpkin puree
1 diced onion
3 diced garlic cloves
1 seeded chipotle in adobe sauce
¼ cup uncooked red lentils run through a food processor
¼ cup walnuts run through a food processor
1 teaspoon salt
1 teaspoon black pepper

1 teaspoon cinnamon
¼ teaspoon nutmeg

Directions:

1. Turn on the Instant Pot's "sauté" setting and cook the garlic and onion for about 3-4 minutes.
2. When brown and fragrant, toss in all the spices, including the chipotle pepper, and stir.
3. Pour in the water and veggie broth, along with the potatoes, apples, pumpkin puree, and ground lentils and walnuts.
4. Choose the "Manual" setting and select a 4-minute cook time on "high pressure."
5. When the beep sounds, hit "Cancel" or unplug the cooker.
6. Wait 10 minutes for the pressure to come down by itself,
7. Before opening, release any leftover pressure.
8. Open up the lid and blend the soup, either with an immersion hand blender, or by carefully pouring it into a blender.
9. When smooth, serve right away!

Nutritional Info:
Total calories - 147
Protein – 5g
Carbs - 26.5g
Fiber - 4.2g
Fat - 3.7g

Favorite Vegan Curried Sorghum

Servings: 4
Preparation time: 10 minutes

Cooking time: 1 hour

Ingredients:
- 3 cups water
- 1 cup sorghum
- 1 cup coconut milk
- Salt to the taste
- 3 tablespoons rice wine vinegar
- ½ teaspoon chili powder
- 1 tablespoon curry powder
- 2 cups carrots
- ½ cup golden raisins
- ¼ cup green onion, finely chopped
- 2 teaspoons palm sugar

Directions:

1. Put sorghum in your instant pot and mix it with the water and salt to the taste.
2. Cook on High for 1 hour and then release pressure naturally for 10 minutes.
3. In a bowl, mix palm sugar with coconut milk, vinegar, salt to the taste, curry powder and chili powder and stir well.
4. Drain sorghum, transfer it to a bowl, add coconut milk mix, carrots, onions and carrots, toss to coat, divide amongst plates and serve right away.

Enjoy!

Nutritional Information:

Calories 300,
Fat 6g
Carbs 20f
Fiber 12f
Protein 23g

Garlic Lentils Kidney Bean Stew

Serves: 6
Time: About 25 minutes

Ingredients:

1.5 pounds of diced sweet potatoes
4 cups veggie broth
2, 15-ounce cans of cooked kidney beans (drained and rinsed)
28-ounces of diced tomatoes (with liquid)
1, 15-ounce can of full-fat coconut milk
1 cup of dried brown lentils
½ cup chopped cilantro
2 minced garlic cloves
1 big diced onion
1 can green chilis
2 tablespoons red curry paste
2 tablespoons chili powder
1 tablespoon lime juice
1 teaspoon sea salt

Directions:

1. Select the "Sauté" setting on the Instant Pot and add garlic and onion.
2. When the aromatics are soft, add the sweet potatoes and stir for a few minutes.
3. Press "Cancel" and add the rest of the ingredients.
4. Secure the lid.
5. Choose "Manual" and a cook time of 10 minutes on "high pressure."
6. When the timer beeps, hit "Cancel" again and wait 10 minutes.
7. Quick-release any remaining pressure.
8. Stir and serve right away!

Nutritional Info:

Total calories - 111
Protein – 5g
Carbs – 23g
Fiber – 5g
Fat - 8 g

Tasty Chili Taco Mix

Serves: 8
Time: Overnight + about 45 minutes

Ingredients:

1 pound soaked dried pinto beans
3 cups water
2 chopped garlic cloves
1 chopped medium-sized onion
2 whole dried red chilis
2 tablespoons tomato paste
1 minced green pepper
2 teaspoons oregano
2-3 teaspoons chili powder
½ teaspoon ground cumin
Salt

Directions:

1. The beans should be soaked overnight. The night before you plan on making this recipe, rinse the beans and cover them with water. Drape a cloth towel over the bowl and store on the counter.
2. The next day, drain the beans
3. Pour 3 cups of water into your Instant Pot and add the beans, along with the garlic, onion, oregano, chilies, and cumin.
4. Close the lid.

5. Select "Manual" and choose 5 minutes at "high pressure."
6. When ready, unplug the cooker and wait 10 minutes for the pressure to decrease naturally.
7. Open the cooker and take out the dried chilies.
8. Add the remaining ingredients and cook without the lid for another 20-30 minutes in order for the flavors to deepen.
9. Serve in a corn tortilla or on top of fresh lettuce.

Nutritional Info:

Total calories - 215
Protein - 12.9g
Carbs - 39.5g
Fiber – 10g
Fat -   8g

Mustard Spaghetti Squash Lasagna

Serves: 6
Time: 1 hour, 30 minutes

Ingredients:

3 pounds spaghetti squash
8-ounces sliced mushrooms
1 ½ cups spaghetti sauce
1 minced garlic clove
Salt and pepper to taste

1, 14-ounce package of extra-firm tofu (not silken)
2 peeled garlic cloves
2 tablespoons nutritional yeast
1 cup packed fresh basil

1 cup plain nut milk
¼ cup raw cashews
¼ cup nutritional yeast
2 tablespoons cornstarch
1 tablespoon lemon juice
½ teaspoon dry mustard

Directions:

1. Begin by pressure-cooking the squash. Cut it in half lengthwise and remove the seeds.
2. Pour 1 cup of water into your Instant Pot and lower in the steamer basket.
3. Put the squash in the basket.
4. Close the cooker.
5. Select "Manual," and then "high pressure" for 8 minutes.
6. Unplug the cooker and quick-release when time is up, and cool before removing the squash.
7. Scrape the spaghetti strands using a fork and store in a colander that's resting over a bowl.
8. Heat a stovetop saucepan and toss in the chopped garlic, mushrooms, and 1 tablespoon of water.
9. Stir and cover. Stir every minute or so for 3 minutes.
10. Take off the lid and cook until the liquid evaporates.
11. Season and set aside for now.
12. Put the 2 peeled garlic cloves in a food processor and chop.
13. Add the rest of the ingredients in the second ingredient list and process till creamy and smooth.
14. Using a blender, pour everything in the third ingredient list and smooth.
15. Time to assemble. Pour in ¼ cup of the spaghetti sauce along with ¼ cup of veggie stock in the pressure cooker. Put ½ of the spaghetti squash right on top.
16. Spoon the tofu filling over the squash and spread, so it's even.
17. Add mushrooms and then half of the cashew "cheese" sauce on top.
18. Add the rest of the squash and then the rest of the spaghetti sauce.
19. Close the Instant Pot lid.
20. Select "Manual" and cook for just 5 minutes on "low pressure." You're really just heating everything up.
21. When the timer beeps, let the pressure come down naturally for 10 minutes.
22. Open the cooker and pour the rest of the cashew "cheese" on top.
23. Let the lasagna rest for a few minutes before serving.

Nutritional Info:

Total calories - 254
Protein - 18.3g
Carbs - 30.5g
Fiber - 3.3g
Fat -   8.4g

Healthy Red Cabbage Salad

Servings: 4
Preparation time: 5 minutes
Cooking time: 5 minutes

Ingredients:
- 2 cups red cabbage, shredded
- 1 tablespoon canola oil
- Salt and black pepper to the taste
- ¼ cup white onion, finely chopped
- 2 teaspoons red wine vinegar
- ½ teaspoon palm sugar

Directions:
1. Put shredded cabbage in your instant pot, add some water, cover and cook on High for 5 minutes.
2. Release pressure naturally, drain water and transfer it to a salad bowl.
3. Add salt, pepper to the taste, onion, oil, palm sugar and vinegar, toss to coat and serve right away.
Enjoy!

Nutritional value: calories 110, fat 1g, carbs 6g, fiber 2.2g, g; protein 1.1 g

Mushroom Walnut Cabbage Rolls

Servings: 6
Preparation time: 15 minutes
Cooking time: 35 minutes

Ingredients:
- 1 tablespoon extra virgin olive oil
- 1 cup brown rice, uncooked
- 9 and ½ cups water
- 3 cups mushrooms, chopped
- 1 yellow onion, chopped
- 2 garlic cloves, minced
- Salt and black pepper to the taste
- 12 green cabbage leaves
- ½ teaspoon walnuts, finely chopped
- ½ teaspoon caraway seeds
- A pinch of cayenne pepper
- Tomato sauce for serving

Directions:
1. Put 1 and ½ cups water and the rice in your instant pot, cover and cook on High for 15 minutes.
2. Release pressure automatically, rinse rice under cold water, drain it well and put it in a bowl.
3. Heat up a pan with the oil over medium high heat, add onion, mushrooms and garlic, stir and cook for 5 minutes.
4. Add caraway, walnuts, salt, pepper, and cayenne, pour over rice and stir very well.
5. Pour 8 cups water in a pot, bring to a boil over medium high heat, add cabbage leaves, cook for 1 minute, drain and rinse them under cold water.
6. Arrange them on a working surface, place 1/3 cup rice mix in the middle of each, roll them, seal edges and place them in your instant pot.
7. Add 1 inch water, cover and cook on High pressure for 10 minutes.
8. Release pressure, divide them on plates and serve them with some tomato sauce on top.

Enjoy!

Nutritional Information:
Calories 283
Fat 10g
Carbs 30g
Fiber 6g
Protein 5 g

Coconut Black-Eyed Peas + Kale Bowl

Serves: 6
Time: About 50 minutes

Ingredients:

5 cups water + 2 tablespoons water
1 ½ cups of rinsed, dried black-eyed peas
1 tablespoon chopped garlic
1 tablespoon chopped ginger root + 2 teaspoons chopped ginger root
1 tablespoon coconut aminos
2 minced garlic cloves
½ teaspoon salt
¼ teaspoon red pepper flakes

2 cups brown rice
2 ½ cups water

1 big bunch of kale, with stems removed and leaves chopped up
1 minced garlic clove
1 chopped, small onion
½ chopped red bell pepper
¼ cup water
1 tablespoon coconut aminos

Directions:

1. Pour 5 cups of water into the Instant Pot.
2. Add the peas, 1 tablespoon of garlic, 1 tablespoon of ginger, and ½ teaspoon of salt.
3. Secure the lid and select "Manual," and then cook for 10 minutes at "high pressure."
4. When ready, unplug the cooker and wait 10 minutes before quick-releasing any remaining pressure.
5. Drain the peas, leaving 1 cup of the cooking liquid.
6. Take out a saucepan and pour the 2 tablespoons of water into it.
7. Heat over the stove.
8. Add 2 teaspoons of ginger root and the 2 cloves of garlic.
9. After two minutes of cooking, add ⅓ cup of the pea cooking liquid, the beans, 1 tablespoon coconut aminos, and red pepper flakes.
10. Now is a good time to make the brown rice. To make brown rice in the Instant Pot, pour in 2 ½ cups of water with 2 cups of brown rice.
11. Close the lid and choose "Manual," and then 22 minutes on "high pressure."
12. Let this simmer for 20-3o minutes, without a liquid. If the peas start to dry out, add more of their cooking liquid.
13. The rice should be done now. The pot will automatically go to "keep warm." Keep this position for 10 minutes before hitting "cancel" and quick-releasing any leftover steam. You can keep the rice in the cooker for now.
14. Take out another skillet and add the onion.
15. Cook until it starts to brown, and then add garlic and the red bell pepper.
16. Add the kale and ¼ cup of water and cover.
17. after 3-6 minutes, the kale should still be very green, but tender.
18. Take the skillet off the hot burner and add 1 tablespoon coconut aminos.
19. Serve the peas with the kale and rice. Sriracha is a good condiment.

Nutritional Information

Total calories - 186
Protein - 12.5g
Carbs - 34.4g
Fiber - 6.2g
Fat - 1 g

Special Basil Tomato Zucchini Dish

Servings: 3
Preparation time: 10 minutes
Cooking time: 10 minutes

Ingredients:
- 1 tablespoon vegetable oil
- 1 pound colored cherry tomatoes
- 2 yellow onions, chopped
- 1 cup tomato puree
- Salt and black pepper to the taste
- 2 garlic cloves, minced
- 6 zucchinis, chopped
- A drizzle of olive oil
- 1 bunch basil, finely chopped

Directions:
1. Heat up a pan with the vegetable oil over medium high heat, add onions, stir and sauté those for 5 minutes.
2. Transfer this to your instant pot, add zucchini, tomatoes, salt and pepper and tomato puree, cover and cook on High for 5 minutes.
3. Release pressure naturally, add garlic and basil, more salt and pepper if needed and a drizzle of olive oil.
4. Toss to coat, divide amongst plates and serve.

Nutritional value: calories 70, fat 1g, carbs 6g, fiber 2.8gg; protein 2g

Detox Vegetable Mix Dish

Servings: 4
Preparation time: 10 minutes

Cooking time: 10 minutes

Ingredients:
- 1 eggplant, cut in medium chunks
- ¼ cup extra virgin olive oil
- 1 yellow bell pepper, cut in thin strips
- 2 zucchinis, cut in small pieces
- Salt and black pepper to the taste
- 2 potatoes, chopped
- 1 yellow onion, cut in wedges
- 10 cherry tomatoes, cut in halves
- 2 tablespoons pine nuts
- 1 tablespoon capers, drained
- 1 tablespoon raisins
- 1 cup water
- ¼ cup olives, pitted and roughly chopped
- 1 bunch basil leaves, chopped

Directions:
1. Put eggplant pieces in a strainer, sprinkle salt, leave them aside for a few minutes, press them to get rid of the liquid and transfer them to your instant pot.
2. Add olive oil, potatoes, onion, zucchinis, bell pepper, tomatoes, capers, pine nuts, raisins, olives, half of the basil and the water, cover pot and cook on High for 7 minutes.
3. Release pressure, add salt and pepper to the taste, the rest of the basil, stir gently, divide amongst plates and serve.

Enjoy!

Nutritional value:
Calories 131,
Fat 7.3g
Carbs 16g
Fiber 4.7g
Protein 3.5g

Coconut Chili Sweet Potato Peanut Butter Soup

Serves: 4
Time: 10-15 minutes

Ingredients:

3 big sweet potatoes, cubed
3 chopped garlic cloves
1 chopped onion
15-ounce can of diced tomatoes (liquid saved)
14-ounce can of full-fat coconut milk
4-ounce can of green chilis
2 cups veggie broth
½ cup peanut butter
1 tablespoon lime juice
½ teaspoon allspice
¼ teaspoon ground cilantro

Directions:

1. Turn on the Instant Pot and hit "Sauté."
2. Pour in a little oil and cook the garlic and onion, stirring, until soft.
3. Hit "Cancel."
4. Add the rest of the ingredients and stir.
5. Lock the lid.
6. Press "Manual" and adjust time to 4 minutes on "high pressure."
7. When the timer beeps, hit "Cancel" again and wait for the pressure to decrease naturally.
8. Stir.
9. Puree until smooth and serve!

Nutritional Information:
Total calories - 286

Protein – 8g
Carbs – 29g
Fiber – 6g
Fat - 16g

Tomato Beans Stew

Servings: 10
Preparation time: 15 minutes
Cooking time: 1 hour and 10 minutes

Ingredients:
- 2 carrots, chopped
- 1 plantain, chopped
- 1 pound red beans, dry
- Salt and black pepper to the taste
- 1 tomato, chopped
- 2 green onions stalks, chopped
- 1 small yellow onion, diced
- ¼ cup cilantro leaves, chopped
- 2 tablespoons vegetable oil

Directions:
1. Put the beans in your instant pot, add water to cover, cook on High for 35 minutes and release pressure for 10 minutes naturally.
2. Add plantain, carrots, salt and pepper to the taste, cover instant pot again and cook on High for 30 more minutes.
3. Meanwhile, heat up a pan with the vegetable oil over medium high heat, add yellow onion, stir and cook for 2 minutes.
4. Add tomatoes, green onions, some salt and pepper, stir again, cook for 3 minutes more and take off the heat.
5. Release pressure naturally from your instant pot, divide cooked beans amongst plates, top with tomatoes and onions mix, sprinkle cilantro at the end and serve right away.
   Enjoy!

Nutritional value: calories 70, fat 3.1, carbs 9.6, fiber 1, sugar 3.6, protein 2.5

Tamari Tofu & Veggies Dish

Servings: 4
Preparation time: 10 minutes
Cooking time: 5 minutes

Ingredients:
- 1 yellow onion, thinly sliced
- 6 big mushrooms, sliced
- 3 teaspoons tamari
- 8 ounces tofu, soft and cut in small cubes
- ½ cup red bell pepper
- ½ cup green beans
- ¼ cup veggie stock
- Salt and white pepper to the taste

Directions:
1. Heat up a pan over medium high heat, add mushrooms and onions, stir and brown for 2 minutes.
2. Add tamari and tofu and cook for 2 more minutes.
3. Transfer everything to your instant pot, add the stock, cover pot and cook on High for 3 minutes.
4. Release pressure quick, add green beans and the bell pepper, cover and cook on High for 1 minute more.
5. Release pressure again, add salt and pepper to the taste, stir, divide amongst plates and serve hot. Enjoy!

Nutritional Info: Calories 113 ;Fat 6.2g;Carbs 9g;Fiber 1.5g;Protein 6.8g

Ginger Tomato Mushroom Dish

Servings: 4
Preparation time: 10 minutes
Cooking time: 15 minutes

Ingredients:
- 8 ounces shiitake mushrooms, minced
- 4 ounces white mushrooms, minced
- 1 and ¼ cups veggie stock
- ½ cup red onion, finely chopped
- ½ cup celery, chopped
- ½ cup carrot, chopped
- 5 garlic cloves, minced
- 1 tablespoon ginger, grated
- Salt and black pepper to the taste
- ¼ teaspoon oregano, dry
- 28 ounces canned tomatoes, chopped
- 1 and ½ teaspoons turmeric, ground
- ¼ cup basil leaves, chopped
- Spaghetti squash for serving

Directions:
1. In your instant pot, mix ¼ cup veggie stock, mushrooms, onion, celery, carrot, ginger and garlic, stir and cook on Sautee mode for 5 minutes.
2. Add the rest of the stock, tomatoes, salt, pepper, turmeric and oregano, stir, cover and cook on High for 10 minutes.
3. Release the pressure, turn instant pot to Sauté mode again and cook for 5 more minutes.
4. Add basil, divide on plates and serve with some spaghetti squash. Enjoy!

Nutritional value: calories 70, fat 3.8g, carbs 5.7g, fiber 1.4g, protein 3.1g

Almond Milk Corn With Lime Sauce

Servings: 4
Preparation time: 10 minutes
Cooking time: 10 minutes

Ingredients:

- 4 ears corn
- 1 and ½ cups water
- 2 tablespoons nutritional yeast
- 2 tablespoons hemp hearts
- ½ cup almond milk
- 1 tablespoon brown rice flour
- Salt and black pepper to the taste
- A pinch of cayenne pepper
- 1 garlic clove, crushed
- 1 tablespoon lime juice
- Chopped cilantro for serving
- 1 jalapeno, chopped for serving

Directions:
1. Put a steaming basket in your instant pot, add corn, add the water, cover and cook on High for 4 minutes.
2. Release pressure, take corn out and arrange it on plates.
3. In your kitchen blender, mix almond milk with hemp, yeast, flour, garlic, salt and pepper and blend well.
4. Pour this into a small pan, heat up over medium high heat, add cayenne and lime juice, stir and cook 3-4 minutes.
5. Take sauce off heat, add cilantro and jalapeno, stir and drizzle over corn. Enjoy!

Nutritional value: Calories 67, Fat 3g, Carbs 6g, Fiber 1g, Protein 4.7g

Rich N' Delicious Vegan Lasagna

Servings: 6
Preparation time: 10 minutes
Cooking time: 40 minutes

Ingredients:
- 1 squash, cut in halves and seedless
- 1 cup water

- 1 tablespoon water
- 1 garlic clove, minced
- 8 ounces mushrooms, sliced
- 1 cup spinach,
- 1 and ½ cups vegan spaghetti sauce
- Salt and black pepper to the taste

For the filling:
- 2 garlic cloves
- 14 ounces firm tofu
- Salt and cayenne pepper to the taste
- 2 tablespoons nutritional yeast
- 1 cup basil, chopped

For the cheese sauce:
- ¼ cup cashews
- 1 cup soy milk
- ¼ cup nutritional yeast
- 2 tablespoons cornstarch
- 1 tablespoon lemon juice
- A pinch of salt
- ½ teaspoon dry mustard

Directions:
1. Place squash halves in your instant pot in a steamer basket, add the water, cover and cook on High for 8 minutes.
2. Release pressure, scoop squash flesh into a bowl and leave aside for now.
3. Heat up a pan over medium heat, add mushrooms, 1 minced garlic clove and 1 tablespoon water, stir, cover and cook for 3 minutes.
4. Add salt and pepper to the taste, stir and take off the heat.
5. In your food processor, mix 2 whole garlic cloves with tofu, basil, 2 tablespoons yeast, salt and cayenne pepper, blend well, pour into a bowl and leave aside for now.
6. Clean your food processor, add soy milk, ¼ cup yeast, cashews, cornstarch, lemon juice, salt, pepper and dry mustard, blend very well and also leave aside.
7. Clean your instant pot, spread half of the squash, press well on the bottom.
8. Add mushroom filling over squash and spread evenly.
9. Then add the vegan soy and cashews sauce and also spread.
10. Add rest of the squash flesh and spread evenly and top with the vegan spaghetti sauce.

11. Cover instant pot and cook on High for 15 minutes.
12. Release pressure, divide lasagna amongst plates and serve after 15 minutes.

Enjoy!

Nutritional Information:
Calories 254 ;Fat 8.4g;Carbs 30g;Fiber 3.3g;Protein 18g

Curry Pineapple sweet veggie dish

Servings: 4
Preparation time: 10 minutes
Cooking time: 1 hour and 10 minutes

Ingredients:
- 1 cup black eyed peas, dry and soaked
- 1 cup brown lentils
- 3 tablespoons extra virgin olive oil
- 1 yellow onion, chopped
- 3 cups water
- ½ cup cashew butter mixed with 1 tablespoon water
- ½ teaspoon turmeric
- Salt and black pepper to the taste
- ½ teaspoon cumin
- ¼ teaspoon cinnamon
- 2/3 cup pineapple chunks

Directions:
1. Put the lentils in your instant pot, add ¼ cup water, cook on High for 30 minutes, release pressure naturally, transfer to a bowl and leave them aside for now.
2. Put the peas in your instant pot, add 2 cups water, coon on High for 30 minutes, release pressure naturally, transfer them to another bowl and leave them aside for now.
3. Heat up a big pan with the oil over medium high heat, add onion, stir and cook for 2-3 minutes.

4. Add turmeric, salt, pepper, cumin, cinnamon, peas and lentils, stir well and cook for 3 minutes more.

5. Add cashew butter, the rest of the water and the pineapple, stir and cook for 4-5 minutes more.

6. Divide amongst plates and serve right away. Enjoy!

Nutritional Information :Calories 330 ;Fat 11.2g;Carbs 43g;Fiber 17g ;Protein 15.8 g

Instant Pot Chickpeas Dish

Servings: 8
Preparation time: 10 minutes
Cooking time: 20 minutes

Ingredients:
- 16 ounces chickpeas, soaked overnight and drained
- Salt and black pepper to the taste
- 3 cups coconut milk
- 1 teaspoon garlic, minced
- 1 cup cherry tomatoes, cut in halves
- ¾ pound sweet potatoes, cut in small chunks
- 1 tablespoon curry paste
- 1 tablespoon curry powder
- 1 teaspoon ginger, minced
- ½ cup basil leaves, finely chopped
- ¼ cup coriander, finely chopped
- 20 prunes, chopped
- 1 tablespoon soy sauce

Directions:
1. Put the chickpeas in your instant pot, add garlic, coconut milk, sweet potatoes, curry powder and paste, tomatoes, coriander, salt, pepper and ginger.
2. Stir, cover and cook on High for 20 minutes.
3. Release pressure naturally, stir chickpeas mix and add prunes, basil and some soy sauce.

4. Stir again everything, divide amongst plates and serve. Enjoy!

Nutritional value: calories 164, fat 1g, carbs 36.7g, fiber 6g, protein 4.4g

Creamy Butternut Squash Soup

Prep Time: 15 minutes;
Cook Time: 15 minutes
Ingredients:
- 1 tablespoon olive oil
- 1 large onion, roughly chopped
- Salt and pepper, to taste
- 4 pounds butternut squash, peeled, seeded and cubed
- ½-inch piece fresh ginger, peeled and roughly sliced
- 4 cups vegetable stock
- ½ cup toasted pumpkin seeds

Directions:
1. Set the pressure cooker to "Sauté", heat the olive oil and toss in the chopped onion, salt and pepper. Sauté until the onion is tender.
2. When tender, add about half of the cubed butternut squash. Let it brown for about 10 minutes, stirring occasionally.
3. Toss in the rest of the butternut squash, sliced ginger and vegetable stock.
4. Lock the lid of the pressure cooker and cook for 15 minutes at high pressure.
5. When done, release the pressure naturally.
6. Once it slightly cools off, puree the soup.
7. Sprinkle with toasted pumpkin seeds before serving.

Nutrition Info: Calories: 338; Total Fat: 12g; Carbs: 49.8g; Dietary Fiber: 10.3g

Thyme Tomato Soup

Prep Time: 10 minutes; Cook Time: 15 minutes
Ingredients:
- 1 tablespoon vegetable oil

- 1 tablespoon vegan butter
- 1 large onion, finely chopped
- 2 gloves garlic, crushed
- 3 pounds fresh tomatoes, coarsely chopped
- 2 tablespoon fresh thyme, finely chopped
- 1 teaspoon salt
- ½ cup vegetable stock

Directions:
1. Heat the pressure cooker by using the "Sauté" function. Heat the oil and vegan butter and when the butter melts, toss in the chopped onion and garlic. Sauté for about 3 to 4 minutes.
2. Add the chopped tomatoes, fresh thyme and season with salt. Pour in the vegetable stock, stir and seal the lid on. Cook for 15 minutes at high pressure, then release the pressure naturally.
3. Puree the soup in a food processor and put it though a fine-mesh strainer. Re-heat the soup if necessary and serve warm.

Nutrition Info:
Calories: 149; Total Fat: 7.7g; Protein: 2.7g; Carbs: 16.4g; Dietary Fiber: 2.9g;

Soy Milk Butternut Pumpkin Soup

Prep Time: 20 minutes; Cook Time: 5 minutes

Ingredients:
- 1 tablespoon vegan butter
- 1 butternut pumpkin, diced
- 1 potato, diced
- 1 brown onion, chopped
- 3 cups vegetable stock
- 4 bay leaves
- 1 apple, peeled, cored and grated
- 2 cups soy milk

Directions:
1. Heat the pressure cooker by using the "Sauté" function. Add the butter and, once it is melted, toss in the diced pumpkin, potato and onion. Cook over low heat, occasionally stirring, until the onion is slightly browned.

2. Pour in the vegetable stock and add the bay leaves.
3. Seal the lid and cook for 5 minutes at high pressure.
4. Release the pressure naturally and open the lid. Stir in the apple and cook with the lid off for about 10 minutes.
5. Take out the bay leaves and transfer the soup to a blender. Pour in the soy milk and blend until the soup is nicely creamy. Serve Warm

Nutrition Info: Calories: 226; Total Fat: 6.6g; Protein: 6.3g; Carbs: 35.2g; Dietary Fiber: 5.3g;

Fresh Mint Creamy Barley Soup

Prep Time: 15 minutes; Cook Time: 15 minutes

Ingredients:
- 1 ½ tablespoons vegan butter
- 1 large onion, chopped
- 3 tablespoons pearl barley, rinsed
- 5 cups vegetable stock
- 3 cups plain soy yogurt, lightly beaten
- 2 tablespoons chopped fresh mint

Directions:
1. Heat the pressure cooker by using the "Sauté" function. Melt the vegan butter, add the chopped onion and sauté until the onion is translucent.
2. Add the barley and vegetable stock.
3. Seal the lid and cook for 15 minutes at high pressure.
4. Release pressure naturally, remove the lid and let the soup cool off slightly.
5. Transfer it to a soup bowl and place it in the refrigerator to cool completely. Stir in 3 cups of soy yogurt and fresh mint.
6. Serve the soup chilled.

Nutrition Info: Calories: 189 Total Fat: 8.3g; Protein: 5.7g; Carbs: 25.4G; Dietary Fiber: 2.5g;

Taco Soup

Prep Time: 10 minutes; Cook Time: 7 minutes
Ingredients:
- 1 large onion, diced
- 3 cloves garlic, minced
- 2 (15-ounce) cans of black beans, drained and rinsed
- 2 (15-ounce) cans of diced tomatoes, not drained
- 2 (15-ounce) cans of tomato sauce
- 3 cups water
- 1 cup frozen corn
- 1 cup chopped fresh spinach
- ¼ cup cilantro, diced
- ½ tablespoon cumin

Directions:
1. Heat the pressure cooker by using the "Sauté" function. Add the diced onion and minced garlic. Sauté for 3 to 4 minutes.
2. Stop the sautéing and toss in the black beans, tomatoes, tomato sauce, water, frozen corn, spinach, cilantro and cumin. Stir well.
3. Seal the lid and cook for 3 minutes at high pressure.
4. When done, allow the pressure to release naturally. Serve warm

Nutrition Info: Calories: 341; Total Fat: 2.2g; Protein: 15.9g; Carbs: 45.4g; Dietary Fiber: 16.7g;

Mustard Seeds Spinach Lentil Soup

Prep Time: 20 minutes; Cook Time: 15 minutes

Ingredients:
- ½ cup channa dal / Bengal gram, soaked in water for 1 hour
- 3 cloves garlic
- Salt, to taste
- 1 cup water
- 1 tablespoon olive oil
- 1 teaspoon mustard seeds

- 1 medium onion, sliced
- 2 cups fresh spinach, chopped

Directions:
1. Drain the soaked Bengal gram and place it in the pressure cooker, along with the garlic, salt and 1 cup of water.
2. Cook at high pressure for 15 minutes.
3. Heat the olive oil in a pan, toss in the mustard seeds and cook until they splutter. Then add the sliced onion and sauté for about a minutes.
4. Add the fresh spinach and sauté until the spinach is wilted. Add the cooked gram into the pan and stir well. Let it cook together for about 10 minutes.

Nutrition Info: Calories: 178; Total Fat: 11.2g; Protein: 5.1g; Carbs: 14.1g; Dietary Fiber: 2.7g;

Turmeric Pumpkin Bean and Chickpea Stew

Prep Time: 20 minutes; Cook Time: 40 minutes

Ingredients:
- 1 cup dried cannellini beans, soaked overnight
- 1 cup chickpeas, soaked overnight
- 6 cups water
- 3 medium onions, chopped
- 2 cloves garlic, minced
- 4 medium tomatoes, chopped
- 2 cups raw pumpkin, peeled and cubed
- 1 teaspoon paprika
- ¼ teaspoon turmeric
- Salt and pepper, to taste

Directions:
1. Drain the soaked cannellini beans and chickpeas. Place them and the 6 cups of water in the pressure cooker. Bring to high pressure and let it cook for 12 minutes. Let the pressure to come down naturally.
2. In the meantime, heat a pan and sauté the onions for about 3 to 4 minutes. Toss in the garlic and chopped tomatoes. Let it cook for about 10 minutes.
3. Pour the tomatoes, raw cubed pumpkin, paprika, turmeric, salt and pepper to the beans and let it simmer over medium heat for about 30 minutes, until the pumpkin is perfectly tender.

Nutrition Info: Calories: 178; Fat: 1.7G; Protein: 11.7g; Carbs: 26.8G; Fiber: 14.3g;

Peanut Potato Stew

Prep Time: 10 minutes; Cook Time: 25 minutes

Ingredients:
- 1 onion, chopped
- 2 teaspoons fresh ginger, minced
- 1 teaspoon fresh garlic, minced
- 2 teaspoons ground cumin
- ¼ teaspoon ground cinnamon
- 2 (14.5-ounce) cans diced tomatoes
- 2 sweet potatoes, peeled and cubed
- 2 (14.5-ounce) cans chickpeas, drained and rinsed
- 1 ½ cups vegetable broth
- 1 pound green beans, cut in 1 inch pieces
- ¼ cup natural peanut butter

Directions:
1. Heat the pressure cooker by using the "Sauté" function. Toss in the chopped onion and about 2 tablespoons of water and cook for about 8 minutes. Add minced ginger, garlic, cumin and cinnamon. Cook for 1 more minute while stirring.
2. Add in the diced tomatoes, sweet potatoes, chickpeas and vegetable broth. Cook at high pressure for 5 minutes. When done, quick-release the pressure.
3. Add in the green beans and peanut butter. Return to heat, cover but don't seal the lid, and cook for about 10 minutes. Quick-release the pressure when done.

Nutrition Info: Calories: 323; Fat: 6.6G; Protein: 14.2g; Carbs: 42.5g; Fiber: 14.7g;

Kidney Beans Chickpea Lentil Stew

Prep Time: 20 minutes; Cook Time: 7 minutes

Ingredients:

- 1 tablespoon olive oil
- 1 medium onion, finely chopped
- 1 garlic clove, minced
- 1 cup tomato puree
- 1 cup split chickpeas
- 1 cup brown lentils, soaked
- 1 cup kidney beans, soaked
- 1 cup chopped spinach, tightly packed
- Salt and pepper, to taste

Directions:
1. Heat the olive oil in the pressure cooker by using the "Sauté" function. Add the chopped onion and minced garlic. Sauté the onion until it becomes translucent.
2. Pour in the tomato puree and simmer everything for about 10 minutes.
3. Add the split chickpeas, soaked lentils and kidney beans.
4. Seal the lid and cook for 7 minutes at high pressure.
5. Release the pressure naturally. Open the lid and toss in the chopped spinach. Cook for another 5 minutes with the lid removed.
6. Season with salt and pepper. Serve with bread or steamed rice.

Nutrition Info: Calories: 278; Fat: 7.3g ; Protein: 19.4g; Carbs: 23.3G; Fiber: 21.2g;

Yummy Cannellini Stew

Prep Time: 20 minutes; Cook Time: 7 minutes

Ingredients:
- 2 cups dry Cannellini beans, soaked overnight
- 2 teaspoons olive oil
- 1 medium onion, diced
- 3 cloves garlic, minced
- 1 cup diced potatoes
- 6 cups vegetable broth
- 2 bay leaves
- 2 cups diced tomatoes
- ¼ cup fresh basil, chopped
- 1 tablespoon lemon juice

Directions:
1. Heat the olive oil in the pressure cooker by using the "Sauté" function. Add the chopped onion and sauté for 2 minutes. Toss in the minced garlic and sauté for 1 more minute.
2. Add in the diced potatoes, vegetable broth, bay leaves and drained beans.
3. Seal the lid and cook for 7 minutes at high pressure.
4. Allow the pressure to release naturally.
5. Open the lid and remove the bay leaves.
6. Puree the soup with a hand blender.
7. Turn the heat to medium, add the diced tomatoes and cook for about 5 minutes with the lid off.
8. Turn the heat off and toss in the chopped basil and lemon juice.
9. Serve warm.

Nutrition Info: Calories: 438; Fat: 2.9G; Protein: 25.4g; Carbs: 64G; Fiber: 17.5g;

Green Chilies Spinach Curry

Prep Time: 10 minutes; Cook Time: 1 minute

Ingredients:
- ½ cup split pigeon peas / tour dal
- 1 ½ cup spinach, finely chopped
- 2 cups of water
- Salt, to taste
- ½ cup grated coconut
- ½ teaspoon turmeric powder
- 2 cloves garlic
- 2 green chilies
- ½ teaspoon cumin seeds
- 1 teaspoon oil
- 1 teaspoon mustard seeds

- 2 dried red chilies
- 1 tomato, chopped

Directions:
1. Place the pigeon peas, fresh spinach, water and salt into the pressure cooker, seal the lid and cook for 1 minute. Release the pressure naturally.
2. In the meantime, blend together the coconut, turmeric powder, garlic, green chilies and cumin seeds to form a paste.
3. Pour the paste into the cooked dal and boil, with the lid open, on a low flame.
4. Heat the oil in a pan, add the mustard seeds and red chilies. Once the seeds begin to splutter, toss in the chopped tomato and sauté until the tomato turns mushy.
5. Mix the tomato into the cooked dal and stir well. Wait for the curry to thicken up, then remove it from heat and serve while still hot. Serve with: Steamed rice

Nutrition Info: Calories: 102; Fat: 2.8g ; Protein: 5.2g; Carbs: 10.2G; Fiber: 5.9g;

Garlic Carrot and Lentil

Prep Time: 15 minutes; Cook Time: 10 minutes

Ingredients:
- 5 tablespoons grated coconut
- 2 green chilies
- 1/3 cup split pigeon pea, soaked in water for 30 minutes
- 1 cup chopped carrots
- 1 onion, chopped
- 1 medium tomato, chopped
- 2 large garlic cloves, minced
- ¼ teaspoon turmeric powder
- ½ teaspoon mustard seeds
- 1 teaspoon olive oil

Directions:
1. Grind the grated coconut with green chilies and some water to a paste. Set aside.

2. Drain the soaked pigeon pea. Add the chopped carrots, peas, onion, tomato, garlic and turmeric powder in the pressure cooker, cover with 1 cup of water and cook for 10 minutes at high pressure.
3. Release the pressure naturally, remove the lid and slightly mash the contents.
4. Heat the olive oil in a pan, toss in the mustard seeds and fry until they splutter. Then, add the cooked vegetables and stir well.
5. Pour in ¾ cup of water and let everything simmer for 4 to 5 minutes. Once it thickens, remove from the heat and serve immediately.

Nutrition Info: Calories: 335; Fat: 26G; Protein: 5.3g; Carbs: 15.5G; Fiber: 10.2g;

Masala Curry Potato Chickpea

Prep Time: 10 minutes; Cook Time: 20 minutes
Ingredients:
- 3 tablespoons olive oil
- 4 teaspoons cumin seeds
- 1 large onion, finely sliced
- 4 teaspoons crushed garlic
- 2 teaspoons garam masala (extra for a spicier dish)
- 2 teaspoons ground turmeric
- 2 (15-ounce) cans chickpeas, rinsed well and drained
- 2 (14-ounces) cans diced tomatoes
- 3 large potatoes, peeled and cubed
- ½ cup water
- Salt, to taste

Directions:
1. Heat the olive oil in the pressure cooker by using the "Sauté" function. Toss in the cumin seeds and cook them for about 30 seconds. Then, add in the onion and sauté for another 5 minutes.
2. Stir in the crushed garlic, garam masala and turmeric.
3. Add the canned chickpeas, diced tomatoes, cubed potatoes, water and salt.
4. Bring the cooker to high pressure and cook for 15 minutes on medium heat. Release the pressure naturally and serve with some steamed rice.

Nutrition Info: Calories: 346; Fat: 9.7g   Protein: 11.5g; Carbs: 49.4g; Dietary Fiber: 9.8g;

Coconut Mustard Black Chickpeas

Prep Time: 15 minutes; Cook Time: 15 minutes

Ingredients:
- 1 cup black chickpeas, soaked overnight
- 3 cups water
- 1 cup fresh grated coconut
- 3 dried red chili
- 1 teaspoon mustard seeds
- 1 onion, finely chopped
- 1 tablespoon grated ginger
- 2 tomatoes, finely chopped
- 3 teaspoons cooking oil
- Salt, to taste

Directions:
1. Soak the chickpeas the night before. Drain them well, put them in the pressure cooker, cover with 3 cups of water and cook for 15 minutes at high pressure.
2. Heat 1 teaspoon of oil in a pan and fry the grated coconut and red chili until the coconut starts to turn light brown.
3. Transfer the coconut and chili to a blender and blend to make a smooth paste. If necessary, add some water.
4. Heat 2 teaspoons of oil in a pan and toss in the mustard seeds. When the seeds begin to crackle, toss in the chopped onion and grated ginger. Sauté for 2 to 3 minutes.
5. Add the curry leaves and sauté for few more seconds. Toss in the chopped tomatoes and sauté for a few additional minutes. Mash the tomatoes slightly with a ladle.
6. Stir in the cooked chickpeas, coconut paste and salt.
7. Cover with a lid and let it simmer for a few more minutes, while stirring occasionally. Serve garnished with coriander leaves.

Nutrition Info: Calories: 334; Fat: 15.9G; Protein: 12.2g; Carbs: 27.5G; Fiber: 12.4g;

Ginger Green Peas Masala Curry

Prep Time: 15 minutes; Cook Time: 15 minutes

Ingredients:
- ½ cup dried green peas, soaked overnight
- 2 tablespoons grape seed oil
- 1 red onion, chopped
- 2 cloves garlic, minced
- 1 teaspoon grated ginger
- 3 Thai green chilies
- 8 curry leaves
- 1 teaspoon red chili powder
- ½ teaspoon cumin powder
- 2 tomatoes, chopped
- ½ cup coconut milk
- Salt, to taste

Directions:

1. Rinse and drain the soaked green peas. Cook the in the pressure for 15 minutes at high pressure.
2. In the meantime, heat 1 tablespoon of the grape seed oil in a pan, toss in the chopped onion, garlic, ginger and green chilies. Sauté for about 3 to 4 minutes. Remove from the heat, let it cool and grind it into a smooth paste.
3. Heat the remaining 1 tablespoon of oil, add the curry leaves and the ground mixture. Season with the red chili and cumin powder. Stir and cook for 3 to 4 minutes more.
4. Toss in the chopped tomatoes and cook until the tomatoes soften. Season with salt.
5. Pour in the coconut milk and the green peas with the water they were cooking in.
6. Let everything boil through once more before removing from the heat.

Nutrition Info: Calories: 295; Fat: 15.6G; Protein: 12.9g; Carbs: 25.6G; Fiber: 13.9g;

Thai Coconut Chickpeas Dish

Prep Time: 5 minutes; Cook Time: 18 minutes
Ingredients:
- 1 ½ cups dried chickpeas, soaked
- 1 teaspoon minced garlic
- ¾ pound sweet potatoes, peeled and cubed
- 1 cup coarsely chopped plum tomatoes
- 3 cups coconut milk
- 1 tablespoon mild curry powder
- ¼ cup minced fresh coriander
- 2 tablespoons tamari soy sauce
- ½ cup minced fresh basil

Directions:
1. Drain the chickpeas and place them in the pressure cooker. Add the minced garlic, sweet potatoes, tomatoes, coconut milk, curry powder and fresh coriander.
2. Lock the lid on and bring to high pressure. Cook for 18 minutes and let the pressure come down naturally.
3. Remove the lid, make sure the chickpeas are tender, add the soy sauce and fresh basil and stir well.

Nutrition Info: Calories: 380; Fat: 16.2g   Protein: 19.5g; Carbs: 52.2g; Fiber: 33g;

Instant Pot Paprika Broccoli Burgers

Servings: 6
Preparation time: 10 minutes
Cooking time: 40 minutes

Ingredients:

- ½ cup pink lentils, soaked and drained
- 1 cup broccoli florets
- ½ cup tomato, chopped
- 1/3 teaspoon garlic powder
- ¾ cup water
- Salt to the taste
- 1 and ½ cups pinto beans, already cooked
- 1 teaspoon chipotle powder
- ¼ teaspoon cumin powder
- ½ teaspoon paprika
- A pinch of cayenne pepper
- 1 tablespoon parsley, chopped
- 4 drops lemon juice
- ¼ cup red onion, chopped
- 3 tablespoons chickpea flour

Directions:
1. Put lentils in your instant pot, add salt, water and tomato and cook on High for 7 minutes.
2. Release pressure, add broccoli, cover and cook on High for 10 more minutes.
3. Release pressure again, discard water if needed, put everything in a bowl and mash with a fork
4. Add pinto beans after you've mashed them a bit with a fork as well, garlic powder, chipotle powder, cumin powder, paprika, cayenne, parsley, onion, lemon juice, flour and more salt to the taste and stir everything,
5. Shape patties, arrange them on a lined baking sheet, introduce in the oven 400 degrees F for 10 minutes.
6. Flip patties and cook for 10 minutes more.
7. Serve on buns with your favorite vegan toppings.

Enjoy!

Nutritional value: calories 170, fat 5.1g, carbs 16g, fiber 2.1g, protein 6g

Special Cinnamon Couscous Patties

Servings: 6
Preparation time: 10 minutes
Cooking time: 12 minutes

Ingredients:
- ½ teaspoon sesame oil
- 1 cup couscous, rinsed
- ¼ cup red bell pepper, finely chopped
- ½ cup red onion, finely chopped
- Salt and black pepper to the taste
- 1 and ½ cups veggie stock
- ½ teaspoon cinnamon, ground
- ¼ teaspoon, coriander, ground
- 2 tablespoons wine vinegar
- 1 tablespoons flaxseed mixed well with 2 tablespoons water
- ½ cup brown rice flour
- Vegetable cooking spray

Directions:
1. Set your instant pot on Sauté mode, add sesame oil and heat it up, add red bell pepper and onion, stir and cook for 4 minutes.
2. Add couscous, stock, salt, pepper, coriander, vinegar and cinnamon, cover pot and cook everything on High for 3-4 minutes.
3. Release pressure naturally, fluff couscous and transfer it to a bowl.
4. Add flaxseed mixed with the water and stir everything.
5. Shape 6 burgers, dust them with rice flour, spray some cooking oil on them, put them in a heated pan, cook them for 4 minutes on high heat, flip and cook the for 4 minutes more.
6. Serve these burgers with your favorite vegan toppings.
Enjoy!

Nutritional value: calories 150, fat 1g, carbs 25g, fiber 5g, protein 6g

Instant Pot Coconut Creamy Spinach

Prep Time ~20 mins
Serves: 4
Ingredients:
1 lb. spinach, thoroughly washed
1 tbsp. garlic powder
1 cup coconut milk
1 tbsp. each salt
Extra virgin olive oil

Directions:
-Place a steamer in your instant pot and add spinach
-Set your Instant Pot to Sauté – More
-Add 2 cups of water
-Cover with glass lid and allow to steam for 10 mins
-Remove spinach and empty Instant Pot
-Add coconut milk to your Instant Pot and set on Sauté – More
-Add salt, garlic powder and spinach, cover
-Cook for another 10 mins

Nutrition Information: Calories: 126   ; Fat: 9 G; Protein: 6 G; Carbs: 7 g

Healthy Almond Vegetable Curry

Prep Time: 10 minutes; Cook Time: 10 minutes

Ingredients:
- 1 red onion, chopped
- 3 potatoes, diced
- 2 sweet potatoes, diced
- 2 green peppers, chopped
- 1 pound split chickpeas, rinsed
- 2 cups split green peas
- 6 tablespoons mild curry paste

- 1/3 cup unsweetened coconut milk
- ¼ cup water
- ¾ chopped toasted almonds
- 25 g chopped coriander

Directions:

1. Heat the pressure cooker by using the "Sauté" function and toss in the chopped onion. Sauté for about 5 minutes.
2. Add in the diced potatoes, sweet potatoes, peppers, split chickpeas and green peas, curry paste, coconut milk and water.
3. Close the lid and cook for 5 minutes at high pressure. When done, use the quick release method.
4. Garnish with toasted almonds and chopped coriander before serving.

Nutrition Info: Calories: 541; Fat: 8G; Protein: 23.9g; Carbs: 29.1g Fiber: 4.7g;

Yummy Opt Squash

Prep Time: 10 minutes; Cook Time: 12 minutes

Ingredients:
- ½ cup Chana Dal, soaked in water for 30 minutes
- 4 teaspoons vegetable oil
- ¼ teaspoon black mustard seeds
- 4 ½ cup opo squash, peeled and diced
- ½ tomato, diced
- 1 teaspoon turmeric
- 3 teaspoon ground cumin-coriander powder
- 2 tablespoons dark brown sugar
- ¼ teaspoon salt
- ¼ cup water

Directions:
1. Drain Chana Dal.

2. Heat the oil in the pressure cooker by using the "Sauté" function. Toss in the black mustard and fry for a minute or so.
3. Add the diced opo squash, drained Chana Dal, diced tomato, turmeric, ground cumin-coriander powder, dark brown sugar, salt and water. Stir well.
4. Seal the lid and cook for 12 minutes at high pressure. Allow the pressure to come down naturally. Serve hot with naan or rice.

Nutrition Info: Calories: 276; Fat: 17.8g ; Protein: 6.7g; Carbs: 28.7G; Fiber: 1.2g;

Sprig Sage Butternut Squash Risotto

Prep Time: 15 minutes; Cook Time: 5 minutes
Ingredients:
- 4 cups diced butternut squash
- 2 tablespoons olive oil
- 2 sprigs sage, leaves removed
- 4 garlic cloves, whole
- 2 cups Arborio rice
- ¼ cup white wine
- 4 cups water
- 2 teaspoons sea salt

Directions:
1. Heat the pressure cooker by using the "Sauté" function. Add in the olive oil, sage and garlic. Sauté for a few minutes, then remove the whole garlic cloves and set them aside.
2. Place half of the butternut squash cubes into the pressure cooker and coat them with olive oil.
3. Sauté the cubes for about 4 minutes, without stirring.
4. Add the rice and toast it for 3 to 5 minutes. Pour in the wine and let it evaporate. Then add the remaining butternut squash, the toasted garlic cloves, 4 cups of water and salt.
5. Seal the lid on and cook for 5 minutes at high pressure.
6. When done, let the pressure release naturally.

Nutrition Info: Calories: 319; Fat: 7.1G; Protein: 5.1g; Carbs: 27.4g Fiber: 1g;

Onion Asparagus Arborio Rice

Prep Time: 10 minutes; Cook Time: 18 minutes

Ingredients:
- 1 pound asparagus
- 4 cups water
- 1 tablespoon olive oil
- 1 medium red onion, chopped
- 2 cups Arborio rice
- ¼ cup dry white wine
- 1 teaspoon salt
- ½ teaspoon lemon juice

Directions:
1. Trim the asparagus and chop the stems in roundels. Chop off the tips and set them aside.
2. Toss the stems into the pressure cooker and cover them with 4 cups of water.
3. Seal the lid and cook for 12 minutes at high pressure. Quick-release the pressure.
4. Open the lid and remove the contents.
5. Heat the pressure cooker by using the "Sauté" function and add the olive oil and chopped onion. Sauté until it becomes translucent.
6. Add the rice and cook for about 3 to 5 minutes. Pour in the white wine and cook until all of the liquid evaporates.
7. Pour in the cooked asparagus, along with all the cooking liquid and the reserved asparagus tips, season with salt and stir well.
8. Cook for 6 minutes at high pressure, then let the pressure release naturally.
9. Drizzle with lemon juice before serving.

Nutrition Info: Calories: 300; Fat: 3.6G; Protein: 7.2g; Carbs: 36.7G; Fiber: 2.9g;

Delicious Mash Potato

Serves: 6
Preparation Time: 15 minutes

Ingredients:
- 3 lbs. potatoes, clean and diced
- 4 tbsp. half and half
- 2 tbsp. vegan butter
- 1 cup vegetable broth
- 1/4 tsp. pepper
- 3/4 tsp. salt

Directions:
1. Place steamer rack in the instant pot then pour vegetable broth.
2. Add potatoes and seal pot with lid.
3. Cook on manual high pressure for 8 minutes.
4. Release pressure using quick release method then open lid carefully.
5. Transfer potatoes in large mixing bowl and mash with masher.
6. Add half and half, butter, pepper and salt. Mix well until combine.
7. Serve hot and enjoy.

Nutritional Info: Calories 210; Fat 5.5 g; Carbohydrates 36.3 g; Protein 5.0 g

Mustard Chili Cabbage Sabzi

Serve: 2-3
Prep Time: 20 minutes; Cook Time: 15 minutes
Ingredients:
- 4 cups chopped cabbage
- ¼ cup dry chickpeas, soaked overnight
- 1 green chili, sliced

- ¼ teaspoon turmeric powder
- Salt, to taste
- 2 tablespoons olive oil
- 1 teaspoon mustard seeds
- 1 teaspoon cumin seeds
- 1 spring curry leaves

Directions:
1. Drain the chickpeas, place them in the pressure cooker and cook for 15 minutes at high pressure.
2. Heat the olive oil, toss in the mustard seeds, cumin seeds and curry leaves and sauté for a minute or 2.
3. Toss in the green chilies and chopped cabbage. Cook for 5 minutes, open the lid, and add the chickpeas, turmeric and salt. Stir well, cover with a lid and cook for 5 more minutes. Serve warm.

Nutrition Info: Calories: 231; Fat: 17.8G; Protein: 6.9g; Carbs: 14.1G; Fiber: 11.8g;

Tasty Vegan Corn Burger

Servings: 6
Prep time: 10 minutes; Cook time: 20 minutes

Ingredients:
- 6 corns on the cob, cut in halves
- 3 ounces tomatoes, chopped
- 1 teaspoon green chili paste
- 1 teaspoon red chili paste
- ¼ pounds vegan cheese, grated
- Salt to the taste
- 1 teaspoon vegetable oil
- Burger buns

Directions:

1. Place corn in your instant pot in a steamer basket, add some water, cover the pot and cook on High for 10 minutes.

2. Release pressure, grate corn, put it in a bowl, add cheese and stir well
3. set your clean instant pot on Sauté mode, add oil, heat up add green and red chili paste, tomatoes and salt, stir and cook for 5 minutes.
4. Spread this mix on burger buns, place them on a lined baking sheet, introduce in the oven at 350 degrees F, bake for 5 minutes and serve with the tomato sauce you've made on top. Enjoy!

Nutritional Info: calories 140, fat 8g, carbs 14g, fiber g1, protein 3g

Gluten-free Instant Pot Mushroom Patties

Servings: 6
Preparation time: 10 minutes
Cooking time: 15 minutes

Ingredients:
- 1 tablespoon canola oil
- 1 garlic clove, minced
- 3 green onions, minced
- 1 yellow onion, minced
- ½ teaspoon cumin
- 15 ounces canned pinto beans, drained
- ¾ cup mushrooms, chopped
- 1 teaspoon parsley leaves, chopped
- Salt and black pepper to the taste
- A drizzle of olive oil for frying

Directions:
1. Set your instant pot on Sauté mode, add canola oil, heat it up, add garlic and yellow onion, stir and cook for 5 minutes.
2. Add mushroom, green onions, salt, pepper and cumin, stir, cover and cook on Low for 5 minutes.
3. Release pressure, transfer mushrooms mix to a bowl and leave it aside to cool down.
4. Put the beans in your food processor, blend a few times and add them to mushroom mix.
5. Add more salt and pepper to the taste and parsley and stir well.

6. Shape patties, heat up a pan with some olive oil over medium high heat, add burgers, cook for 3 minutes on each side and serve them.
Enjoy!

Nutritional Info: calories 155, fat 4g, carbs 12g, fiber 4g, protein 14g

Garlic Amaranth Black Eyed Peas

Prep Time: 20 minutes; Cook Time: 25 minutes

Ingredients:
- 1.5 cups dry black eyed peas, soaked overnight
- 1 tablespoon olive oil
- 1 teaspoon cumin seeds
- 1 teaspoon cinnamon
- ½ onion, chopped
- 2 cloves garlic, minced
- 1 tomato, diced
- 1 teaspoon red chili powder
- 1 teaspoon turmeric powder
- Salt, to taste
- 1-2 cups of water
- 1 bunch amaranth greens

Directions:

1. Drain black eyed peas and cook them in the pressure cooker for 5 minutes at high pressure.
2. Heat the olive oil in a pan and toss in the cumin seeds and cinnamon.
3. When they begin to sputter, add the chopped onion and minced garlic. Sauté until the onion turns translucent.
4. Toss in the diced tomato, chili powder, turmeric and salt. Cook for 5 to 6 minutes.
5. Add the water and cooked black eyed peas, stir well and bring it to a boil.

6. Add the amaranth greens, cover with a lid and cook for 5 to 6 minutes. Serve warm.

Nutrition Info: Calories: 284; Fat: 8.7G; Protein: 16g; Carbs: 32.4G; Fiber: 8.9g;

Onion Lentil Risotto & Arborio Rice

Prep Time: 5 minutes; Cook Time: 5 minutes
Serve: 3
Ingredients:
- 1 tablespoon olive oil
- 1 medium onion, chopped
- 1 celery stalk, chopped
- 1 cup dry lentils, soaked overnight
- 1 cup Arborio rice
- 2 garlic cloves, minced
- 3 ¼ cups vegetable stock

Directions:
1. Heat the olive oil in the pressure cooker by using the "Sauté" function. Add the chopped onion and sauté until it becomes translucent.
2. Then add the chopped celery and sauté for another minute.
3. Add the rice and minced garlic and sauté for 1 to 2 minutes. Pour in the vegetable stock, seal the lid and cook for 5 minutes at high pressure.
4. When done, release the pressure naturally.
5. Serve immediately.

Nutrition Info: Calories: 335; Fat: 5.7G; Protein: 15.1g; Carbs: 44.7G; Fiber: 15.4g;

Simple Lemon Broccoli

Prep Time: 5 minutes; Cook Time: 2 minutes
Serve: 4

Ingredients:
- 2 pounds fresh broccoli, cut into florets
- Juice of ½ lemon
- ½ cup water
- Salt and pepper, to taste

Directions:
1. Place the broccoli, lemon juice, water, salt and pepper in the pressure cooker.
2. Seal the lid and cook for 2 minutes at high pressure.
3. Release the pressure naturally and remove the broccoli from the pressure cooker.
4. Let the broccoli cool off before serving.

Nutrition Info: Calories: 136; Fat: 00G; Protein: 16g; Carbs: 11.5G; Fiber: 11g;

Grilled Zucchini With Chickpeas Quinoa

Prep Time: 20 minutes; Cook Time: 60 minutes
Serve: 3

Ingredients:

- ½ cup chickpeas, dry
- 2 cups water
- 1 teaspoon olive oil
- 1 teaspoon salt
- 1 zucchini, sliced
- 1 cup dry quinoa, soaked overnight
- Salt, to taste
- 1 tablespoon olive oil, divided
- ¼ cup white and green onions
- 2 green chilies

- 2 cloves garlic, crushed
- ½ cup tomatoes
- 1 cup dill leaves

Directions:

1. Place the dry chickpeas in the pressure cooker, cover with water and cook for 40 minutes at high pressure. Release the pressure naturally.
2. When done, drain the water and pat the chickpeas dry.
3. Preheat the oven to 350 degrees F and layer the chickpeas on a baking tray. Drizzle them with 1 teaspoon of olive oil, season with salt and roast in the oven for 15 to 20 minutes. Allow them to cool off completely.
4. In the meantime, grill the sliced zucchini for about 3 minutes per side.
5. Drain the quinoa, place it in a pan, along with some salt and ½ tablespoon of olive oil and cook until all the water evaporates. Turn the heat off, cover with a lid and let it sit for about 10 minutes. Fluff the cooked quinoa with a fork.
6. Heat ½ tablespoon of olive oil in a pan, toss in the chopped onions, chilies and garlic. Sauté for 1 minute, then add the chopped tomatoes and sauté until the tomatoes turn soft.
7. Remove from the heat, add the dill leaves and stir well. Toss in the cooked quinoa, chickpeas and zucchini and stir everything very well.
8. Serve immediately.

Nutrition Info: Calories: 268; Fat: 7.6G; Protein: 10.8g; Carbs: 34.3G; Fiber: 11g;

Garlic Mushroom Risotto

Prep Time: 5 minutes; Cook Time: 20 minutes
Serve: 2
Ingredients:
- 1 onion, chopped
- 2 cups mushrooms, chopped

- 3 cloves garlic, minced
- 1 cup risotto rice
- 2 cups vegetable broth
- Salt and pepper, to taste

Directions:
1. Heat the pressure cooker by using the "Sauté" function and toss in the chopped onion.
2. Cook for a few minutes, until the onion becomes translucent.
3. Add in the chopped mushroom and minced garlic and cook for another 5 to 8 minutes.
4. Add the rice and let it cook for 2 more minutes. Pour in the vegetable broth and season with salt and pepper.
5. Seal the lid on and let it cook for 8 minutes at high pressure. Release the pressure naturally when done.
6. Serve warm.

Nutrition Info: Calories: 359; Fat: 1.3G; Protein: 9.1g; Carbs: 37.9G; Fiber: 3g;

Instant Pot Lentils Burgers

Servings: 8
Preparation time: 15 minutes
Cooking time: 40 minutes

Ingredients:
- 2 teaspoons ginger, grated
- 1 cup mushrooms, minced
- 1 cup yellow onion, minced
- 1 cup red lentils, rinsed
- 2 and ½ cups veggie stock
- 1 and ½ sweet potatoes, chopped
- Vegetable cooking spray
- ¼ cup parsley, finely chopped
- ¼ cup hemp seeds
- ¼ cup cilantro, finely chopped

- 1 tablespoon curry powder
- 1 cup quick oats
- 4 tablespoons brown rice flour
- Salt and pepper to the taste

Directions:
1. Set your instant pot on Sautee more, add onion, mushroom and ginger, stir and cook for 3 minutes.
2. Add stock, sweet potatoes and lentils, cover pot and cook on High for 6 minutes.
3. Release pressure naturally, transfer lentils mix to a bowl and leave aside for 15 minutes.
4. Mash lentils mix, add parsley, curry powder, salt and pepper, hemp seeds and cilantro and stir well.
5. Add oats and rice flour and stir again well.
6. Shape 10 burgers with your wet hands, arrange them on a baking sheet after you've sprayed it with some vegetable cooking oil, introduce them in the oven at 375 degrees F and bake for 10 minutes.
7. Flip burgers, bake them for 10 more minutes, take them out of the oven, leave to cool down a bit and serve.

Enjoy!

Nutritional value: calories 140, fat 8g, carbs 15g, fiber 4.7g, protein 11g

Flaxseed Black Bean Burgers

Servings: 5
Preparation time: 15 minutes
Cooking time: 35 minutes

Ingredients:

- 1 cup black beans, soaked for 3 hours
- 1 tablespoon flaxseed+1 tablespoon water

- 1 red onion, chopped
- 3 tablespoon vegetable oil
- ½ cup quick oats
- ½ teaspoon cumin
- 2 teaspoons chipotle powder
- Salt to the taste
- 2 garlic cloves, minced
- 2 teaspoons lemon zest, grated
- Burger buns for serving
- Red cabbage, thinly sliced for serving

Directions:

1. Drain beans, place them in your instant pot, and add water to cover them, cook on High for 20 minutes, release pressure quick, drain the beans again, put them in a bowl, crush them with a fork and leave aside for now.
2. Heat up a pan with 1 tablespoon oil over medium high heat, add onion, stir and cook for 3 minutes.
3. Add garlic, stir and cook for 3 more minute.
4. Take this mix off heat, leave aside to cool down and add to the bowl with the beans.
5. Add flaxseed mixed with 1 tablespoon water, oats, cumin, chipotle powder, salt to the taste and lemon zest and stir everything well.
6. Shape 5 burgers with your wet hands and place them on a working surface.
7. Heat up a pan with the rest of the oil over medium high heat, add burgers, cook for 3 minutes, flip, cook them for 3 more minutes, transfer them to paper towels and drain grease.
8. Divide on burger buns, add red cabbage and serve.

Enjoy!

Nutritional Info: calories 251, fat 9.3g, carbs 3g2, fiber 7.3g, protein 10.5g

Amazing Mushroom Spinach Lasagna

Servings: 6
Preparation time: 10 minutes

Cooking time: 40 minutes

Ingredients:
- 1 squash, cut in halves and seedless
- 1 cup water
- 1 tablespoon water
- 1 garlic clove, minced
- 8 ounces mushrooms, sliced
- 1 cup spinach,
- 1 and ½ cups vegan spaghetti sauce
- Salt and black pepper to the taste

For the filling:
- 2 garlic cloves
- 14 ounces firm tofu
- Salt and cayenne pepper to the taste
- 2 tablespoons nutritional yeast
- 1 cup basil, chopped

For the cheese sauce:
- ¼ cup cashews
- 1 cup soy milk
- ¼ cup nutritional yeast
- 2 tablespoons cornstarch
- 1 tablespoon lemon juice
- A pinch of salt
- ½ teaspoon dry mustard

Directions:
1. Place squash halves in your instant pot in a steamer basket, add the water, cover and cook on High for 8 minutes.
2. Release pressure, scoop squash flesh into a bowl and leave aside for now.
3. Heat up a pan over medium heat, add mushrooms, 1 minced garlic clove and 1 tablespoon water, stir, cover and cook for 3 minutes.
4. Add salt and pepper to the taste, stir and take off the heat.
5. In your food processor, mix 2 whole garlic cloves with tofu, basil, 2 tablespoons yeast, salt and cayenne pepper, blend well, pour into a bowl and leave aside for now.
6. Clean your food processor, add soy milk, ¼ cup yeast, cashews, cornstarch, lemon juice, salt, pepper and dry mustard, blend very well and also leave aside.
7. Clean your instant pot, spread half of the squash, press well on the bottom.

8. Add mushroom filling over squash and spread evenly.
9. Then add the vegan soy and cashews sauce and also spread.
10. Add rest of the squash flesh and spread evenly and top with the vegan spaghetti sauce. Cover instant pot and cook on High for 15 minutes.
12. Release pressure, divide lasagna amongst plates and serve after 15 minutes.

Nutritional Info: calories 254, fat 8.4g, carbs 30g, fiber 3.3g, protein 18 g

Cumin Moroccan Black Eyed Peas

Prep Time: 10 minutes; Cook Time; 40 minutes
Serves: 4;

Ingredients:
- 1 ½ cups dried black eyed peas, soaked
- 2 tomatoes, sliced
- 1 large onion, sliced
- 3 cloves of garlic, minced
- 4 tablespoons chopped fresh parsley
- 1 teaspoon salt
- 1 teaspoon ground cumin
- 2 teaspoons sweet paprika
- 1 teaspoon ginger
- ¼ cup olive oil
- 3 ½ cups water
- Salt and pepper, to taste

Directions:
1. Drain the black eyed peas and add all the ingredients into the pressure cooker. Cover with 3 ½ cups of water.
2. Seal the lid on and cook for 5 minutes at high pressure, until the peas are tender.
3. Once the consistency of the beans is saucy and no longer watery, season with some salt and pepper and serve.

Nutrition Info: Calories: 238; Fat: 13.6g ; Protein: 8.7g; Carbs: 18.5G; Fiber: 5.4g;

Vegan Sheppard's Pie

Servings: 4
Preparation time: 10 minutes
Cooking time: 30 minutes

Ingredients:
- 26 ounces potatoes, cubed
- Water for the potatoes
- 2 tablespoons soy milk
- 2 tablespoons vegan margarine
- A drizzle of vegetable oil
- 1 celery stick, chopped
- 1 carrot, chopped
- Salt and black pepper to the taste
- 3 ounces red lentils, already cooked
- 14 ounces canned tomatoes, chopped
- 4 ounces veggie stock

Directions:

1. Put the potatoes in your instant pot, add water to cover and cook them on High for 10 minutes.
2. Release pressure quick, drain potatoes, transfer them to a bowl, add soy milk and vegan margarine and mash them very well.
3. Heat up a pan with the oil over medium high heat, add celery and carrot, stir and cook for 2 minutes.
4. Add lentils, stock, tomatoes, salt and pepper to the taste, stir and cook for 10 minutes.
5. Transfer this mix on the bottom of your cleaned instant pot, add mashed potatoes and spread evenly, cover pot and cook on High for 6 minutes.
6. Release pressure, divide amongst plates and serve.
Enjoy!

Nutritional Info: calories 230, fat 0.5g, carbs 33g, fiber 8g, protein 13.2g

Mexican Style Corn With Lime Sauce

Servings: 4
Preparation time: 10 minutes
Cooking time: 10 minutes

Ingredients:
- 4 ears corn
- 1 and ½ cups water
- 2 tablespoons nutritional yeast
- 2 tablespoons hemp hearts
- ½ cup almond milk
- 1 tablespoon brown rice flour
- Salt and black pepper to the taste
- A pinch of cayenne pepper
- 1 garlic clove, crushed
- 1 tablespoon lime juice
- Chopped cilantro for serving
- 1 jalapeno, chopped for serving

Directions:

1. Put a steaming basket in your instant pot, add corn, add the water, cover and cook on High for 4 minutes.
2. Release pressure, take corn out and arrange it on plates.
3. In your kitchen blender, mix almond milk with hemp, yeast, flour, garlic, salt and pepper and blend well.
4. Pour this into a small pan, heat up over medium high heat, add cayenne and lime juice, stir and cook 3-4 minutes.
5. Take sauce off heat, add cilantro and jalapeno, stir and drizzle over corn. Enjoy!

Nutritional Info: calories 67, fat 3g, carbs 6g, fiber 1g, protein 4.7g

Spinach Sweet Potato Risotto

Prep Time: 15 minutes; Cook Time: 8 minutes
Serves: 4;

Ingredients:
- 1 medium sweet potato, peeled and diced
- 4 shallots, finely diced
- 2 cloves garlic, minced
- 3 ½ cups vegetable broth
- 1 ½ cups rice
- 1 tablespoon sage, finely minced
- ¼ teaspoon turmeric
- 1 ½ cups green beans, chopped
- 1 cup spinach, chopped

Directions:

1. Preheat the oven to 410 degrees F. Line a baking sheet with parchment paper.
2. In a large bowl, toss the sweet potatoes with 2 tablespoons of vegetable broth.
3. Layer the potatoes on the baking sheet and roast them in the preheated oven for 10 to 15 minutes. Flip them over and roast for another 5 minutes.
4. In the meantime, heat the pressure cooker by using the "Sauté" function. Toss in the diced shallots and sauté for about 2 to 3 minutes.
5. Add the minced garlic and cook for another 30 seconds. Pour in ¼ cup of the vegetable broth.
6. Add the rice, the remaining vegetable broth, sage and turmeric. Lock the lid on and set the pressure cooker to high pressure. Let it cook for 5 minutes.
7. Quickly and release the pressure, remove the lid and stir. Toss in the green beans and fresh spinach, lock the lid on again and let the vegetables steam with the rice for about 3 minutes.
8. Stir in the roasted sweet potato before serving.

Nutrition Info: Calories: 288; Fat: 0.9G; Protein: 6.4g; Carbs: 32.5G; Fiber: 3.3g;

Ginger Moroccan Pumpkin Lentils

Prep Time: 15 minutes; Cook Time: 35 minutes
Serves: 4;

Ingredients:
- 1 ½ cups green lentils, rinsed
- ¼ cup olive oil
- 2 medium onions, chopped
- 3 large tomatoes, sliced
- 4 cloves garlic, minced
- ¼ cup chopped fresh parsley
- 1 tablespoon paprika
- 2 teaspoons cumin
- 2 teaspoons ginger
- 1 teaspoon salt
- ½ teaspoon turmeric
- 8 cups water
- 2 pounds pumpkin, uncooked and cubed
- 3 carrots, diced

Directions:

1. Put the green lentils into the pressure cooker. Add the olive oil, chopped onions, sliced tomatoes, minced garlic, parsley, paprika cumin, ginger, salt and turmeric. Pour in 8 cups of water.
2. Bring to high pressure and let it cook for about 20 minutes.
3. Interrupt the cooking and add the cubed pumpkin and carrots. Also add more water if necessary.
4. Bring back to pressure and let it cook for another 15 minutes.
5. Garnish with some fresh parsley before serving.

Nutrition Info: Calories: 413; Fat: 14G; Protein: 16.2g; Carbs: 43.6G; Fiber: 18.3g;

Garlic Spinach Pasta

Servings: 4
Preparation time: 5 minutes
Cooking time: 15 minutes

Ingredients:
- 1 pound spinach
- 1 pound fusilli pasta
- 2 garlic cloves, crushed
- 2 garlic cloves, chopped
- A drizzle of olive oil
- Salt and black pepper to the taste
- ¼ cup pine nuts, chopped
- Vegan cheese, grated for serving

Directions:
1. Set instant pot on Sautee, add olive oil and heat it up.
2. Add spinach and crushed garlic, stir and cook for 6-8 minutes.
3. Add pasta, salt and pepper to the taste, some water to cover pasta, stir and cook on Low for 6 minutes.
4. Release pressure, add chopped garlic and pine nuts, stir, divide amongst plates and serve with grated vegan cheese on top.

Enjoy!

Nutritional Info: calories 200, fat 1g, carbs 6g, fiber 1g, protein 6g

Kale Pasta with Pinto Beans

Prep Time: 15 minutes; Cook Time: 60 minutes
Serves: 8;

Ingredients:
- 2 cups dried pinto beans, soaked overnight
- 6 cups water
- 1 medium onion, chopped
- 2 ribs celery, chopped

- 7 cloves garlic, minced and divided
- 26 ounces chopped tomatoes, canned
- 3 teaspoons dried basil leaves, divided
- 2 teaspoons dried oregano, divided
- 2 teaspoons salt
- 2 cups small pasta
- 6 cups chopped kale
- 3 tablespoons nutritional yeast

Directions:

1. Drain and rinse the soaked pinto beans.
2. Heat the pressure cooker by using the "Sauté" function. Toss in the chopped onion and cook until it becomes translucent. Add the chopped celery and 3 minced garlic cloves. Let it cook for 2 more minutes.
3. Add in the chopped tomatoes, 2 teaspoons dried basil and 1 teaspoon dried oregano. Heat while stirring constantly.
4. Add in the drained pinto beans, 6 cups of water and salt.
5. Lock the lid on, bring to high pressure and let it cook for 10 minutes. Then let the pressure to come down naturally. If you are not sure whether the beans are perfectly tender, quick-release the pressure, check the beans and let them cook for another few minutes, if necessary.
6. Once they are tender, add the 4 remaining garlic cloves, 1 teaspoon of basil and 1 teaspoon of oregano.
7. Add the pasta and cook on medium heat using the sauté function until the pasta is almost al dente.
8. Toss in the chopped kale, turn the heat off and cover with a lid. Let the kale sit for about 5 minutes.
9. Before serving, sprinkle with nutritional yeast.

Nutrition Info: Calories: 313; Fat: 1.3g; Protein: 15.6g; Carbs: 45.8G; Fiber: 12.1g;

Delicious Garlic Veggies Dish

Servings: 4
Preparation time: 10 minutes
Cooking time: 15 minutes

Ingredients:

- 8 ounces shiitake mushrooms, minced
- 4 ounces white mushrooms, minced
- 1 and ¼ cups veggie stock
- ½ cup red onion, finely chopped
- ½ cup celery, chopped
- ½ cup carrot, chopped
- 5 garlic cloves, minced
- 1 tablespoon ginger, grated
- Salt and black pepper to the taste
- ¼ teaspoon oregano, dry
- 28 ounces canned tomatoes, chopped
- 1 and ½ teaspoons turmeric, ground
- ¼ cup basil leaves, chopped
- Spaghetti squash for serving

Directions:

1. In your instant pot, mix ¼ cup veggie stock, mushrooms, onion, celery, carrot, ginger and garlic, stir and cook on Sautee mode for 5 minutes.
2. Add the rest of the stock, tomatoes, salt, pepper, turmeric and oregano, stir, cover and cook on High for 10 minutes.
3. Release the pressure, turn instant pot to Sauté mode again and cook for 5 more minutes.
4. Add basil, divide on plates and serve with some spaghetti squash. Enjoy!

Nutritional value: calories 70, fat 3.g8, carbs 5.7g, fiber 1.4g, protein 3.1g

Simple Vegan Penne Rigatta

Servings: 5

Preparation time: 10 minutes
Cooking time: 20 minutes

Ingredients:
- 15 ounces penne pasta
- 1 yellow onion, thinly sliced
- 2 garlic cloves, minced
- 12 mushrooms, thinly sliced
- 1 zucchini, thinly sliced
- A splash of sherry wine
- 1 shallot, finely chopped
- A pinch of basil, dried
- A pinch of oregano, dried
- Salt and black pepper to the taste
- 1 tablespoon olive oil
- 1 cup veggie stock
- 2 cups water
- 5 ounces tomato paste
- 2 tablespoons soy sauce

Directions:
1. Set your instant pot on Sauté mode, add oil and heat it up.
2. Add shallot, onion, a pinch of salt and pepper, stir and cook for 3 minutes.
3. Add garlic, stir and sauté for 1 minute more.
4. Add mushrooms, zucchini, basil and oregano, stir and cook 1 more minute.
5. Add sherry wine, veggie stock, water and soy sauce and stir.
6. Also add your penne, the tomato paste, more salt and pepper to the taste, stir, cover the instant pot and cook on High for 5 minutes.
7. Release pressure for 5 minutes, divide pasta amongst plates and serve. Enjoy!

Nutritional Info: calories 250, fat 13g, carbs 12g, fiber 1g, protein 3g

Mexican Bell Peppers Mixed Beans

Prep Time: 15 minutes; Cook Time: 36 minutes

Serves: 6;

Ingredients:

- 1 pound dry pinto beans
- 2 tablespoons olive oil
- 4 cups water
- 1 large onion, chopped
- 1 large Poblano pepper, chopped
- 1 large green bell pepper, chopped
- 1 large red bell pepper, chopped
- 1 tablespoon minced garlic
- 2 teaspoons dried oregano
- 3 cups vegetable broth
- 2 large avocados, diced
- ¼ cup fresh squeezed lime juice
- 1 small red onion, finely chopped
- 1 medium-sized Poblano pepper, finely chopped

Directions:
1. Place the pinto beans, 1 tablespoon of olive oil and 4 cups of water into the pressure cooker. Cook at high pressure for 30 minutes. When done, let the pressure release naturally.
2. In the meantime, heat the other tablespoon of olive oil, toss in the chopped onion, Poblano pepper, green bell pepper and red bell pepper and sauté for about 5 minutes. Add the minced garlic and oregano and sauté for 2 more minutes.
3. Toss the diced avocados with lime juice and stir in the chopped red onion and Poblano pepper.
4. Drain the beans, discard the cooking water and place the beans back into the pressure cooker, along with the sautéed pepper mixture. Pour in 3 cups of vegetable broth and cook at high pressure for 6 minutes. When done, use the quick-release method to release the pressure.
5. Serve the beans with the prepared salsa sauce.

Nutrition Info: Calories: 455; Fat: 12.9G; Protein: 18.2g; Carbs: 34G; Fiber: 17.1g;

Simple Potato Salad

Prep Time: 5 minutes; Cook Time: 5 minutes
Serves: 4;

Ingredients:
- 1 ½ cups water
- 3 pounds red potatoes, diced
- ½ medium red onion, finely chopped
- 3 tablespoons white wine vinegar
- Salt, to taste
- 3 tablespoons olive oil
- 1 bunch parsley, finely chopped

Directions:
1. Prepare the pressure cooker with water and trivet.
2. Place the diced red potatoes in the steamer basket and lock the lid. Cook for 5 minutes at high pressure.
3. In the meantime, mix the chopped onion with white wine vinegar and some salt in a medium bowl.
4. When the potatoes are done, release the pressure naturally and then transfer the potatoes into the bowl with the onion. Drizzle with olive oil.
5. When the salad has cooled to room temperature, stir in the chopped parsley and serve right away.

Nutrition Info: Calories: 395; Fat: 11G; Protein: 7.9g; Carbs: 44.9G; Fiber: 6.3g;

Chili Ginger Mixed Vegetable

Prep Time: 10 minutes; Cook Time: 10 minutes
Serves: 4;

Ingredients:
- 3 tablespoons olive oil
- 1 teaspoon cumin seeds
- 4 cloves garlic, minced
- 3 cardamom seeds
- 1 onion, chopped
- 1 teaspoon ginger garlic paste
- 1 green chili
- 2 carrots, peeled and cubed
- ¾ cup fresh green peas
- 2 cups basmati rice
- 3 cups water
- Salt to taste

Directions:

1. Heat the pressure cooker by using the "Sauté" function. Heat the olive oil, cumin seeds, minced garlic and cardamom. Sauté for about a minute, toss in the chopped onion, ginger garlic paste and green chili. Sauté for another minute.
2. Add the carrots and green peas. After another minute of sautéing, add the basmati rice.
3. Sauté for 2 minutes and cover with 3 cups of water. Season with salt.
4. Cook for about 10 minutes at high pressure.
5. Before serving, fluff it with a fork.

Nutrition Info: Calories: 437; Fat: 11.6G; Protein: 8.1g; Carbs: 70.8G; Fiber: 5g;

Instant Pot Broccoli Carrots Casserole

Servings: 4
Preparation time: 10 minutes
Cooking time: 10 minutes

Ingredients:
- 3 tablespoons vegetable oil
- 1 teaspoon lemon juice
- ¼ cup bread crumbs
- 1 and ¾ cup water
- 1 tablespoon parsley, finely chopped
- 1 pound carrots, cut in thin matchsticks
- 1 pound broccoli
- Salt and black pepper to the taste

Directions:
1. Heat up a pan with the oil over medium high heat, add bread crumbs, stir and cook until they become golden.
2. Transfer them to a bowl, add parsley and lemon juice, stir well and leave aside for now.
3. In your instant pot, mix carrots with broccoli, salt and pepper to the taste, add the water, cover and cook on High for 10 minutes.
4. Release pressure naturally, drain veggie and divide them amongst plates.
5. Sprinkle bread crumbs mix all over them and serve right away.

Nutritional value: calories 170, fat 5g, carbs 13g, fiber 5.6g, protein 20g

Tasty Red Cabbage Salad

Servings: 4
Preparation time: 5 minutes
Cooking time: 5 minutes

Ingredients:
- 2 cups red cabbage, shredded
- 1 tablespoon canola oil
- Salt and black pepper to the taste
- ¼ cup white onion, finely chopped
- 2 teaspoons red wine vinegar
- ½ teaspoon palm sugar

Directions:

1. Put shredded cabbage in your instant pot, add some water, cover and cook on High for 5 minutes.
2. Release pressure naturally, drain water and transfer it to a salad bowl.
3. Add salt, pepper to the taste, onion, oil, palm sugar and vinegar, toss to coat and serve right away.
Enjoy!

Nutritional value: calories 110, fat 1g, carbs 6g, fiber 2.2g, protein 1.1g

Brown Rice Cabbage Rolls

Servings: 6
Preparation time: 15 minutes
Cooking time: 35 minutes

Ingredients:

- 1 tablespoon extra virgin olive oil
- 1 cup brown rice, uncooked
- 9 and ½ cups water
- 3 cups mushrooms, chopped
- 1 yellow onion, chopped
- 2 garlic cloves, minced
- Salt and black pepper to the taste
- 12 green cabbage leaves
- ½ teaspoon walnuts, finely chopped
- ½ teaspoon caraway seeds
- A pinch of cayenne pepper
- Tomato sauce for serving

Directions:
1. Put 1 and ½ cups water and the rice in your instant pot, cover and cook on High for 15 minutes.
2. Release pressure automatically, rinse rice under cold water, drain it well and put it in a bowl.

3. Heat up a pan with the oil over medium high heat, add onion, mushrooms and garlic, stir and cook for 5 minutes.
4. Add caraway, walnuts, salt, pepper, and cayenne, pour over rice and stir very well.
5. Pour 8 cups water in a pot, bring to a boil over medium high heat, add cabbage leaves, cook for 1 minute, drain and rinse them under cold water.
6. Arrange them on a working surface, place 1/3 cup rice mix in the middle of each, roll them, seal edges and place them in your instant pot.
7. Add 1 inch water, cover and cook on High pressure for 10 minutes.
8. Release pressure, divide them on plates and serve them with some tomato sauce on top.
Enjoy!

Nutritional Info: calories 283, fat 10f, carbs 30f, fiber 6f, protein 5f,

Simple Brussels sprouts

Serves: 4
Preparation Time: 10 minutes

Ingredients:
- 1 lb. Brussels sprouts
- 4 tbsp. pine nuts
- 1 cup water
- Olive oil
- Pepper
- Salt

Directions:

1. Pour water into the instant pot.
2. Add Brussels sprouts in steamer basket and place basket in the pot.
3. Seal pot with lid and cook on manual high pressure for 3 minute.
4. Release pressure using quick release method then open lid carefully.

5. Season with pepper, salt and olive oil.
6. Sprinkle pine nuts and serve.

Nutritional Info: Calories 107; Fat 6.3 g; Carbohydrates 11.4 g; Protein 5.0 g

Delicious Garlic Chickpeas

Serves: 2
Preparation Time: 45 minutes

Ingredients:
- 1 cup dried chickpeas, rinse
- 2 bay leaves
- 3 garlic cloves
- 4 cups water

Directions:

1. Add chickpeas, bay leaves, garlic and water in instant pot.
2. Seal pot with lid and select bean function for 35 minutes.
3. Allow to release pressure naturally then open lid.
4. Serve warm and enjoy.

Nutritional Info Calories 371; Fat 6.1 g; Carbohydrates 62.1 g; Protein 19.6 g

Stuffed Bell Peppers

Servings: 8
Total Time Taken: 50 minutes
Ingredients

2/3 cup quinoa, rinsed
2 tablespoons Amaranth
1 medium-sized onion, peeled and chopped
1 medium-sized zucchini, trimmed and grated
2 teaspoons minced garlic
1 teaspoon ground cumin
2 tablespoons currants
2 tablespoons sunflower seeds, lightly toasted
2 tablespoons chopped parsley
2 medium-sized tomatoes, diced
75g vegan cheese, grated
4 large green bell peppers
2 tablespoons olive oil
1 teaspoon salt
½ teaspoon ground black pepper

Directions

1. In a 6-quarts instant pot place quinoa and amaranth, and pour in 1 cup water.
2. Plug in and switch on the instant pot, then secure with lid and position pressure indicator.
3. Select manual option, adjust cooking time on timer pad to 2 minutes and let cook. Instant pot will take 10 minutes to build pressure before cooking timer starts.
4. When the timer beeps, switch off the instant pot and let pressure release naturally for 10 minutes and then do quick pressure release.
5. In the meantime, place a medium-sized non-stick skillet pan over medium heat and add oil. When the oil is heated, add onion and zucchini and cook for 5 minutes or until tender, stir frequently.
6. Add cumin and garlic and continue cooking for 1 minute and then remove the pan from heat.
7. When the timer beeps, switch off the instant pot and let pressure release naturally for 10 minutes and then do quick pressure release. Then uncover pot and fluff quinoa with a fork.
8. Transfer onion mixture in a large bowl, add tomato, parsley, currants, sunflower seeds, cooked grains, cheese, salt and black pepper. Stir until combined.
9. Cut each pepper in half, remove and discard seeded, Fill peppers with prepared grain mixture.
10. Pour 1 cup water into the instant pot and insert a steamer basket. Place peppers into the basket.

11. Plug in and switch on the instant pot, then secure with lid and position pressure indicator.

12. Select manual option, adjust cooking time on timer pad to 15 minutes and let cook. Instant pot will take 10 minutes to build pressure before cooking timer starts.

13. When the timer beeps, switch off the instant pot and let pressure release naturally for 10 minutes and then do quick pressure release.

14. Then uncover the pot, sprinkle cheese over peppers and close the lid for few minutes until cheese melt completely. Serve peppers warm.

Nutritional Information Per Serving: 311 Cal, 9 g total fat; carb. 4.1 g fiber, 14.4 g protein.

Tasty Tofu Curry

Servings: 4
Total Time Taken: 30 minutes

Ingredients
10 fluid ounces coconut milk, full-fat
1 tablespoon curry powder
2 tablespoons peanut butter
1 tablespoon garam masala
2 cups cubed green bell pepper
2 teaspoons salt
8 ounces tomato paste
1 cup cubed onion
2 teaspoons mince garlic
1 cup diced tofu, firm

Directions
1. In a food processor or blender place all the ingredients except tofu and pulse until smooth.

2. Place tofu in a 6 quarts instant pot and then top with prepared sauce.

7. Plug in and switch on instant pot, secure with lid and position pressure indicator. Select manual option, adjust cooking time on timer pad to 4 minutes and let cook. Instant pot will take 10 minutes to build pressure before cooking timer starts.

8. When the timer beeps, switch off the instant pot and then do quick pressure release.

3. Uncover pot and stir and serve immediately.

Nutritional Info: 297 Cal, 23 g total fat; carb. 6 g fiber, 16.4 g protein.

Yummy Bolognese Lentil

Serving: 5
Total Time Taken: 35 minutes

Ingredients
1 cup black lentils, rinsed
3 medium-sized carrots, peeled and diced
28 ounce chopped fire-roasted tomatoes
1 medium-sized white onion, peeled and diced
2 teaspoons garlic, minced
10-ounce tomato paste
1 teaspoon salt
½ teaspoon ground black pepper
¼ teaspoon red pepper flakes
2 tablespoons Italian seasoning
2 tablespoons apple cider vinegar
32 fluid ounce water

Directions

1. Into a 6-quarts instant pot, place all the ingredients and stir until combined.
2. Plug in and switch on the instant pot, secure pot with lid.
3. Then position pressure indicator, select manual option and adjust cooking time on timer pad to 15 minutes and let cook. Instant pot will take 10 minutes to build pressure before cooking timer starts.
4. When the timer beeps, switch off the instant pot and let pressure release naturally for 10 minutes and then do quick pressure release.
5. Uncover the pot, stir until just mixed and serve immediately.

Nutritional Info: 122 Cal, 2 g total fat 21.8 g carb. 5 g fiber, 5 g protein.

Healthy Plant-based lentil pasta

Servings: 4
Total Time Taken: 60 minutes

Ingredients
½ cups green lentils, rinsed
28 ounce crushed fire-roasted tomatoes
1 teaspoon salt
2 teaspoons dried thyme
1 small bay leaf
8 fluid ounce vegetable broth
20-ounce water
1 pound whole-grain pasta, uncooked

Directions
1. Into a 6-quarts instant pot place lentils, thyme, bay leaf and vegetable broth, and stir until combined.
2. Plug in and switch on the instant pot, then secure pot with lid. Position pressure indicator, select manual option and adjust cooking time on timer pad to 6 minutes and let cook at high pressure. Instant pot will take 10 minutes to build pressure before cooking timer starts.
3. When the timer beeps, switch off the instant pot and let pressure release naturally for 10 minutes and then do quick pressure release.
4. Then uncover the pot, pour in water and stir in tomatoes, salt and pasta until well mixed.
5. Switch on the instant pot, then secure with lid, select manual option and adjust cooking time on timer pad to 5 minutes and let cook.
6. Serve immediately.

Nutritional Info: 427 Cal, 5.6 g total fat 46 g carb. 15 g fiber, 17.4 g protein

Asian Onion Sesame Tofu

Serving: 4
Total Time Taken: 25 minutes

Ingredients
1 pound tofu, cubed
1 cup diced sweet potato
1 medium-sized carrot, peeled and chopped
2 cups snow peas, cut in half
2 cups sliced white onion
1 ½ teaspoon minced garlic
2 tablespoons tahini paste
2 tablespoons tamari
2 tablespoons sriracha sauce
1 tablespoon apple cider vinegar
2 teaspoons toasted sesame oil
1/3 cup vegetable broth
2 tablespoons sesame seeds
2 tablespoons chopped scallion

Directions
1. Plug in and switch on a 6-quarts instant pot, add oil and let heat. Then add carrot, sweet potato and onion and sauté for 3-5 minutes or until it begins to tenderize.
2. Then stir in garlic and 1 tablespoon sesame seeds and continue cooking for 1 minute. If sauté/simmer option isn't available then follow these steps in a skillet and then add the mixture to the instant pot.
3. Press cancel, add tofu, vinegar, tamari, pour in broth and secure pot with lid.
4. Then position pressure indicator, select manual option and adjust cooking time on timer pad to 3 minutes and let cook. Instant pot will take 10 minutes to build pressure before cooking timer starts.
5. When the timer beeps, switch off the instant pot and do quick pressure release.
6. Then uncover the pot, stir in peas and cover pot again with lid. Let sit for 3 minutes.

7. Uncover pot, then stir pepper sauce along with tahini and garnish with remaining sesame seeds and scallions. Serve immediately.

Nutritional Info: 416 Cal, 16 g total fat 20 g carb. 5 g fiber, 32 g protein.

Satisfying Parsnip Potato Soup

Serving: 3
Total Time Taken: 40 minutes

Ingredients

1 medium-sized potato
1 medium-sized parsnip
1 apple
2 medium-sized onions, peeled and diced
1 ½ teaspoons minced garlic
1 teaspoon ground black pepper
2 tablespoons olive oil
14 fluid ounce vegetable broth
¼ cup chopped walnuts

Directions

1. Plug in and switch on a 6-quarts instant pot, select sauté/simmer option, add oil and let heat.
2. Then add onion and garlic and let cook for 5-7 minutes or until soft. If sauté/simmer option isn't available then follow the above step in a skillet and then add the mixture to the instant pot.
3. In the meantime, peel a potato, parsnip, and apple. Core apple and cut into bite size pieces along with potato and parsnip.
4. Press cancel, add potato, parsnip and apple and remaining ingredients except for walnuts and then secure pot with lid.
5. Position pressure indicator, select manual option and adjust cooking time on timer pad to 5 minutes and let cook. Instant pot will take 10 minutes to build pressure before cooking timer starts.
6. When the timer beeps, switch off the instant pot and let pressure release naturally for 10 minutes and then do quick pressure release.

7. Then uncover the pot, stir until just mixed and puree mixture with an immersion blender. If soup is thin, simmer for 5-10 minutes using sauté/simmer option.
8. Ladle soup into serving bowls, garnish with walnuts and serve immediately.

Nutritional Info: 186 Cal, 4 g total fat 26 g carb. 6 g fiber, 3 g protein.

Healthy Rice Dish

Serving: 4
Total Time Taken: 30 minutes

Ingredients
1 medium-sized cauliflower, grated
4 ounce cubed pineapple
2 cups rice
1 teaspoon salt
2 teaspoons olive oil
2 ½ cups water

Directions
1. In a 6-quarts instant pot place all the ingredients and stir until mix.
2. Plug in and switch on the pot, select rice option and secure pot with lid. Then position pressure indicator and let cook on default time. Instant pot will take 10 minutes to build pressure before cooking timer starts.
3. When the timer beeps, switch off the instant pot and let pressure release naturally for 10 minutes and then do quick pressure release.
4. Uncover the pot, stir and then transfer to a serving dish. Serve immediately.

Nutritional Info: 193 Cal, 3 g total fat 35 g carb. 5g fiber, 5 g protein.

Vegan Corn Bread

Serving: 5
Total Time Taken: 40 minutes

Ingredients
½ stick vegan butter, melted
1 tablespoon flax seed meal
1 1/3 cup cornmeal
2/3 cup all-purpose flour, sifted
1 teaspoon salt
2/3 cup brown sugar
2 tablespoons applesauce, unsweetened
2 ½ teaspoons apple cider vinegar
1 cup almond milk
3 tablespoons water
½ teaspoon baking soda

Directions
1. In a small bowl combine flax seeds and water and set aside for 10 minutes.
2. In the meantime whisk together almond milk and lemon juice and set aside for 5 minutes or until curdles form. Then stir in baking soda and set aside until required.
3. In a large bowl using a hand mixer cream together butter and sugar, then whisk in applesauce and flax seed mixture until combined. Gradually whisk in almond milk mixture until combined.
4. Into the milk mixture, add flour, cornmeal, and salt and with a spoon stir until incorporated.
5. Take a round pan with a flat-bottom, big enough to fit inside the instant pot, generously grease with oil and then fill it 2/3 full with prepared cornbread mixture.
6. Into a 6-quarts instant pot pour 1 cup water and then insert a trivet. Place cake pan on the trivet and secure pot with lid.
7. Plug in and switch on the pot, select manual option, adjust timing to 20 minutes and position pressure indicator. Instant pot will take 10 minutes to build pressure before cooking timer starts.
8. When the timer beeps, switch off the instant pot and do quick pressure release.

9. Uncover pot, carefully remove baking dish and let the cake cool on wire rack before taking out to serve.

Nutritional Info: 183 Cal, 6 g total fat ;27 g carb., 1.6 g fiber, 4.3 g protein.

Maple Cinnamon Apple Lentils

Serving: 4
Total Time Taken: 30 minutes

Ingredients
1 cup red lentils, soaked for 30 minutes
2 medium-sized apples, cored
1 tablespoon ground cinnamon
1 teaspoon turmeric powder
¼ teaspoon ground cinnamon
1 teaspoon ground cloves
1 tablespoon maple syrup
1 cup coconut milk, divided
3 cups red rooibos tea, brewed

Directions

1. Drain lentils and place in a 6-quarts instant pot along with remaining ingredients except for maple syrup and milk.
2. Stir until combine, then plug in and switch on the instant pot.
3. Secure pot with lid, then position pressure indicator and adjust cooking time on timer pad to 2 minutes and let cook. Instant pot will take 10 minutes to build pressure before cooking timer starts.
4. When the timer beeps, switch off the instant pot and let pressure release naturally for 10 minutes and then do quick pressure release.
5. Then uncover the pot, stir until well mixed and then divide equally among serving bowl. Serve with a generous amount of milk and maple syrup.

Nutritional Info: 168 Cal, 1 g total fat ;34 g carb., 11 g fiber, 9 g protein.

Conclusion

Thank you again for downloading this book! Hopefully you've tried and enjoy the Instant Pot delicious recipes in this book

Enjoy your healthy mouth-watering instant pot and master your cooking at the same time.

If you enjoyed this book, then I'd like to ask you for a favor, would you be kind enough to leave a review for this book on Amazon? It'd be greatly appreciated!

Thank you and good luck!

Printed in Poland
by Amazon Fulfillment
Poland Sp. z o.o., Wrocław